Modern German Poetry

Titles in the CRITICAL COSMOS series include

AMERICAN FICTION
American Fiction to 1914
American Fiction 1914–1945
American Fiction 1946–1965
American Fiction 1966–1986
American Jewish Literature
American Women Novelists and Short Story Writers
Black American Fiction
Harlem Renaissance

AMERICAN DRAMA, POETRY, AND PROSE
American Drama to 1945
American Drama 1945–1986
American Poetry through 1914
American Poetry 1915–1945
American Poetry 1946–1965
American Poetry 1966–1986
American Prose and Criticism to 1865
American Prose and Criticism 1865–1944
American Prose and Criticism 1945–1986
American Women Poets
Black American Poetry

BRITISH LITERATURE TO 1880
British Drama 1660–1900
British Medieval Literature
Eighteenth Century Fiction
Eighteenth Century Prose and Criticism
Elizabethan Fiction and Prose
Elizabethan Poetry
Elizabethan and Jacobean Drama
English Romantic Fiction and Prose
English Romantic Poets
Seventeenth Century Poetry
Seventeenth Century Prose
Victorian Fiction
Victorian Poetry
Victorian Prose

FRENCH LITERATURE
French Drama: The Renaissance to 1915
French Fiction: The Renaissance to 1915
French Poetry: The Renaissance to 1915
French Prose and Criticism through 1789
French Prose and Criticism, 1790 to World War II
French Prose and Criticism, World War II to the Present
Modern French Drama
Modern French Fiction
Modern French Poetry

GERMAN LITERATURE
German Drama: The Renaissance to 1915
German Fiction to 1915
German Poetry: The Renaissance to 1915
German Prose and Criticism to 1915
Modern German Drama
Modern German Fiction
Modern German Poetry
Modern German Prose and Criticism

MODERN BRITISH AND COMMONWEALTH LITERATURE
Anglo-Irish Literature
British Modernist Fiction 1920–1945
British Prose 1880–1914
British World War I Literature
Canadian Fiction
Canadian Poetry and Prose
Commonwealth Poetry and Fiction
Contemporary British Drama 1946–1986
Contemporary British Fiction 1946–1986
Contemporary British Poetry
Contemporary British Prose
Edwardian and Georgian Fiction 1880–1914
Edwardian and Georgian Poetry 1880–1914
Modern British Drama 1900–1945
Modern British Poetry and Prose

AFRICAN, LATIN AMERICAN, AND OTHER EUROPEAN LITERATURE
African Anglophone Literature
Dadaism and Surrealism
European Medieval Literature
Italian Drama
Italian Fiction: The Renaissance to the Present
Italian Poetry: The Renaissance to the Present
Jewish Literature: The Bible to 1790
Jewish Literature 1790–1945
Modern African Literature
Modern Jewish Literature
Modern Latin American Fiction
Modern Scandinavian Literature
Modern Spanish and Latin American Poetry
Russian Drama
Russian Fiction
Russian Poetry
Scandinavian Literature to 1915
Soviet Fiction
Spanish Fiction to 1927
Spanish Poetry to 1927

THE CRITICAL COSMOS SERIES

Modern German Poetry

Edited and with an introduction
by *HAROLD BLOOM*
Sterling Professor of the Humanities
Yale University

CHELSEA HOUSE PUBLISHERS
New York ◇ *Philadelphia*

© 1989 by Chelsea House Publishers, a division
of Main Line Book Co.

Introduction © 1988 by Harold Bloom

Printed and bound in the United States of America

10 9 8 7 6 5 4 3 2 1

∞The paper used in this publication meets the minimum
requirements of the American National Standard for
Permanence of Paper for Printed Library Materials,
Z39.48–1984.

Library of Congress Cataloging-in-Publication Data
Modern German poetry.
   (The Critical cosmos series)
   Bibliography: p.
   Includes index.
   1. German poetry—20th century—History and
criticism.   I. Bloom, Harold.   II. Series: Critical cosmos.
PT552.M64   1988   831'.91'09   87–8063
ISBN 1–55546–087–9

Contents

Doppelgänger Motif and Two-Voiced Poem
in the Works of Hans Magnus
Enzensberger   217
William S. Sewell

Editor's Note

This book brings together a representative selection of the best criticism available in English upon the principal modern German poets from Rilke to the present, thus excluding such figures as George and Hofmannsthal, who are included in the previous volume of this series. Because standard translations do not exist for some of these poets, originals remain untranslated where the critics have left them so. I am grateful to Barbara Vinken for her devoted labor as a researcher for this volume.

My introduction concerns Rilke, by common consent the major German poet of our century, and seeks to counter Paul de Man's influential deconstruction of Rilke's figurative language. De Man's essay is reprinted here, after Erich Heller's thematic study of Nietzsche's influence upon Rilke's similar revisionary stance towards prior modes of thought and feeling.

Two articles by Michael Hamburger follow, the first a general survey of the Expressionist mode in modern German poetry, the second on Gottfried Benn, Expressionist who degenerated into a racist.

Georg Trakl, who seems to me the best of modern German poets, superior even to Rilke and Hofmannsthal, is considered in two essays, the first by the philosopher Heidegger, who traces in Trakl's language a "going under" to the "yet concealed evening land." That revisionary language of descent is uncovered also by Brigitte Peucker, who celebrates Trakl's extraordinary triumph over belatedness, his transumption of Hölderlin and other precursors.

Bertolt Brecht, dramatist and Marxist revolutionary, is the subject of two commentaries by Reinhold Grimm, one studying Brecht's dialectic between politics and the aesthetic and the other his war quatrains. The prose poems of Günter Eich are analyzed by Anselm Haverkamp, who judges them to be miniature masterpieces of irony in our belated time.

Paul Celan, worthy inheritor of Trakl and a gnomic seer in the Jewish

Kabbalist tradition, is examined as an exemplar of the aphoristic, mystical mode by Joachim Schulze, while John Felstiner explores Celan's poetics by means of translation.

The equally tragic Ingeborg Bachmann is studied by James K. Lyon as a mythologist of the private life. William S. Sewell concludes this volume with an account of the image of the double in the poetry of Hans Magnus Enzensberger, widely regarded as the leading German poet of his generation.

Introduction

I

Can there be *poetic* structures of transcendence? A brilliant but neglected study by Justus George Lawler, *Celestial Pantomime* (1979), treated structural patterns as varied as chiasm and parentheses, refrains and oscillatory imagery, and found them to be valid forms for representing transcendence. The question thus becomes: Can the most ambitious and accomplished poetry be written at all, if its structures do not somehow try to represent transcendence? If poetry is completely identical with figuration, how can it survive rhetorical self-consciousness when such rhetoricity is carried beyond all limits? Indeed, carried far enough, the poem becomes, as Lawler said, a *canon* "in the musical sense of a contrapuntal melody that derives from the dominant theme . . . a sonic chiastic structure reflecting the duality, deception, or confusion expressed in the rhetorical statements." Can such a structure persuade us, even for a moment, to believe in a fiction, even with what Wallace Stevens called the nicer knowledge of belief, which is that what one believes in is not true?

No poet of our century, none at least of overwhelming achievement, surpasses Rainer Maria Rilke in those rhetorical gestures that dare "to affirm and to promise, as few others do, a form of existential salvation that would take place in and by means of poetry." I quote from the late Paul de Man's formidably brilliant essay on Rilke's tropes in *Allegories of Reading,* a definitive study of some of the cognitive limits of figurative language. De Man's critique (first published in French, in 1972) has haunted my own rereadings of Rilke for some fifteen years now, though I will argue against some of its procedures and conclusions here. But I would not dispute de Man's final sentences in his essay:

> The promise contained in Rilke's poetry, which the commentators, in the eagerness of their belief, have described in all its severe

1

complexity, is thus placed, by Rilke himself, within the dissolving perspective of the lie. Rilke can only be understood if one realizes the urgency of this promise together with the equally urgent, and equally poetic, need of retracting it at the very instant he seems to be on the point of offering it to us.

One reason I would not dispute this is that it would be just as valid, and yet no more or less valid, if one substituted the name of Shelley or of Whitman or of Hart Crane, or of almost any visionary poet, for the name of Rilke. Deconstruction alas is after all a kind of double-entry bookkeeping. Draw a severe line down the center of a page in your ledger, and call that line the *aporia*, or trope of doubt. Head the left-hand column "rhetoric as trope" and the right-hand column "rhetoric as persuasion." Then enter every figuration first on the left hand, then on the right, discount both, and you will be left only with that line down the middle, which is where you began. But what has happened to those ensembles of tropes that we call poems by Rilke and by Shelley, by Whitman and by Hart Crane?

Yet Paul de Man's strictures upon Rilke are haunting, if only because Rilke must be the most pretentious of modern visionary poets in nearly all of his too-frequent affirmations. It did not wait for de Man to protest this aspect of Rilke; the young Samuel Beckett, reviewing an English translation of Rilke, annihilated the poet's spiritual self-deceptions, his mistaking of his own tropes as transcendental realities:

> Such a turmoil of self-deception and naif discontent gains nothing in dignity from that prime article of the Rilkean faith, which provides for the interchangeability of Rilke and God. . . . He has the fidgets, a disorder which may very well give rise, as it did with Rilke on occasion, to poetry of a high order. But why call the fidgets God, Ego, Orpheus and the rest?

That rhetorical question is not going to be bettered. No one (except possibly de Man) would be uneasy with Rilkean affirmations if they presented themselves as the cry of the human, rather than transcendent, verities. The poetic and critical issue, I take it, is Rilkean authority. He was not a wisdom writer, offering us the sagacity of Ecclesiastes or of Dr. Johnson, nor does he have the gnomic intensity of Trakl or of Celan. He sought the prophetic stance of his heroic precursor, Hölderlin, but prophets are hard to accept in our century, and Rilke will not bear too close a comparison to Hölderlin, or to William Blake. De Man, who did not really like Rilke's poetry at all, rather astonishingly preferred Rilke's very late poems, particularly those written in French! Slight as these are, they suggested to de Man a Rilkean affinity to poets themselves more deconstructive, as it were:

> These poems are by necessity brief and enigmatic, often consisting of one single sentence. One might well consider them to be Rilke's

most advanced poetic achievement. It is through them that he is related to poets such as Trakl or Celan. The figure stripped of any seduction besides that of its rhetorical elasticity can form, together with other figures, constellations of figures that are inaccessible to meaning and to the senses, located far beyond any concern for life or for death in the hollow space of an unreal sky.

I feel the force of this, but can I know what it means? Is it also "inaccessible to meaning and to the senses"? Has the critic writing this truly renounced any claim to extratextual authority? Has he, as well as Rilke, relied too much upon what he calls "the determining figure . . . of chiasmus, the crossing that reverses the attributes of words and of things"? Despite these questions, which de Man always welcomed in arguments between us, I do not know how to refute de Man's most damaging arguments against Rilke, which are concentrated in a single long paragraph:

Chiasmus, the ground-figure of the *New Poems*, can only come into being as the result of a void, of a lack that allows for the rotating motion of the polarities. As long as it is confined to objects, this structural necessity may seem harmless enough: the declining motion of a fountain or of a ball, the reflection of a mirror or the opening of a window casement have, in themselves, nothing of pathos about them. But Rilke's figuration must also involve subject/object polarities, precisely because it has to put in question the irrevocability of this particularly compelling polarity. This implies the necessity of choosing as figures not only things but personal destinies or subjective experiences as well, with the avowed purpose of converting them into impersonal over-things, but without being able (or wanting) to prevent that the subjective moment first function on the level of meaning. However, these experiences, like the figural objects, must contain a void or a lack if they are to be converted into figures. It follows that only negative experiences can be poetically useful. Hence the prevalence of a thematics of negative experiences that will proliferate in Rilke's poetry: the insatiability of desire, the powerlessness of love, death of the unfulfilled or the innocent, the fragility of the earth, the alienation of consciousness—all these themes fit Rilke's rhetoric so well, not because they are the expression of his own lived experience (whether they are or not is irrelevant) but because their structure allows for the unfolding of his patterns of figuration. And just as the kinetic totalization had to encompass rising and falling motions into one single trope, or just as the reflective totalization must include both sides of the mirror, so the totalization of subjective experience must lead to a positive assertion that only chiasmus can reveal. The reversal of a negativity into a promise, the ambivalent thematic strategy of the *Duino Elegies*, allows for a linguistic play that is analogous to that in the most discreet of the *New Poems*. They call, however, for a very different tone, whose pathos, fervor, and exaltation make one forget the formal and fictional nature of the unity they celebrate. It is inevitable that the *Elegies* are being read as messianic poems: all their thematic assertions confirm this claim, and it is borne out by the virtuosity of the figuration. Yet the promise asserted by these texts is grounded in a play of language that can only come about because the poet has renounced any claim to extra-textual authority. In conformity with a paradox that is inherent in all literature, the poetry gains a maximum of convincing power at the very moment that it abdicates any claim to truth. The *Elegies* and the *Sonnets* have been the main source of evidence in trying to prove the adequation of Rilke's rhetoric to the truth of his affirmations, yet his notion of figural language eliminates all truth-claims from his discourse.

Is it true that chiasmus is not possible without a void, a lack? I would prefer as more descriptive the observation of Justus Lawler, who finds "man's confusion" at the center of the whirl of antinomies, at the intersection of male and female, finite and infinite, experience and innocence restored. A human confusion is not a void or a lack, but a plethora that cannot be mastered. Chiasm meant completion to some of the ancients, but was primarily a figure of elaboration in the Renaissance. Sonic chiasm, in which Rilke abounds, is most extraordinary in Milton's *Paradise Lost*, where Lawler studies it, following hints from Kenneth Burke. Milton's Satan scarcely can orate without chiasm, because duplicity is his mode and confusion his necessary condition. Divisiveness, rather than lack or void, is what attends and stimulates chiasmus into being, and Rilke is the great modern poet of divisiveness within one's being, and so the Milton of our century.

II

A more amiable (though no less rigorous) view of Rilke than de Man's would show us a poet who has the audacity to represent his own confusions, between finite and infinite, as the chiasms that are his maturest poems. This is to say that the prose-Rilke, as it were, was willing to call them confusions, but the poet-Rilke was found by the chiasms that enshrine confusions memorably, even inevitably. Consider the First Elegy of *Duino Elegies*. In a series of interpretive letters, Rilke sonorously and pretentiously magnifies his human confusions so that a critic can begin to wonder if the poet ever knew what he thought he was writing about. We receive a celebrated series of noble idealizations:

Affirmation of *life-AND-death* turns out to be one in the Elegies.
. . . Everywhere transience is plunging into the depths of Being.
. . . We wildly collect the honey of the visible, to store it in the

great golden hive of the invisible. . . . To show the *identity* of dreadfulness and bliss. . . . Death is the *side of life* that is turned away from us and not illuminated. . . .

And so on. If the First Elegy had only the rhetorical authority of these fidgets, then Beckett would be totally vindicated, and de Man's skepticism would be sustained. Fortunately Rilke's poetry is very different from his interpretive prose:

> Freilich ist es seltsam, die Erde nicht mehr zu bewohnen,
> kaum erlernte Gebräuche nicht mehr zu üben,
> Rosen, und andern eigens versprechenden Dingen
> nicht die Bedeutung menschlicher Zukunft zu geben;
> das, was man war in unendlich ängstlichen Händen,
> nicht mehr zu sein, und selbst den eigenen Namen
> wegzulassen wie ein zerbrochenes Spielzeug.
> Seltsam, die Wünsche nicht weiterzuwünschen. Seltsam,
> alles, was sich bezog, so lose im Raume
> flattern zu sehen. Und das Totsein ist mühsam
> und voller Nachholn, daß man allmählich ein wenig
> Ewigkeit spürt.—Aber Lebendige machen
> alle den Fehler, daß sie zu stark unterscheiden.
> Engel (sagt man) wüßten oft nicht, ob sie unter
> Lebenden gehn oder Toten. Die ewige Strömung
> reißt durch beide Bereiche alle Alter
> immer mit sich und übertönt sie in beiden.

(Of course, it is strange to inhabit the earth no longer,
to give up customs one barely had time to learn,
not to see roses and other promising Things
in terms of a human future; no longer to be
what one was in infinitely anxious hands; to leave
even one's own first name behind, forgetting it
as easily as a child abandons a broken toy.
Strange to no longer desire one's desires. Strange
to see meanings that clung together once, floating away
in every direction. And being dead is hard work
and full of retrieval before one can gradually feel
a trace of eternity.—Though the living are wrong to believe
in the too-sharp distinctions which they themselves have
    created.
Angels [they say] don't know whether it is the living
they are moving among, or the dead. The eternal torrent
whirls all ages along in it, through both realms
forever, and their voices are drowned out in its thunderous
    roar.)

                    (translated by Stephen Mitchell)

The crucial word is *seltsam*, "strange," a remarkable litotes or understatement, here a trope of the Sublime. Angels become the agents of chiasmus here, moving through the intersections of confusion, between the living and the dead. Our human confusion becomes the angelic element in us, by an irony that is mordantly persuasive. The central trope is the most memorable here: *"Und das Totsein ist mühsam* (And being dead is hard work)."* That is rather in the spirit of Maud Gonne's sister, who remarked to the poet of "Adam's Curse" that "it's hard work being beautiful, Mr. Yeats."

Is this an instance of what Paul de Man called "the reversal of a negativity into a promise, the ambivalent thematic strategy of the *Duino Elegies*"? I hardly hear promise or affirmation in Rilke's sublimely wry passage, which seems to be wholly characteristic of the *Elegies*. Rilke's interpretive prose promises and affirms incessantly, and his exegetes promise and affirm after him. But the *Elegies* are beautifully evasive, rather resembling the Wallace Stevens of "The Owl in the Sarcophagus" and "The Rock," another modern poet who writes of death through the perpetual trope of chiasmus. The Angel of the *Duino Elegies* is very different from the Angel of Stevens's *Notes toward a Supreme Fiction*, but both are tropological messengers of evasion, of the gestures that make Sublime poems, rather than the promises and affirmations that cannot sustain a rigorous deconstructive analysis.

Rilke and Nietzsche: Orpheus, Dionysus and the Revision of Thought and Feeling

Erich Heller

Rilke may be to Nietzsche what Orpheus is to Dionysus; and Rilke's Orpheus and Nietzsche's Dionysus are brother deities, by virtue of that peculiar adjustment to more modern attitudes of the soul which was forced upon Greek mythology by the spiritual need and hunger of modernity. But before we establish this equation, we shall have to attend to what else they have in common.

They are both initiates in the alchemy of loneliness and suffering. Rilke as well as Nietzsche discovers the fountainhead of joy in the very heart of the land of sorrow. Happiness for them is not, as it was for Schopenhauer, in the absence of pain; it is the fruit of so radical an acceptance of suffering that abundant delight springs from its very affirmation. For the denial of pain means the denial of existence. Existence is pain, and joy lies not in non-existence, as Schopenhauer would have it, but in its tragic transfiguration. This is the theme of Nietzsche's *Birth of Tragedy* as well as of *Zarathustra* and of *The Will to Power*, where it is treated with ever growing assurance by a man, it is well to remember, who wrote to a friend: "The terrible and all but incessant torture of my life makes me thirst for the end. . . . As far as agony and renunciation are concerned, my life during these last years is a match for that of any ascetic at any time. . . . Yet no pain has been able or shall be able to tempt me into giving false testimony about life as I recognize it." And this recognition is praise. From the darkest night of the soul rises Zarathustra's "Trunkenes Lied," his Dionysian song of the deep suffering of the world, which is yet surpassed in depth by that rapture of delight which wills, not that the world with its pain should pass away, but that it should last for ever:

From *The Disinherited Mind*. © 1959 by Meridian Books.

doch alle Lust will Ewigkeit—,
—will tiefe, tiefe Ewigkeit!—

an eternity not of joy (as Nietzsche is so often misunderstood to mean) but
of the world *with* all its sorrow, transfigured in the act of willing it.

If we bear in mind what has been said about the difference in tone
and gesture between Rilke and Nietzsche, there remains hardly a single
element in Nietzsche's acceptance and transformation of suffering that
could not also be found in Rilke. Indeed, the parallels appear to be exact.
As early as his *Tuscan Diary* he writes: "To think that I myself was once
among those who suspect life and distrust its power. Now I would love it
at all events. . . . Whatever of it is mine . . . I would love with tenderness,
and would bring to ripeness within myself all possibilities that its possession
offers to me." And much later, in the Tenth Elegy, we encounter what is
an elegiac version of the theme of *The Birth of Tragedy*: Rilke's Klage, the
embodiment of Lamentation, guiding the dead youth through the country
of her ancestors with its mines of sorrow, until they reach the terminus
where Klage and youth must part, that gorge

> wo es schimmert im Mondschein:
> die Quelle der Freude. In Ehrfurcht
> nennt sie, sagt: "Bei den Menschen
> ist sie ein tragender Strom."

> (where it gleams in the moonlight:
> the source of Joy. With awe
> she names it, says "Among men
> it is a carrying stream.")

And not even an intonation alien to Nietzsche's, but *merely* the presence
of the Angels seems (and merely *seems*) to render the beginning of Rilke's
Tenth Elegy unsuitable as an epitaph for Nietzsche:

> Dass ich dereinst, an dem Ausgang der grimmigen Einsicht,
> Jubel und Ruhm aufsinge zustimmenden Engeln.
> Dass von den klargeschlagenen Hämmern des Herzens,
> keiner versage an weichen, zweifelnden oder
> reissenden Saiten.

> (Some day, emerging at last from the vision of terror,
> may I burst into jubilant praise to assenting Angels.
> May no one of the clear-struck keys of the heart
> fail to respond through alighting on slack or doubtful
> or rending strings!)

Nietzsche, who for so long believed that he was a musician as well as
a philosopher, once composed a "Hymn to Life," the text of which is—

strangest of biographical coincidences—by Lou Salomé. In *Ecce Homo* he says that he chose it because its last lines possess greatness; their meaning is that suffering is no argument against life: "Hast du kein Glück mehr übrig mir zu geben, wohlan! noch hast du deine Pein. . . ." It is a bad poem. The future lover of the poetess would have done better. If Nietzsche discovered some greatness in those verses, persuaded no doubt by the theme of praise, the great persuasion of the *Sonnets to Orpheus* would have overwhelmed him.

For instance, the sonnet "Singe die Gärten, mein Herz, die du nicht kennst." It almost sounds like Lou's "Hymn to Life" set to music by Rilke (though perhaps in this sonnet the music is actually not very much better than Nietzsche's):

> Meide den Irrtum, dass es Entbehrungen gebe
> für den geschehnen Entschluss, diesen: zu sein!
> Seidener Faden, kamst du hinein ins Gewebe.
>
> Welchem der Bilder du auch im Innern geeint bist
> (sei es selbst ein Moment aus dem Leben der Pein),
> fühl, dass der ganze, der rühmliche Teppich gemeint ist.

> (Do not believe you will be deprived
> of something by your resolution: to *be*.
> Silken thread, you have entered the weaving.
>
> With whatever pattern you are inwardly blended
> [and be it a scene from the story of Agony],
> feel that the whole, the praiseworthy carpet is meant.)

And the sonnet which begins with the beautiful lines:

> Nur im Raum der Rühmung darf die Klage
> gehn, die Nymphe des geweinten Quells

> (Only in the realm of Praise may Lamentation move,
> naiad of the wept fountain)

is indeed Rilke's "Trunkenes Lied," the lyrical echo of Zarathustra's Dionysian song. For in this song too sorrow transcends itself in the *knowing* certainty of jubilation, raising to the skies a constellation of immaculate joy:

> Jubel weiss, und Sehnsucht ist geständig,—
> nur die Klage lernt noch; mädchenhändig
> zählt sie nächtelang das alte Schlimme.
>
> Aber plötzlich, schräg und ungeübt,
> hält sie doch ein Sternbild unsrer Stimme
> in den Himmel, den ihr Hauch nicht trübt.

(1.8)

(Triumph knows, and Longing makes confession,—
Lamentation learns: in nightly session
counts, with maiden-hands, old tribulation.

Then, however inexpertly limned,
lifts our voices in a constellation
to the sky her breathing has not dimmed.)

Delighted as Nietzsche would have been by these sonnets, would he necessarily have recognized Orpheus as their divine inspiration? He himself was preoccupied with gods of fuller status: with Dionysus and Apollo. His early *Birth of Tragedy* interpreted the Attic drama as the outcome of an age-old struggle which these two gods waged within the Greek soul. In tragedy, at last, the two hostile gods came together and concluded peace: Dionysus, the god of chaotic ecstasy, rapturously abandoning all claims to form and shape, all individuality, to the amorphous oneness of life; and Apollo, the god with the lyre at whose call all things were arrested within their own contours and their own articulate order. Would Europe, after the end of the "tragic" period of Greece, ever again know such reconciliation, and achieve so profound a harmony between the deepest and most conflicting impulses of the human soul? Shall we ever create an order which is not, as all our orders are, at the expense of the fullness of life, but its richest unfolding; a pattern which is not imposed upon chaos, but overreaching and surpassing it, its beauty still tremulous with the ancient terror? Or is the ancient god of ecstasy doomed to an ignominious existence in the murky corners of sin and depravity, and the god of order to be imprisoned in the petrified structure of classicism and morality? Or *shall* Dionysus and Apollo be united again, as they were in Attic tragedy?

Such were the youthfully enthusiastic questions which Nietzsche asked in his *Birth of Tragedy*. At the time his equally enthusiastic answer was: the old gods have risen again; they live in the work of Richard Wagner. It was to prove an agonizingly provisional answer. Perhaps Rilke's Orpheus would have made good the promise that Wagner's Parsifal broke.

The attempt of scholars to unravel the complex of historical reminiscences, images, insights, feelings that make up the story of Dionysus, Apollo and Orpheus in modern German literature and thought, and then to relate it to what may be the Greek reality of these divine creatures, is as heroic as it is doomed to failure. For a scholar's guarded steps cannot possibly keep pace with the rush and dance of the passions of the mind swirling around those names and arrested only for brief moments in innumerable figurations. Nietzsche, from *The Birth of Tragedy* onwards, is seeking spiritual employment in the service of a god who is a synthesis of Dionysus and Apollo. In this composite Nietzschean deity, Apollo, it is true, more and more loses his name to the other god, but by no means the power of his artistic creativeness, for ever articulating the Dionysian chaos in distinct shapes, sounds and images, which are Dionysian only because they are still aglow with the heat of the primeval fire. At the end of his

Will to Power, that is, at the end of the life of his mind, Nietzsche once more returned to the antagonism within the Greek soul between the Dionysian and Apolline, and once more celebrated the triumph of a god who wrests the utmost of glorifying beauty from the monstrous terror of chaotic passions. This triumphant god, far from suffering the chill of classicism, has, as it were, Apollo's eyes and the heart of Dionysus. In Nietzsche's mature years the real opposition is not Dionysus versus Apollo, but the Apolline Dionysus versus Christ.

And Rilke? In a letter from Rome, written probably in the spring of 1904, eighteen years before the *Sonnets to Orpheus* (it is the last-known letter using undisguised Nietzschean terms), Rilke indulges in a kind of eschatological vision of Apollo's ultimate triumph over the chaotic dominion of Dionysus. The phrases of this letter have not only the ring, but almost the precise wording of Nietzsche's evocations of Apollo-Dionysus. It is chaos itself, says Rilke, which, at the end of days, will stand transformed into "a million ripe, fine and golden forms," an "Apolline product, fermented into maturity and still radiant with its inner glow." And nothing could be more Nietzschean than "the wakeful, lucid enthusiasm" of Rilke's Apolline world.

This is the eschatology of an artist; of an artist, at that, whose business is not merely to heighten by his own creations the beauty of a world, beautiful and significant in itself, but to *create* himself the only beautiful and significant world that there is or can be. It is astonishing and instructive to see how long an idea, present right at the beginning of a poet's career, takes to mature into great poetry. We may also observe how this same idea, originally part of a quasi-historical or Darwinian theory about the development of man, becomes in the end the timeless assertion, not of a future state, but of existence itself. In 1898 Rilke notes in the *Tuscan Diary*: "Not for all time will the artist live side by side with ordinary men. As soon as the artist—the more flexible and deeper type among them— becomes rich and virile, as soon as he *lives* what now he merely *dreams*, man will degenerate and gradually die out. The artist is eternity protruding into time." In the *Sonnets to Orpheus* this eternity not merely protrudes, it has arrived. It *is* the world itself; a world which exists in and through song alone. Song is existence—"Gesang ist Dasein." A god could easily achieve it: "Für den Gott ein Leichtes." But if there are no gods? Then we must become gods ourselves. We? We who hardly *are*? "Wann aber *sind* wir?" Indeed, man must transform and transfigure himself; and in transfiguring himself he will be the redeemer and transfigurer of all existence: *"der Verklärer des Daseins."*

This dialogue, made up of verbatim quotations from Rilke and Nietzsche, is about the Orpheus of the sonnets. The other name of this "Verklärer des Daseins"—the formula is Nietzsche's—is Dionysus Apollo:

> Du aber, Göttlicher, du, bis zuletzt noch Ertöner,
> da ihn der Schwarm der verschmähten Mänaden befiel,

hast ihr Geschrei übertönt mit Ordnung, du Schöner,
aus den Zerstörenden stieg dein erbauendes Spiel.
. . . .

O du verlorener Gott! Du unendliche Spur!
Nur weil dich reissend zuletzt die Feindschaft verteilte,
sind wir die Hörenden jetzt und ein Mund der Natur.

(1.26)

(You that could sound till the end, though, immortal
    accorder
seized by the scorn-maddened Maenads' intemperate throng,
wholly outsounded their cries when in musical order
soared from the swarm of deformers your formative song.
. . . .
O you god that has vanished! You infinite track!
Only because dismembering hatred dispersed you
are we hearers to-day and a mouth which else Nature would
    lack.)

This composite deity is still more obviously present in the following sonnet, in which allusions to Rilke's imagined family history, repeated in the Third Elegy, are merged in a kind of Dionyso-Apolline anthropology of universal significance:

Zu unterst der Alte, verworrn,
all der Erbauten
Wurzel, verborgener Born,
den sie nie schauten.

Sturmhelm und Jägerhorn,
Spruch von Ergrauten,
Männer im Bruderzorn,
Frauen wie Lauten. . . .

Drängender Zweig an Zweig,
nirgends ein frier. . . .
Einer! o steig . . . o steig. . . .

Aber sie brechen noch.
Dieser erst oben doch
biegt sich zur Leier.

(1.17)

(Undermost he, the earth-bound
root of uprearing
multitudes, source underground,
never appearing.

Helmet and hunting-horn,
words of the ageing,
rage between brothers-born,
women assuaging.

Branch on branch, time on time,
vainly they spire. . . .
One free! Oh, climb . . . oh, climb. . . .

One, though the others drop,
curves, as it scales the top,
into a lyre.)

There are also sonnets in which the image of Orpheus could, without imposing the slightest strain on either the poem or our imagination, fade out altogether, making room for Zarathustra himself; for instance, the sonnet which begins

Rühmen, das ist's! Ein zum Rühmen Bestellter,
ging er hervor wie das Erz aus des Steins
Schweigen. Sein Herz, o vergängliche Kelter
eines den Menschen unendlichen Weins.

(1.7)

(Praising, that's it! As a praiser and blesser
he came like the ore from the taciturn mine.
Came with his heart, oh, transient presser,
for men, of a never-exhaustible wine.)

and, still more so, the sonnet

Wolle die Wandlung. O sei für die Flamme begeistert

(2.12)

(Choose to be changed. With the flame be enraptured)

in which almost every word—"Wandlung," "Flamme," "jener entwerfende Geist, welcher das Irdische meistert," "Was sich ins Bleiben verschliesst, schon ists das Erstarrte," "Hammer" and "Härtestes"—belongs as its most unmistakable property to Zarathustra's prophetic household, although there can be no doubt that they have come into Rilke's possession through perfectly legitimate channels. The seal on the deed is authentic. It shows a lonely priest in a ruined cathedral. The roof is off. Through the vast opening comes down what looks a little like the traditional image of the Holy Ghost. But as it is blurred and indistinct, this may be too hasty an interpretation, merely suggested by the cathedral. It may also be rain. As it descends through the open roof of a ruin, we might perhaps just call it "openness" (*das Offene*). This seems to be confirmed by the words which are printed around the circumference of the seal. They say: "Denn offen ist es bei dir und hell (Where you are at home, everything is open and light)," and "Mit allen Augen sieht die Kreatur das Offene (With all its eyes the creature-world beholds the open)."

The last sentence is the beginning of Rilke's Eighth Elegy; but the first was spoken by Zarathustra on coming home to his lonely cave. Once more he has left the noisy town—one is irresistibly tempted to say, the "Leid-Stadt" of Rilke's Tenth Elegy:

> wo in der falschen, aus Übertönung gemachten
> Stille, stark, aus der Gussform des Leeren der Ausguss,
> prahlt, der vergoldete Lärm, das platzende Denkmal.
> O wie spurlos zerträte ein Engel ihnen den Trostmarkt,
> den die Kirche begrenzt, ihre fertig gekaufte:
> reinlich und zu und enttäuscht wie ein Postamt am Sonntag

>> (where, in the seeming stillness of uproar outroared,
>> stoutly, a thing cast out from the mould of vacuity,
>> swaggers that gilded fuss, the bursting memorial.
>> How an Angel would tread beyond trace their market of
>>   comfort,
>> with the church alongside, bought ready for use: as tidy
>> and disappointed and shut as the Post on a Sunday)

for Rilke's is as exact a description as Nietzsche gives of the town that Zarathustra has left behind in order to converse with his own solitude:

> "Here you are at home with yourself," he says. . . . "Here all things come to your speech, caressing and flattering, for they wish to ride on your back. And you yourself are riding on many a symbol towards many a truth. . . .
> "Here the words and word-shrines of everything that is open up before you; everything that is desires to become word; everything that will become desires to learn from you how to speak."

Rilke too was to travel on many a symbol, yielded by the word-shrines of things, towards many of Zarathustra's truths. Rilke's youthful *Tuscan-Diary* version of Zarathustra's secret sessions with "die Dinge" is as follows: " . . . I feel that more and more I am becoming the disciple of things (not merely their listener), a disciple who adds, through comprehending questions, intensity to their answers and confessions, and who, enticing them to spend their advice and wisdom, learns how to reward their generous love with the disciple's humility."

The aspect of things changes in the new "openness" of Nietzsche's, of Rilke's solitude. Within the perspective of this expanded, and yet, as we shall see, more radically confined space, it appears that neither things nor names have ever been really known. With a new consciousness and perception gained, they must be christened anew, baptized, as it were, into a new Church. For another dimension of speech has been thrown open, and all things desire to hear their names once more, uttered in a voice resonant enough to fill the new spaces. Said as they used to be said, words fall flat in these changed acoustical conditions.

What happened to the *form* and *shape* of things at the beginning of the Renaissance seems now to happen to their *names*. With the third dimension *consciously* perceived as an essential aspect of vision, all objects demanded to be seen and painted afresh, and indeed quite new ones called out for recognition. Zarathustra's words of the things that "come to your speech, caressing and flattering, for they wish to ride on your back," would, with a change from speech to canvas, have made good sense to the first of the great Renaissance painters. If the medieval madonnas and angels seemed to complain that they cut poor figures in their two-dimensional flatness, at the same time an abundance of other images pressed upon the painters' imagination, claiming their right to significance in the new field of vision. Pillars, towers, gates, trees, jugs and windows demanded to be *seen* with an intensity as never before—"wie selber die Dinge niemals innig meinten zu sein."

Rilke's new dimension is inwardness. As they came to Zarathustra with their novel claims, so the things approach Rilke, asking to be taught how to become words and how to make themselves truly felt in the widened space; and in return they show him that this is precisely his real task in the world: to assimilate them into the new inward dimension:

> —Sind wir vielleicht *hier*, um zu sagen: Haus,
> Brücke, Brunnen, Tor, Krug, Obstbaum, Fenster,—
> höchstens: Säule, Turm . . . aber zu *sagen*, verstehs,
> oh zu sagen *so*, wie selber die Dinge niemals
> innig meinten zu sein.

> (—Are we, perhaps, here in order to say: House,
> Bridge, Fountain, Gate, Jug, Peartree, Window,—
> at most: Pillar, Tower? . . . but to *say*, remember,
> oh, to say this so as never the things themselves
> meant so intensely to be.)

(Ninth Elegy)

It has often been said of both Nietzsche and Rilke that they were masters of new nuances, the one of thought, and the other of feeling. True, they both felt that their souls and minds were at the mercy of sensations and revelations so subtle as had never been received before; that they were instruments on which the wind of unsuspected spaces played its first tentative tunes. In this unexplored space, which is, as it were, made up of the "empty distances" *between* and *around* our normal concepts of thought and feeling, lies our "wirklicher Bezug," our *real* "relatedness" to what really *is*. Like a hymn of spiritual friendship, addressed to Nietzsche, sounds Rilke's sonnet:

> Heil dem Geist, der uns verbinden mag;
> denn wir leben wahrhaft in Figuren.
> Und mit kleinen Schritten gehn die Uhren
> neben unserm eigentlichen Tag.
>
> Ohne unsern wahren Platz zu kennen,
> handeln wir aus wirklichem Bezug.
> Die Antennen fühlen die Antennen,
> und die leere Ferne trug.
>
> (1.12)
>
> (Hail, the spirit able to unite us!
> For we truly live our lives in symbols,
> and with tiny steps move our clocks,
> beside our real, actual day.
>
> Without knowing our true place
> we yet act from real relatedness.
> Antennae feel antennae,
> and the empty distance carries.)

And Nietzsche's response:

> Jenseits des Nordens, des Eises, des Heute,
> jenseits des Todes,
> abseits:
> *unser* Leben, *unser* Glück!
> Weder zu Lande
> noch zu Wasser
> kannst du den Weg
> zu den Hyperboreern finden:
> von *uns* wahrsagte so ein weiser Mund.
>
> (Beyond the North, the ice, the present day,
> beyond death,
> away from it:
> *our* life, *our* bliss!
> Neither by land nor by sea
> can you find the way
> to the Hyperboreans:
> it was of *us* that the mouth of wisdom thus
>   prophesied.)

And the solitary figure of Rilke in the Piccola Marina of Capri, feeling and hardly surviving the

uraltes Wehn vom Meer,
welches weht
nur wie für Urgestein,
lauter Raum
reissend von weit herein.

(primeval waft from the sea,
that wafts
only as if for primeval stone,
pure space rushing
in from afar.)

easily merges with that of Nietzsche, leaning over a bridge in the brown Venetian evening:

Meine Seele, ein Saitenspiel,
. . . unsichtbar berührt

(My soul, a play of strings
. . . touched by an invisible hand)

words which might be followed by Rilke's

Und welcher Geiger hat uns in der Hand?
O süsses Lied.

(And who is the minstrel that holds us in his hand?
O sweet song.)

Yet these are only lyrical prolegomena or accompaniments to the real theme: the radical revision of all frontiers within human experience. The full realization of this theme comes to both of them in ecstatic states of inspiration. Both Nietzsche and Rilke knew they were inspired, irresistibly commanded to write, the one *Zarathustra* and the other *Duino Elegies*. Theirs are the only personal accounts we possess in modern literature of states of inspiration. The reports are almost interchangeable, except that Nietzsche's, written at some distance from the experience itself, is more sober than are Rilke's breathless announcements of victory. "Has anyone, at the end of the nineteenth century, any clear idea of what poets of more vigorous ages called *inspiration*?" asks Nietzsche in the *Zarathustra* chapter of his *Ecce Homo*, and continues: "If one were in the least superstitious, one would not know how to reject the suggestion that one is merely an incarnation, merely a mouthpiece, merely a medium of superior powers." Of "days of enormous obedience," speaks Rilke, of "a storm of the spirit" which threatened to annihilate the body. "O that I was allowed to survive to this day, through everything. Wonder. Grace." Both Nietzsche and Rilke felt that the very physical surroundings which were the chosen scenes of these Pentecosts were hallowed places. The tenderness with which Nietzsche describes his walks on the hillsides of Genoa and through the Mediterranean pinewoods along the Bay of Santa Margherita, where Zarathustra accompanied him, is equalled by Rilke's stepping out into the cold moonlight, when he had survived the onrush of the Elegies, and stroking the walls of the "little castle Muzot" "like an old animal."

This is not the way mere nuances are discovered. The word nuance presupposes an order of firmly established ideas and objects between which an indefinite number of subtly-coloured shades may playfully mediate, whereas Nietzsche's and Rilke's sensibilities tend towards a radical denial of that very principle of separation—philosophically speaking, the *principium individuationis*, within a world perceived under the dual aspects of immanence and transcendence—on which our intellectual perception has been based throughout the centuries. Nietzsche denounces its results with regard to our thought as that "barbarism of concepts" which we are still far from fully realizing, and Rilke its effects on our feeling as that pauperism of the heart which makes us outcasts among angels, men and beasts alike, distressed vagabonds of the crudely interpreted world—

> dass wir nicht sehr verlässlich zu Haus sind
> in der gedeuteten Welt.

For all men make the mistake of *distinguishing* too sharply—

> . . . Aber Lebendige machen
> alle den Fehler, dass sie zu stark unterscheiden.
> (First Elegy)

But this is an elegiac understatement of the real denunciation implicit in Rilke's mature work, which is that our traditional way of distinguishing is false throughout the whole range of our fundamental distinctions between transcendence and immanence, God and man, man and things, external reality and inwardness, joy and suffering, communion of love and separation, life and death—a list to which Nietzsche's main contribution is: good and evil. "To presuppose the *oneness* of life and death," Rilke writes, one year after *Duino Elegies* and *Sonnets to Orpheus*, and again, "to know the *identity* of terror and bliss . . . is the essential meaning and idea of my two books."

We observed them, each in his own way, working, thinking and feeling towards a radical revision of the frontiers between traditionally articulated concepts of thought and, as it were, units of feeling. There remains the question of how and why they came to undertake such a stupendous labour of thought and feeling—*Herzwerk*, "work of heart," as Rilke called it. The answer was given for both of them by Nietzsche: because God is dead. And God was so powerful, efficient and secretive a landlord that to look after His Estate all by ourselves involves us in great difficulties. What under

His management used to be clearly defined spheres are now objects of confused and conflicting claims. Much that we were powerfully persuaded to accept as true dissolves into sheer illusion. For all the land appears to have been heavily mortgaged. We have lived in splendour, but the splendour was merely loaned. Payment was due on the death of God, and the unknown transcendental creditor lost little time in claiming it. A tremendous effort has to be exacted to restore the glory.

Both Nietzsche and Rilke have made themselves administrators of the impoverished estate. The enormous complexity of their works must not deceive us; the structure behind it is consistently simple; it has the simplicity of that immense single-mindedness with which they, consciously or intuitively, dedicated their lives to the one task: to re-assess and re-define all experience in thought and feeling; to show that the traditional modes of thought and feeling, in so far as they were determined, or decisively modified, by Christian transcendental beliefs—and to which of them does this not apply?—had been rendered invalid by the end of religion; to replace them; to overcome the great spiritual depression, caused by the death of God, through new and ever greater powers of glory and praise; to adjust, indeed to revolutionize, thought and feeling in accordance with the reality of a world of absolute immanence; and to achieve this without any loss of spiritual grandeur. "Indeed," writes Nietzsche (to Overbeck, May 21st, 1884), "who can feel with me what it means to feel with every shred of one's being that the weight of all things must be defined anew," and Rilke (to Ilse Jahr, February 22nd, 1923): "God, the no longer sayable, is being stripped of his attributes; they return to his creation"; and in "The Letter from the Young Workman" (reversing the debtor-creditor relationship and presenting the bill to Heaven): "It is high time for the impoverished earth to claim back all those loans which have been raised at the expense of her own bliss for the equipment of some super-future." Nietzsche spoke for himself as well as for Rilke when at the time of writing *Zarathustra* he made the following entry in his notebook: "He who no longer finds what is great in God will find it nowhere—he must either deny or create it." It is the most precise formula for the religiously disinherited religious mind.

Nietzsche and Rilke experienced and explored this situation with the utmost consistency, courageously facing the paradox to which it leads: the paradox of affirming from negation, and creating from denial. For the denial of God involves for both Nietzsche and Rilke the denial of man *as he is*. Even before Zarathustra proclaimed the rule of the Superman, Nietzsche, knowing that man has become "impossible" after doing away with God, "the holiest and mightiest that the world possessed," asked: "Is not the greatness of this deed too great for us? To prove worthy of it, must not we ourselves become gods?" And Rilke said of his *Malte Laurids Brigge* that it almost "proved that this life, suspended in a bottomless pit, is impossible."

How is this impossible life to become possible again? How is the vanished glory issuing from a transcendental god to be recreated by a world gloomily imprisoned in its own immanence? At this point both Nietzsche and Rilke indulge in the same alchemy that we have seen employed in their transmutation of pain and suffering. The idea of even heightening the agony of existence in order to increase the resources from which ultimate bliss will be sustained is familiar to both of them. Nietzsche once quoted Cardanus as having said that one ought to seek out as much suffering as possible in order to intensify the joy springing from its conquest; and Rilke wrote of the "holy cunning of the martyrs," taking "the most concentrated dose of pain" to acquire the immunity of continual bliss. Now again they seek in the greatest possible intensification of immanence salvation from the inglorious prison. They almost invent more and more deprivations of transcendence to heighten the pressure within the hermetic vessel. In that, Nietzsche's Eternal Recurrence and Rilke's "*Ein*mal und nichtmehr," "*Once* and no more," are contrasts merely in verbal expression, but identical in meaning. This identity lies in the emphasis both these symbols place on the *eternity* of the moment here and now, the *irrevocability* of the one and unique opportunity and test of living.

The idea of Eternal Recurrence seeks to bestow the paradox of an eternity of finite time on the transient moment, which Rilke, in his turn, eternalizes in the hermetical flame of inner experience, consuming all that is merely corruptible matter and concreteness in our world and leaving us with an essence as imperishable as it is invisible. Rilke states this theme of his mature work with explicit precision as early as his *Tuscan Diary*: "We need *eternity*; for only eternity can provide space for our gestures. Yet we know that we live in narrow finiteness. Thus it is our task to create infinity within these boundaries, for we no longer believe in the unbounded." And the imaginations of both Nietzsche and Rilke have given birth to symbolic creatures moving with perfect grace and ease in a sphere to which man can attain only in the utmost realization of his spiritual powers. These creatures of immanence, transcending immanence in the achievement of a yet profounder immanence, are Nietzsche's Superman and Rilke's Angel. Both are terrible to man, threatening with annihilation the image that, fondly and lazily, he has built up of himself, an image resting on the illusion of transcendence and now shattered in the great undeceiving: "To create the Superman after we have thought, indeed rendered thinkable, the whole of nature in terms of man himself" and then "to *break all your images of man* with the image of the Superman—this is Zarathustra's will . . . " says one of Nietzsche's notebooks from the time of *Zarathustra*; and Rilke's *Duino Elegies* begin with the invocation of the angelic terror:

> Wer, wenn ich schriee, hörte mich denn aus der Engel
> Ordnungen? und gesetzt selbst, es nähme
> einer mich plötzlich ans Herz: ich verginge von seinem
> stärkeren Dasein

(Who, if I cried, would hear me among the angelic
orders? And even if one of them suddenly
pressed me against his heart, I should fade in the
                strength of his
stronger existence)

(First Elegy)

and

Jeder Engel ist schrecklich. Und dennoch, weh mir,
ansing ich euch, fast tödliche Vögel der Seele,
wissend um euch.

(Every angel is terrible. Still, though, alas!
I invoke you, almost deadly birds of the soul,
knowing of you.)

(Second Elegy)

The supreme realization of immanence and its metamorphosis into
everlasting inwardness is man's task in a world dominated by Rilke's Angel,
in the same way in which Nietzsche conceives Eternal Recurrence as the
terrifying discipline which must break man and make the Superman. Only
he, in the glory of his own strength, joy and power of praise, can *will* again
and again a life which, even if lived only once, must be all but unendurable
to man, as soon as he is exposed to the full impact of its absolute godlessness
and senselessness, and no longer sheltered from it by the ruins of Christianity among which he exists. "I perform the great experiment: who can
bear the idea of Eternal Recurrence? He who cannot endure the sentence,
'There is no redemption,' ought to die out." The Superman is for Nietzsche
what Orpheus is for Rilke: the transfigurer of unredeemable existence, with
the "mystery of its unending repetition issuing from superhuman delight."

Und so drängen wir uns und wollen es leisten,
wollens enthalten in unseren einfachen Händen,
im überfüllteren Blick und im sprachlosen Herzen.
Wollen es werden.

(And so we press on and try to achieve it,
try to contain it within our simple hands,
in the gaze ever more overcrowded and in the speechless
                heart.
Try to become it.)

(Ninth Elegy)

But what we try to achieve here and what overcrowds our gaze and heart—
with "überzähliges Dasein," "Supernumerary existence"—is not the vision
of Eternal Recurrence, but, on the contrary, of

Einmal
jedes, nur *ein*mal. *Ein*mal und nichtmehr. Und wir auch
*ein*mal. Nie wieder. Aber dieses
*ein*mal gewesen zu sein, wenn auch nur *ein*mal:
irdisch gewesen zu sein, scheint nicht widerrufbar.

(Just once,
everything only for once. Once and no more. And
we, too,
once. And never again. But this
having been once, though only once,
having been once on earth—can it ever be cancelled?)
(Ninth Elegy)

Nietzsche's Eternal Recurrence and Rilke's eternally reiterated "Once"
are both the extreme symbols of the determination to wrest the utmost of
spiritual significance from a life that, in traditional terms, has ceased to be
spiritually significant. How to cast eternity from the new mould of absolute
transience, and how to achieve the mode of transcendence within the consciousness of pure immanence, is one of the main concerns of Nietzsche
as well as of Rilke. This problem links Rilke (and, of course, Nietzsche)
with the philosophers of Existence; Heidegger, for instance, is said to have
remarked that his philosophy is merely the unfolding in thought of what
Rilke has expressed poetically; but even without this confession the affinity
would be obvious. What, above all, Rilke and the existentialists have in
common is the experience of the utter exposure and defencelessness of the
frontiers of human existence against the neighbouring void, that area which
was once established as the divine home of souls and is now the unassailable
fortress of the *nihil*, defeating for ever every new and heroic attempt of
man to assert himself in that region: hence Jasper's *Scheitern*, Heidegger's
Geworfensein and, long before them, Kierkegaard's—and even Pascal's—
Angst. The focal point of all existentialist philosophies is this "marginal
situation" of man in the border-districts of immanence and the realization
of the existence of a sphere which seems to invite and yet relentlessly beat
back every attempt at transcendence.

It is this impenetrable void against which Zarathustra hurls his armies
of men, knowing that they will not be victorious, but utterly routed; yet a
few will return in triumph, having gained the strength of supermen in the
purifying defeat. For life is a "Wagnis," a perpetual staking of existence,
man a mere "essay in existence" and lovable only because he is "ein Über-
gang und ein Untergang," at once transition and perdition. The same frontier is the defeat of Malte Laurids Brigge, until the mature Rilke succeeds
in concluding an everlasting truce with the anonymous powers on the other
side—by appropriating their territory "inwardly." Where man knew merely
the terror of the monstrous emptiness beyond, there is now the peace of
"reiner Bezug," "pure relatedness," which is so pure because no real "oth-

erness" enters into it. In this "reiner Bezug" life and death are one. As soon as it is achieved,

> entsteht
> aus unsern Jahreszeiten erst der Umkreis
> des ganzen Wandelns. Über uns hinüber
> spielt dann der Engel.

> (arises
> from our seasons the cycle
> of the entire motion. Over and above us,
> then, there is the Angel's play.)
> (Fourth Elegy)

Or, one is tempted to add, the Superman's dance, the joy of the creatures who have gained eternity in the resigned and yet victorious return to themselves. Rilke, in the Super-Narcissus image of his Angels, at the same time expresses the essence of Nietzsche's race of Supermen who assert their power and beauty in the cycle of Eternal Recurrence:

> . . . die die entströmte eigene Schönheit
> wiederschöpfen zurück in das eigene Antlitz.

> (. . . drawing up their own
> outstreamed beauty into their faces again.)
> (Second Elegy)

It is not correct to say that after the *Duino Elegies* Rilke returned, as some critics suggest, to a "simpler" and "purely lyrical" mode of expression. The apparent simplicity and pure lyricism of the final phase are not different in kind from the simplicity amd lyricism of *Sonnets to Orpheus*. There is, indeed, repose; but it is the repose of a poetry that appears to have settled peacefully on the very pastures which had for so long been the goal of the struggle. If the *Duino Elegies* were the invocation of the Angel, some of the poems that come afterwards sound like the Angel's own poetry; and it is hardly surprising that it could also be said: like the poetry of the Superman. This, indeed, does not make them easier to understand. It is the poetry of achievement, and not the poetry of return. There is little gain in it for those who find the "ideas" of the preceding period disturbing. The ideas are not abandoned, but realized; for instance, in the poem written in 1924:

> Da dich das geflügelte Entzücken
> über manchen frühen Abgrund trug,
> baue jetzt der unerhörten Brücken
> kühn berechenbaren Bug.

> Wunder ist nicht nur im unerklärten
> Überstehen der Gefahr;
> erst in einer klaren reingewährten
> Leistung wird das Wunder wunderbar.

Mitzuwirken ist nicht Überhebung
an dem unbeschreiblichen Bezug,
immer inniger wird die Verwebung,
nur Getragensein ist nicht genug.

Deine ausgeübten Kräfte spanne,
bis sie reichen, zwischen zwein
Widersprüchen. . . . Denn im Manne
Will der Gott beraten sein.

(As the winged ecstasy
has borne you over many an early abyss,
now, with mathematical audacity
build the arches of unheard-of bridges.

Wonder is not merely in the inexplicable
surviving of danger;
only in the clear and purely granted
achievement is the miracle miraculous.

To participate in the indescribable
relating, is not presumption,
ever more intense becomes the pattern,
only being borne along will not suffice.

Stretch your practised powers till they span
the distance between two contradictions,
for the god must find
counsel in the man.)

Or in Rilke's last known poem in German, which, if it is simple, has the inexhaustibly complex simplicity of a sphere so esoteric that it renders it completely untranslatable, defeating even the attempt to give a prose version of it in English. Yet all that has been said here about Rilke and Nietzsche could easily be based on this one poem alone and would need no further support. It is dated August 24th, 1926, four months before Rilke's death, and is dedicated to Erika Mitterer "for the feast of praise":

Taube, die draussen blieb,   ausser dem Taubenschlag,
wieder in Kreis und Haus,   einig der Nacht, dem Tag,
weiss sie die Heimlichkeit,   wenn sich der Einbezug
fremdester Schrecken schmiegt   in den gefühlten Flug.

Unter den Tauben, die   allergeschonteste,
niemals gefährdetste,   kennt nicht die Zärtlichkeit;
wiedererholtes Herz   ist das bewohnteste:
freier durch Widerruf   freut sich die Fähigkeit.

Über dem Nirgendssein   spannt sich das Überall!
Ach der geworfene,   ach der gewagte Ball,
füllt er die Hände nicht   anders mit Wiederkehr:
rein um sein Heimgewicht   ist er mehr.

Both Nietzsche and Rilke, experiencing life as wholly immanent, irrevocable in its transience and unredeemable in its imperfection, stake it on the supreme "Wagnis," the daring experiment: man himself must become the redeemer of existence. This is the ultimate consequence of the Will to Power, or of humanism thought out and felt to its radical conclusion by the *anima naturaliter religiosa*. Nietzsche replaces the mystery of the Incarnation by the Superman, the Will to Power incarnate; and Rilke by the angelic vision of a world disembodied in human inwardness. "We must transform our prayers into blessings," says Nietzsche; and Rilke:

Erde, ist es nicht dies, was du willst: *unsichtbar*
in uns erstehen?—Ist es dein Traum nicht,
einmal unsichtbar zu sein?—Erde! unsichtbar!
Was, wenn Verwandlung nicht, ist dein drängender Auftrag?

(Earth, isn't this what you want: an *invisible*
re-arising in us? Is it not your dream
to be one day invisible? Earth! invisible!
What is your urgent command, if not transformation?)
                                                    (Ninth Elegy)

Only on the discovery of this redeeming mission follows Rilke's final affirmation: "Erde, du liebe, ich will."

Interpreting the Elegies to his Polish translator, Rilke wrote: "*There is neither a Here and Now nor Beyond, but only the great Oneness*, in which the creatures surpassing us, the Angels, are at home. . . . *We are the bees of the Invisible. Nous butinons éperdument le miel du visible, pour l'accumuler dans la grande ruche d'or de l'Invisible.*" And after denouncing the ceaselessly progressing depreciation of the spiritual value of all "things," he continues: "The earth has no other refuge except to become invisible: *in us* . . . only *in us* can this intimate and enduring transformation of the Visible into the Invisible . . . be accomplished. . . . The Angel of the *Elegies* has nothing to do with the angel of the Christian Heaven. . . . He is the creature in whom the transformation of the Visible into the Invisible, which is our task, appears already accomplished. . . ." But for all this, the most illuminating part of Rilke's much-quoted letter is the statement that the ultimate affirmation of life, achieved in the *Elegies*, is sustained by precisely the same awareness that persuaded Malte Laurids Brigge of life's "impossibility." Malte's disgust and the Ninth Elegy's praise spring from an identical source. In other words, the Angel did for Rilke what the Superman did for Nietzsche: he supplied the philosophers' stone with which to make gold from base matter. Yet it appears that of the two Rilke was the more successful alchemist. The letters he wrote after the *Duino Elegies* lavished the precious stuff from the poet's workshop on as many needy as cared to apply for it. Nietzsche, on the other hand, while writing *Zarathustra* and expounding the doctrines of Eternal Recurrence, praise and affirmation, made the following entry in his notebook: "I do not wish to live *again*. How have I borne life? By creating. What has made me endure? The vision of the Superman who *affirms* life. I have tried to affirm it *myself*—but ah!"

These two confessions of Rilke and Nietzsche clinch the whole excruciating problem that besets the spiritually disinherited mind of Europe, and raise anew the question of poetry and truth in an age dispossessed of all spiritual certainties. Without that all-pervasive sense of truth which bestows upon happier cultures their intuition of order and reality, poetry—in company with all the other arts—will be faced with ever increasing demands for ever greater "creativeness." For the "real order" has to be "created" where there is no intuitive conviction that it exists. The story of the rise of the poet from the humble position of a teller of tales and a singer of songs to the heights of creation, from a lover of fancies to a slave of the imagination, from the mouthpiece of divine wisdom to the begetter of new gods, is a story as glorious as it is agonizing. For with every new gain in poetic creativity the world as it is, the world as created without the poet's intervention, becomes poorer; and every new impoverishment of the world is a new incentive to poetic creativeness. In the end the world as it is is nothing but a slum to the spirit, and an offence to the artist. Leaving its vapours behind in audacious flight, his genius settles in a world wholly created by the creator-poet: *Gesang ist Dasein.*

"Only after the death of religion will the imagination be able to luxuriate again in divine spheres," said Nietzsche, perhaps not knowing that in saying it he was merely echoing one of the favourite ideas of the Romantics whom he so much disliked. For it was Friedrich Schlegel who wrote: "Only he can be an artist who has a religion of his own, an original view of infinity," and it was Novalis who added to this dictum the marginal note "The artist is thoroughly irreligious. Hence he can work in the medium of religion as though it were bronze." But the original views of infinity cannot for ever remain unaffected by the spiritual destitution of the finite. There must come a time when owing to excessive mining bronze is devalued and the soil becomes too dry for anything to grow luxuriantly, except in artificial conditions.

Neither Rilke nor Nietzsche praises the praiseworthy. They praise. They do not believe the believable. They believe. And it is their praising and believing itself that becomes praiseworthy and believable in the act of worship. Theirs is a *religio intransitiva.* Future anthropologists may see in it the distinctive religious achievement of modern Europe, the theological equivalent of *l'art pour l'art.* For the time being, it may help us to assess the rank of Rilke as a poet, and to clear up some of the confusion into which we are plunged by dissociating his "great poetry" from his "false ideas."

In a sense Rilke's poetry is as "false" as are his ideas. This sense, however, is not simply derogatory. There is a kind of falseness which, quite legitimately, affords the most refined aesthetic pleasure: at the point, that is, at which consistently sustained artificiality assumes the semblance of spontaneity, and the most elaborate magical procedure the appearance of the naïvely miraculous. In this sense both Rilke's poetry and his ideas show the intrinsic falseness of a self-created reality and a self-induced love for it. In defending a sense and vision of reality different from Rilke's, the critic implicitly upholds, often against his explicit intentions, standards of poetry by which the poetic work of Rilke's mature years stands judged as too eccentric to be really great. Rilke poetically exploits a marginal position, precariously maintained on the brink of catastrophe. The catastrophe, perpetually threatening and only just warded off by the most dazzling acrobatics of soul and mind, is the loss of significant external reality. In the great poetry of the European tradition the emotions do not interpret; they respond to the interpreted world. In Rilke's mature poetry the emotions do the interpreting and then respond to their own interpretation.

All great art (and, for that matter, every human order stabilized by tradition) rests on a fundamentally fixed correspondence between the impact of external experience on man and man's articulate answers. These answers may be given on varying levels of profundity and with varying degrees of precision, but they are all recognizable by, as it were, their basic colour as the more or less right answers. Indeed, the imagination, this kingfisher after new experiences and new articulations, may discover new waters in lands which have long remained inaccessible and unexplored. But there will be a place for them, hitherto left blank, on the maps of the familiar world.

Rilke, however, is the poet of a world of which the philosopher is Nietzsche. Its formations evade all traditional systems of cartography. Doubt has dislodged all certainties. The unnameable is christened and the unsayable uttered. It is a world in which the order of correspondences is violently disturbed. We can no longer be sure that we love the lovable and abhor the detestable. Good does no good and evil no harm. Terror and bliss are one. Life and death are the same. Lovers seek separation, not union. All the sweetness of the visible world is stored in invisible hives.

Unembarrassed greatness is not to be expected from the poetry of such a world. Yet Rilke is uniquely successful in evoking the traditional responses of the emotions to fundamentally new impacts. At his bidding the soul travels as though through familiar land; but on arrival it finds itself in a place where it never meant to be. It is not for nothing that the central position in the *Duino Elegies*—the fifth among the ten—is occupied by *Les Saltimbanques*. There is an acrobatic element in Rilke's poetry itself which tinges its greatness with the hue of the abstruse. For his most superb accomplishment is the *salto mortale* of despair which lands the soul in a "Raum der Rühmung," a sphere of praise, where all the praise is sung in honour of the singer while the voiceless world, deranged and dizzy, is left behind to face the music.

"What was it that Zarathustra once told you? That poets lie too much?—But Zarathustra too is a poet. . . . *We* lie too much." These words of Nietzsche's sound like an anticipated motto to Rilke's letters. For the utter precariousness of Rilke's vision is exposed most painfully in endless prose variations which form a large part of his correspondence. Only a generation of recipients and readers benumbed and befogged by every conceivable spiritual deprivation, and insensitive to the intimate relation between language and authenticity, could accept as genuine spiritual guidance pronouncements which more often than not show the unmistakable stylistic imprint of untruth; of that most dangerous kind of untruth which does not spring from fraudulent intent, but from a self-deception so profound that nothing less powerful than a false inflection, a hollow adjective or a synthetic noun can undeceive us of its hypnotic persuasion. Rilke takes the unending curtain-calls which acknowledge his poetic achievement, in the costume of his inspiration. Then, and only then, the prophecy turns to performance, and the visionary glance seems produced by make-up. But it was Nietzsche, the thinker, not Rilke, the poet, who was obsessed with the problem of the actor-artist, as it was Nietzsche who wrote the lines:

> Dass ich verbannt sei
> von aller Wahrheit!
> Nur *Narr*! Nur *Dichter*!

> (Oh, that I am banished
> from all Truth!
> Mere *fool*! Mere *poet*!)

This fact brings to its paradoxical conclusion an argument that took its bearings from a theory expounding that, while the poet merely makes poetry, it is the thinker who is unequivocally committed to his thought.

"My earliest serious concern was with the relationship between Art and Truth," wrote Nietzsche in 1888, right at the end of his conscious life, in a renewed attempt to understand the mind that in 1870 conceived *The Birth of Tragedy*. "And even now," the meditation continues, "I am seized with holy terror in the face of that dilemma. The belief that informs *The Birth of Tragedy* is a belief in Art, against the background of yet another belief: that it is *impossible to live with Truth*. . . . The will to *illusion* . . . is profounder, more 'metaphysical,' than the will to Truth, Reality and Being." And in *The Will to Power* we read: "For a philosopher it is an abomination to say, 'the Good and the Beautiful are one'; and if he dares to add, 'also the True,' then one ought to beat him. Truth is ugly. . . . We have *Art* in order *not to perish of Truth*." Thus the essential function of art is, according to Nietzsche, to think and feel existence to that conclusion which convinces us of its perfection, "to create perfection and the fullness of life," to "*affirm, bless* and *deify* existence."

This is the perfect definition of Rilke's poetic project. It also marks the summit reached by art and poetry in its steep ascent to the heights of absolute creativeness. At this point the separation between art and reality appears to be complete. Reality is the death of the spirit and art its salvation. Where does truth reside? Is it in the deadly real world or in the saving vision of the artist? The question lingers on the all but imperceptible borderline between delusion and lunacy, between Nietzsche's madness and Rilke's prophetic pose, tenaciously maintained even beyond the confines of poetic inspiration. Nietzsche, believing that truth was insufferable and that poetry was an illusion, continually suspected that at least some of his thought was "merely poetry." Rilke, on the other hand, succeeded most of the time in convincing himself that the thought behind his poetry was the mind of truth. Illusion or truth, Superman or Angel, Will to Power or the Will to Inwardness—in both Nietzsche and Rilke the human mind and imagination are engaged in the ultimate task of creating a world to take the place of the spiritually useless productions of God.

"Indeed, the whole book acknowledges only an artist's meaning behind everything that happens—a 'god' if you like, but certainly only an artist-god . . . desirous of achieving his delight and sovereignty through making things and unmaking them . . . and who, in creating worlds, frees himself from the agony . . . of his inner conflicts. The world . . . seen as the successful salvation of god, as a vision . . . of one who suffers most, one who is the richest in conflicts and contradictions and can only save himself by creating illusion. . . . " The book in question is *The Birth of Tragedy*, thus described by Nietzsche himself in 1886, sixteen years after it was written. A critic could hardly do better in the case of *Duino Elegies* and *Sonnets to Orpheus*.

In January, 1889, Nietzsche, then in Turin, became clinically insane. On the fourth of that month the uncanniest of all calls to Orpheus was posted at the Turin railway station. The note was addressed to Nietzsche's friend, the composer Peter Gast. It ran: "To my maestro Pietro. Sing a new song for me: the world is transfigured and all the heavens rejoice." It was signed "The Crucified."

Sharing with each other the fruits of defeat, inflicted upon all besiegers of the Absolute in a world without Truth, thought ceases to be merely thought and poetry is no longer merely poetry. Song, trying to prove the glory, and thought, determined to dispel the illusion, are adventurers in the same heroic saga. It tells the story of one Tantalus who has deprived the gods of their seats at the banquet. Sitting all by himself at the divinely laid table, he cannot eat without letting them into his own secret: that he does not think well enough of himself to believe in the reality of his triumph. This is their curse, which he cannot escape. Intoxicated with their wine, he glories in their absence; but with the sobriety of his thought returning, he sees the water of life receding before the hollow of his outstretched hand.

It is the redeeming achievement of Nietzsche and Rilke that they have raised, the one in the intensely felt plight of his thought, the other in his intensely meditated poetry, the abysmal contradictions of their age to a plane where doubt and confusion once more dissolve into the certainty of mystery.

Tropes (Rilke)

Paul de Man

Rilke is one of the few poets of the twentieth century to have reached a large and worldwide audience. Even in France, where Yeats, Eliot, Wallace Stevens, Montale, Trakl, or Hofmannsthal are not widely known, Rilke is more read than most of the French poets of this century. More than fifty years after his death, a Rilke myth still lives well beyond the borders of the German-speaking world.

The reasons for this degree of public prominence are not obvious, for Rilke is not an easy or a popular poet. His work resists translation, his themes are intimate, and his discourse often oblique. Yet he has been received with a great deal of fervor, as if what he had to say was of direct concern even to readers remote from him in their language and in their destinies. Many have read him as if he addressed the most secluded parts of their selves, revealing depths they hardly suspected or allowing them to share in ordeals he helped them to understand and to overcome. Numerous biographies, reminiscences, and letters bear witness to this highly personal mode of reception. Rilke seems to be endowed with the healing power of those who open up access to the hidden layers of our consciousness or to a delicacy of emotion that reflects, to those capable of perceiving its shades, the reassuring image of their own solicitude. Rilke has himself often played on the ambiguity of a double-faced relationship toward others, leaving in abeyance which of the two, the poet or his reader, depended on the other to nourish his strength. "I wish to help and expect to be helped. Everyone's eternal mistake is to take me for a healer when, in fact, I am only attracting others, for my own profit, in the trap of a simulated assistance." Rilke confides this self-insight in connection with a love affair, but it summarizes a mood encouraged by some aspects of the work. The

From *Allegories of Reading*. © 1979 by Yale University. Yale University Press, 1979.

initial seduction, the first intimacy between Rilke and his readers almost inevitably occurs as an ambiguous complicity in shared confrontation with "the near-impossibility of living." Some passages of *Malte*, large fragments of the correspondence, the general tonality of *The Book of Hours*, or a somewhat hasty reading of the *Duino Elegies*—all orient the reading in that direction. This tendency, which Rilke did nothing to discourage, contributed much to the formation and the success of the personal myth. It also left extensive traces in Rilke studies: it is sometimes difficult to discover the memory of the original texts under the abundant confessional discourse that it generates in the commentators. Rilke's considerable audience is in part based on a relationship of complicity, on shared weaknesses.

It is not difficult, for a reader alerted to the ambivalences of the relationship between the self and its language, to demystify this seduction. The intersubjective reading grounded in a common sentiment, in the "transparency of the heart," does not allow one to reach the area of Rilke's poetry that is not affected by this demystification. In the case of this poet, readings that start out from the most self-directed passages in the letters, the novels, or the confessional texts fail to uncover the poetic dimension of the work. The reason for this is not the bad faith which Rilke confesses in the letter from which I have just quoted; his poetry does not escape from sympathetic understanding because, under the guise of being solicitous and disinterested, he does not hesitate, at times, to use others rather coldly. The mechanics of this bad faith would be easy to describe and, if they were indeed at the center of his consciousness, they would be an effective way of access to his inner being. But they are in fact peripheral and secondary. It has not been difficult to call into question the image of Rilke as a healer of soul and to prove that he was both less generous in practical and less stable in psychological matters than one might have suspected. Rilke's intimate self remains in fact quite invisible and, far from being its driving force, it tends to vanish from the poetry altogether—which does not mean that this poetry is deprived of a certain mode of inwardness that remains to be defined. But the poet Rilke is less interested in his own person than one might gather from his tone and from his pathos. The narcissism that is often ascribed to him no doubt exists, but on a very different level from that of a reader using him as a reflector for his own inner image. The personal seduction is certainly an important component of the work, but it functions, so to speak, as its zone of maximal opacity. One could approach and interpret a sizeable part of his poetry by way of the negative road that would analyze this seduction. It may be preferable however to try to understand the work in a less antithetical way and to read the poetic texts themselves, rather than letters and confessional prose that may well turn out to be of contingent importance.

On a somewhat more advanced level of understanding, the attractiveness of Rilke stems from his themes. This is obvious, first of all, in the most superficial of ways: the poetry puts on display a brilliant variety of

places, objects, and characters. As in Baudelaire, the categories of the beautiful and the ugly are subsumed, in Rilke, under the common rubric of the
interesting. His poetic universe has something dazzling, as if it consisted
of rare items in a collection or a museum, well set off against the background
of a world that emphasizes their singularity. Repugnant and terrifying
themes have the same seductive power as the numberless objects of beauty
and of light—fountains, toys, cathedrals, cities of Spain and Italy, roses,
windows, orchards—that appear throughout the work. A form of poetic
decorum, itself a mixture of caution and of genuine reserve, holds the
violent images at a distance and prevents them from acquiring a presence
strong enough to undo the fiction or to dislocate the language. No matter
which of the uncanny figures one singles out, be it the epileptic in *Malte*,
the stylite of the *New Poems*, or the sinister acrobats of the Fifth Elegy, one
will always encounter this picturesque and surprising element mixed with
the horror and interposing, between the reader and the theme, the screen
of a language that controls its own representational mastery. Even in what
appears to be Rilke's most personal poem, the poem written a few days
before his death and dealing with his physical pain, the pain remains "em-
bellished" by the virtuosity of a perfectly prepared and executed conceit.

It would be a mistake to dismiss this concern for attractive surfaces all
too hastily as a form of aestheticism. The reference to Baudelaire should
suffice to stress that more is involved. Aesthetic refinement is for Rilke, as
for the author of the *Fleurs du mal*, an Apollonian strategy which allows
him to state what would otherwise be unsayable. On this level of experience, the aesthetics of beauty and of ugliness can no longer be distinguished
from each other. Nor is it possible to think of these seductive surfaces as
merely superficial.

For the thematic attraction also functions on a more generally inclusive
level of understanding. Beyond the brightness of the settings, Rilke's work
dares to affirm and to promise, as few others do, a form of existential
salvation that would take place in and by means of poetry. Few poets and
thinkers of our century have dared to go so far in their affirmations, especially in affirmations that refuse to be anchored in established philosophical or theological certainties, or to have recourse to ethical imperatives
that might directly lead to modes of action. It may seem surprising to
characterize Rilke's work as positive and affirmative when it puts such stress
on the main negative themes of modern consciousness. Rilke has an acute
awareness of the alienated and factitious character of human reality, and
he goes far in his refusal to grant any experience the power to suspend
this alienation. Neither love nor the imagining power of the deepest nos-
talgias can overcome the essential barrenness of the self and of the world.
Severed forever from the plenitudes of self-presence, Rilke's figure of humanity is the frailest and most exposed creature imaginable. He calls man
"the most ephemeral" (Ninth Elegy), "the most fleeting" (Fifth Elegy), the
creature "that is incessantly departing" (Eighth Elegy), and that can never

establish itself in an appeased presence to itself or to the world. The promise that the work contains is therefore anything but facile. But this makes it all the more convincing.

On the thematic level, the existence of this promise is undeniable. The large affirmations of the *Elegies*, gnomic as they are, bear witness to this assertion, all the more so since they promise a salvation that could take place here and now: "Hiersein ist herrlich" ("To be here is glorious" [Seventh Elegy]); "*Hier* ist des *Säglichen* Zeit, *hier* seine Heimat" ("*Here* is the time for the *Tellable, here* is its home" [Ninth Elegy]); "Supernumerous existence / wells up in my heart" (idem). This emphatic *here* designates the poetic text itself and thus affirms that it escapes the fragmentation of number and of time. In the audacity of his assertion, Rilke assumes for poetry the furthest-reaching promise conceivable. The evolution of his own poetry seems to fulfill this promise. After being announced in the *Elegies*, it comes about in the appeased tonality of the later work, the *Sonnets to Orpheus*, and many of the poems written after 1912 and published posthumously. It can be said of these poems that they perform the transition from elegy to hymn, from complaint (*Klage*) to praise (*Rühmen*).

One can understand therefore that Rilke not only claims the right to state his own salvation but to impose it, as it were, on others. The imperative mode that often appears in his poetry ("You must change your life"; "Demand change"; "Sing the world to the Angel" . . .) is not only addressed to himself but asks for the acquiescence of his reader. The exhortation is rooted in an authority confirmed by the possibility of its poetic existence. Far from putting this assurance in jeopardy, the insistence of the negative themes certifies its veracity. A too easily granted promise would be suspect and would not convince, but a promise of salvation that could only be deserved by endless labor and sacrifice, in suffering, renunciation, and death, is a different matter. One can begin to understand Rilke's poetry only if one is willing to entertain this conviction. As for deciding whether it is a legitimate promise, whether it is a truth or a seduction, the question must remain open, not only as a matter of caution but because a rigorous reading must determine whether or not the work itself asks this question.

The interpreters who read Rilke's work as a radical summons to transform our way of being in the world are therefore not misrepresenting him; such a summons is indeed a central theme of the poetry. Some respond to it without reservations. Others have suggested that Rilke is still in the grip of ontological presuppositions which even the most extreme of his experiences cannot reach and that the reversal he demands, difficult as it may be, is still premature and illusory. Rilke's good faith is not being questioned, but his blindness could be demonstrated by the critical analysis of his thought. Heidegger had oriented the reading of Rilke in this direction, in an essay published in 1949 which Rilkean studies have not yet entirely assimilated. But it may be that the positivity of the thematic assertion is not entirely unambiguous and that Rilke's language, almost in spite of its own assertions, puts it in question.

This does not, at first sight, seem to be the case. The advanced level of reflexive self-knowledge that informs Rilke's poetry nowhere conflicts with the mastery of his poetic invention. The meaning of the statement dovetails perfectly with the mode of expression, and since this meaning possesses considerable philosophical depth, poetry and thought here seem to be united in a perfect synthesis.

For that reason, even the best interpretations of Rilke seem to have remained, by and large, on the level of paraphrase, a paraphrase that is often subtle and careful but that does not question the convergence of the meaning with the linguistic devices used to convey it. The statements are rich enough in their content to saturate the full range of meaning. The fact that these highly reflected statements directly implicate language as a con- stitutive category of meaning and thematize some of the lexicological and rhetorical aspects of poetical diction by no means troubles the assumed convergence between statement and *lexis*, between what is being said and the mode of its saying. Rilke's propositions about language are in fact carried out in his poetry, thus allowing one to move freely between poetry and poetics. The possibility of a conflict between both never seems to arise. Thus one of Rilke's commentators can write: "The poetic 'content' and the poetic 'form' are so perfectly united in Rilke's work that it becomes im- possible to object against the value of this poetry in the name of a possible divergence between 'thought' and 'poetry' " [Hermann Mörchen]. Such a divergence is inconceivable because Rilke is claimed to state, in and through his poetry, the very essence of poetry as the truth of this essence. "The true essence of poetry . . . is identical with the structures of its poetic 'content.' " In the author from whom we borrow these formulations, this truth is equated with an existential decision that does not necesarily involve language. But the existential stance must eventually lead to decisions that function on the level of the language, even if these decisions appear to be of secondary importance. The same commentator is naturally led to con- sider formal aspects of the poetry, such as rhyme or metaphor, but he at once curbs their potential autonomy by fully identifying them with the theme they convey: "The fundamental poetic practice, namely the elabo- ration of a metaphorical language, also derives from the experience of suf- fering. The metaphor is an act of identification: the actual suffering of the poet is made 'equal' with that of his symbolic figures." The ontological alienation that Rilke so eloquently evokes would then not implicate lan- guage in any way. Language is the unmediated expression of an unhappy consciousness that it does not cause. This implies that language is entirely ancillary in its relation to a fundamental experience (the pain and the pathos of being) which it merely reflects, but that it is also entirely truthful, since it faithfully reproduces the truth of this pathos. The poet can thus abandon himself without fear to his language, even to its most formal and outward features:

> The logic of sounds [*Lautlogik*] to which the poet yields when he allows himself to be governed by the power of his language can be meaningful only when it stands in the service of the truth which this language uses in order to conserve it. Poetry can be truth only when its trust in language—a trust that is not confined to acoustic affinities but that includes linguistic structures in general, including etymological relationships—is indeed attuned to this justification of existence which language, in the region of its authentic origin, is always in the process of formulating.
>
> [Hermann Mörchen]

With very few exceptions, similar presuppositions underlie the best available critical readings of Rilke. One may well ask whether the poetry indeed shares in the conception of language that is attributed to it. Such a question differs entirely from a concentration on the "form" of Rilke's poetry, in the narrowly aesthetic sense of the term; several careful studies have taken this approach but failed to reach major exegetic results. By suggesting that the properly poetic dimension of Rilke's work has been neglected in favor of his themes, we do not wish to return to the seduction of the forms. The question is rather whether Rilke's text turns back upon itself in a manner that puts the authority of its own affirmations in doubt, especially when these affirmations refer to the modes of writing that it advocates. At a time when the philosophical interest of Rilke's thought has perhaps somewhat declined, the present and future signification of his poetry depends upon the answer to this question.

Rilke's work is often said to be divided by a clear break that corresponds approximately to the passage from *The Book of Hours* to *The Book of Images*; it is also from this moment on that a degree of mastery is achieved and that his manner reaches a certain stability. The break marks an important modification in the metaphorical and dramatic texture of the poetry. The more properly phonic elements are less affected by it. Before and after this date, Rilke persists in giving considerable importance to rhyme, assonance, and alliteration; in this respect, one can hardly speak of a major change, except for a greater degree of refinement and control in the expressive use of acoustic effects of language.

It is not easy to interpret this change. Commentators agree neither on the meaning nor on the evaluation of *The Book of Hours*, and they have difficulty locating it within the corpus of the complete work. Certain characteristics of the situation and of the tone (a prayer addressed to a transcendental entity) seem to prefigure the *Duino Elegies*; the volume also contains the first mention of symbolic objects and privileged words which will later acquire a central importance, whereas many of the other themes of *The Book of Hours* disappear from the later work. The fervor with which the poems address a power that is given the name of "God" raises the question of their theocentric structure, a question that never stops haunting the exegesis of Rilke without, however, receiving a satisfactory answer. Like iron filings under the power of a magnet, the verbal mass turns towards a single object that causes the eclosion of an abundant poetic discourse. The following poem, a typical instance of Rilke's poetry at this time, can both give us some notion of this discourse and serve as an introduction to the general problematics of the work. Since we have to allude to sound elements that cannot be translated, I quote in German:

> Ich liebe dich, du sanftestes Gesetz,
> an dem wir reiften, da wir mit ihm rangen
> du grosses Heimweh, das wir nicht bezwangen,
> du Wald, aus dem wir nie hinausgegangen,
> du Lied, das wir mit jedem Schweigen sangen,
> du dunkles Netz,
> darin sich flüchtend die Gefühle fangen.
>
> Du hast dich so unendlich gross begonnen
> an jenem Tage, da du uns begannst,—
> und wir sind so gereift in deinen Sonnen,
> so breit geworden und so tief gepflanzt,
> dass du in Menschen, Engeln und Madonnen
> dich ruhend jetzt vollenden kannst.
>
> Lass deine Hand am Hang der Himmel ruhn
> und dulde stumm, was wir dir dunkel tun.
>
>   (1:24)

(I love you, gentlest law, through which we yet
were ripening while with it we contended,
you great homesickness we have not transcended,
you forest out of which we never wended,
you song that from our silence has ascended,
you somber net
where feelings taking flight are apprehended.

You made yourself a so immense beginning
the day when you began us too,—and we
beneath your suns such ripeness have been winning
have grown so broadly and deep-rootedly,
that you, in angels, men, madonnas inning,
can now complete yourself quite tranquilly.

Let your right hand on heaven's slope repose
and mutely bear what darkly we impose.)
                                          (trans. J. B. Leishman)

By its setting, which follows the convention of the ode as a series of reiterated apostrophes that are as many metaphors, the poem indeed seems to be fully centered on the entity it attempts to name. But the periphrastic designation is so diverse that it becomes vague: the entity is addressed as "law," "homesickness," "forest," "song," and "net," a sequence that cannot easily be reduced to a common denominator. Moreover, the entity is never itself designated by one of the attributes that properly belong to it. The play of personal pronouns is balanced between "I" (or "we") and "you," thus establishing a nearly perfect symmetry from which the third person is practically excluded; after the "ihm" in the second line, the "ich/ du" or "du/wir" pattern is close to perfect. The object of the apostrophe is only addressed in terms of an activity that it provokes in the addressing subject: if it is said to be a forest, it is only with reference to our behavior towards this forest; the net exists only as an obstacle to *our* flight; law is, per definition, that which governs our behavior and the song is at once identified as *our* song (or silence). The metaphors therefore do not connote objects, sensations, or qualities of objects (there is practically no third person in the grammar of the poem), but refer to an activity of the speaking subject. The dominating center, the "du" of the poem, is present in the poem only to delegate, so to speak, its potential activity to the speaking voice; this becomes the explicit theme of the poem in the two concluding lines. The purpose of the text is not to reunite the two separate entities but to evoke a specific activity that circulates between them.

The poem does not mention this activity by name. It states instead, in its final sentence, that it must remain obscure and invisible: "dunkel tun." That it is called a fulfillment (*Vollendung*) and that the will of the "du" is said to be accomplished by this act does not allow for its definition but repeats in fact the relationship of immanence between the two "persons" that is being staged in the text. A more implicit reading permits however some further specification. The beginning of the poem indicates that the activity in question is first perceived as a constraint and provokes the vain attempts to escape from its power. This is being openly stated in the first two lines and more suggestively evoked in the two following ones: the homesickness is oppressive, but we cannot evade it; there can be no escape from the forest that surrounds us; silence itself cannot prevent us from singing. The sequence culminates in the figure of the net: feelings that try to escape into forgetting or into indetermination are imprisoned and coerced, by this activity, to remain present to us.

But the constraint changes to acquiescence. In the second stanza, the relationship between the "I" and the "you," instead of being paradoxical and dialectical as in the first section, blossoms out in the luminous image of the tree. The promise of the beginning fulfills itself as naturally and harmoniously as the ripening of fruit in the sunshine. The transformation designates the acquisition of a greater mastery in the activity that the poem symbolizes. This mastery is thematically asserted in the reversal that has taken place between the beginning and the end of the poem: the subject that was at first compelled to obey can now act in full freedom and can conform its will to that of the "law." The central will of the poem has been transformed from constraint into a benevolent sun, with only the repetition of the word "dark" ("dunkles Netz," "dunkel tun") as a reminder of the original violence. Besides, the mention of "hand" in the next-to-last line strengthens the impression that we are dealing with an action involving skills that the initially reluctant student now fully masters.

The proof of this mastery can only be hidden in the text. The relationship between the two subjects or grammatical "persons" is so tight that it leaves no room for any other system of relationships. It is their interlacing that constitutes the text. There is therefore nothing in the poem that would entitle us to escape beyond its boundaries in search of evidence that would not be part of it: the freedom that is affirmed at the end is precisely a freedom within bondage that can prevail only because it is tolerated by the authority of the power which allows it to exist. It remains subjected to the single authority, to the single achievement, of the text.

This achievement, however, is primarily phonic in kind. The last stanza, in which the mastery is asserted, is also the one in which effects of euphony reach their highest point of elaboration. The poem comes to rest in the lines

> Lass deine Hand am Hang der Himmel ruhn
> und dulde stumm, was wir dir dunkel tun.

It can easily be verified that, in this last line of verse, there appears rigorously no syllable that does not fulfill an effect of euphony. The main rhymes and assonances ("dulde stumm," "wir dir," "dunkel tun") are interconnected by syllables that are themselves assonant ("und dulde") or alliterated ("was wir") and thus enclose each sound-effect into another, as a larger box can enclose in its turn a smaller one. The mastery of the poem consists in its control over the phonic dimensions of language. A reading of the other poems in *The Book of Monastic Life* confirms this conclusion. The "God" that the poems circumscribe by a multitude of metaphors and changing stances corresponds to the ease that the poet has achieved in his techniques of rhyme and of assonance. It is well known that these poems were written very quickly in a kind of euphoria which Rilke will remember when, more than twenty years later, he will write the *Sonnets to Orpheus*; what the poems celebrate is primarily this euphoria. The metaphors connote in fact a formal potential of the signifier. The referent of the poem is an attribute of their language, in itself devoid of semantic depth; the meaning of the poems is the conquest of the technical skills which they illustrate by their acoustic success.

It may seem preposterous to associate such a near-mechanical procedure with the name of God. Yet, the apparent blasphemy can just as well be considered as the hyperbole of an absolute phonocentrism. A poem of *The Book of Monastic Life* (1:20) asserts the possibility of overcoming death itself by means of euphony, and it fulfills this prophecy in its own texture,

in the "dark interval" (*im dunklen Intervall*) that in its assonance both separates and unites the two words "Tod" (death) and "Ton" (sound). Once
we succeed in hearing the song hidden in language, it will conduct us by
itself to the reconciliation of time and existence. This is indeed the extrav-
agant claim made by these poems when they pretend to designate God by
means of a medium which deprives itself of all resources except those of
sound. Possibilities of representation and of expression are eliminated in
an askesis which tolerates no other referent than the formal attributes of
the vehicle. Since sound is the only property of language that is truly
immanent to it and that bears no relation to anything that would be situated
outside language itself, it will remain as the only available resource. The
Cratylic illusion, which is held by some to constitute the essence of poetry
and which subordinates the semantic function of language to the phonic
one, is doubtlessly at work in *The Book of Monastic Life*. In a manner that is
not yet entirely convincing, this early volume already partakes of the Orphic
myth.

In these texts, in which a measure of technical mastery alternates with
moments of clumsiness, the failure of the claim is as evident as is its presence. In order to give a coherent framework to the sequence of poems,
Rilke is forced to substitute a subject that tells the story of its experience
for the unmediated beauty of the poetic sound. The poems thus acquire a
meaning that does not entirely coincide with their actual intent. They introduce an autonomous subject that moves in the forefront and reduces
the euphony to the function of ornament. In the first version of *The Book
of Monastic Life*, this impression was still heightened by the brief narrative
sections inserted between the poems, like a journal commenting upon the
daily progress of the poet's work. The fact that Rilke was obliged to invent
a fictional character, a monk surrounded by his ritualistic paraphernalia,
well illustrates his inability, at that time, to dispense with the conventional
props of poetic narration. And since the subject is confined to being an
artisan of euphony, it has only a rather thin story to tell. In the two subsequent volumes of *The Book of Hours*, especially in *The Book of Poverty and
of Death*, Rilke abandons the claim to a self-referential diction and returns
to the direct expression of his own subjectivity. The texts lose most of their
formal rigor and acquire the obvious interest of a self-narrating sensibility.
These poems are easy of access and often moving, but measured by Rilke's
final and initial ambition they represent the least exalted moment of his
poetic production. It will take the long labors of *Malte* and of *The New Poems*
to reconquer the impersonality that was proclaimed and lost in *The Book of
Monastic Life*.

While he was writing *The Book of Hours*, Rilke was also working at a
very different kind of poem that would find a place in *The Book of Images*,
itself a work of transition leading up to the masterful *New Poems*. The
development that takes place in these texts is decisive for the entire mature
work. It can be described by the reading of one of the poems characteristic of this period. The poem entitled "Am Rande der Nacht" ("At the

Borderline of the Night") is a somewhat arbitrarily chosen but typical instance:

> Meine Stube und diese Weite,
> wach über nachtendem Land,—
> ist Eines. Ich bin eine Saite,
> über rauschende breite
> Resonanzen gespannt.
>
> Die Dinge sind Geigenleiber,
> von murrendem Dunkel voll;
> drin träumt das Weinen der Weiber,
> drin rührt sich im Schlafe der Groll
> ganzer Geschlechter . . .
> Ich soll
> silbern erzittern: dann wird
> Alles unter mir leben,
> und was in den Dingen irrt,
> wird nach dem Lichte streben,
> das von meinem tanzenden Tone,
> um welchen der Himmel wellt,
> durch schmale, schmachtende Spalten
> in die alten
> Abgründe ohne
> Ende fällt . . .
>
> (1:156)

> (My room and this wide space
> watching over the night of the land—
> are one. I am a string
> strung over wide, roaring resonances.
>
> Things are hollow violins
> full of a groaning dark;
> the laments of women
> the ire of generations
> dream and toss within . . .
> I must tremble
> and sing like silver: then
> All will live under me,
> and what errs in things
> will strive for the light
> that, from my dancing song,
> under the curve of the sky
> through languishing narrow clefts
> falls
> in the ancient depths
> without end . . .)

Instead of being caught in the "somber net" of a pseudo-dialectic between pseudo-subjects, we are at once within a much more familiar poetic landscape. From the beginning, the poem announces itself as naming the unity, the complementarity of an inside/outside polarity: the inner seclusion of the "room" (which introduces a subject by the possessive of "my" room) and the infinitely wide expanse of the night outside. They are decreed to be *one* by categorical assertion, as if this unity were the sudden revelation of a single moment, a specific accord between the self of the poet and the world that surrounds him. But the poem does not remain within the instantaneous stasis of this accord. The initial oneness undergoes a transformation announced in lines 11 and 12: "Ich soll / silbern erzittern." This event triggers a transformation which is experienced as a movement of expansion. It is no longer the static unity of inside and outside that is being asserted, but the metamorphosis of an oppressive and constraining inwardness into a liberating outside world. The positive valorization of the movement is marked by the ascending motion of darkness towards light: ". . . was in den Dingen irrt, / wird nach dem Lichte streben." Upon the synchronic axis of an inside/outside polarity is juxtaposed a dynamic axis which transforms the inside/outside opposition into a successive polarity of the type night/day.

For a reader accustomed to Romantic and post-Romantic poetry, this type of poem is most familiar, both by what it asserts and by the antithetical couples that it sets into play. It tries to evoke and accomplish the synthesis, the unity of a consciousness and of its objects, by means of an expressive act, directed from inside to outside, which fulfills and seals this unity. The subject/object polarity, which remained vague and ambivalent at the beginning, is clearly designated when the poem explicitly confronts the subject, no longer with the indefinite immensity of the first line, but with the objects, the particular things that are contained in this wide space. The unity, which was only asserted as *a priori* at the start, actually occurs before our eyes when the subject, claiming to be the string of a violin, meets and adapts itself perfectly to objects which, in a metaphor that is truly Rilkean in its seductive audacity, are said to be the "body" of this same violin, "Geigenleiber." The totality of the One thus consists of a perfect complementarity: without the sounding board of the violin, the string is devoid of value, but it suffices to bring them together to make the "somber and deep unity" of the world vibrate and shine. Everything seems to confirm that this poem can be considered a later version of the "correspondence" between the inwardness of the subject and the outside world. The exteriority is further confirmed by the assimilation of the sky's immensity, in the first line, to a thing; it is indeed the resonance of its space ("Ich bin eine Saite, / über rauschende breite Resonanzen gespannt") which is transformed in the musical *body* of things ("Die Dinge sind Geigenleiber"). The poem is an example of the most classical of metaphors, conceived as a transfer from an inside to an outside space (or vice versa) by means of an analogical representation. This transfer then reveals a totalizing oneness that was originally hidden but which is fully revealed as soon as it is named and maintained in the figural language. One could stop here, and confine oneself to the discovery of further analogical parallels (such as the convergence of the spatial with the musical theme by way of an erotic connotation—since the body of the violin is that of a woman as well) and especially by stressing the perfect coalescence of the metaphorical narration with the sound-pattern of the poem. The moment of synthesis corresponds exactly to the modulation of the assonances from the ī sound (ten times repeated in the first eight lines) to the ĕ sound (ten times repeated in the four last ones). One should also draw attention to the detailed precision in Rilke's selection of metaphorical analogons.

But if one allows oneself to be guided by the rigorous representational logic of the metaphors, whose clarity of outline indeed distinguishes a poem like this one from those of *The Book of Hours*, then one should follow their guidance to the end. For Rilke's singularity becomes manifest in a displacement that distorts the habitual relationship between theme and figure. The pattern we have just schematized does not appear quite in this shape in the text. The inwardness that should belong, per definition, to the subject is located instead within things. Instead of being opaque and full, things are hollow and contain, as in a box, the dark mass of sentiments and of history. The interiority of the speaking subject is not actively engaged; whatever pathos is mentioned refers to the suffering of others: the woes of women, the ire of historical generations. By a curious reversal, this subjectivity is invested from the start, before the figural transfer has taken place, in objects and in things. This subjective experience is said to be dark to the extent that it is unable, by itself, to find expression; it exists in a condition of error and of blindness ("was in den Dingen irrt") until the subject, the "I" of the poem, confers upon it the clarity of entities that are available to the senses by giving it the attribute of voice. The usual structure has been reversed: the outside of things has become internalized and it is the subject that enables them access to a certain form of exteriority. The "I" of the poem contributes nothing of its own experience, sensations, sufferings, or consciousness. The initial model of the scene is not, as one might think at first, that of an autonomous subject confronting nature or objects, as is the case, for example, in Baudelaire's poem "l'Homme et la mer." The assimilation of the subject to space (as the string of a violin) does not really occur as the result of an analogical exchange, but by a radical appropriation which in fact implies the loss, the disappearance of the subject as subject. It loses the individuality of a particular voice by becoming neither more nor less than the voice of things, as if the central point of view had been displaced into outer things from the self. By the same token, these outer things lose their solidity and become as empty and as vulnerable as we are ourselves. Yet, this loss of the subject's autonomy and of the resilience of the natural world is treated as if it were a positive event, as a passage from darkness to light. It would be mistaken to interpret this light as the clarity of a self-knowledge. In the logic of the figure, it is nothing of the sort: the light is the transformation of a condition of confusion and of nonawareness (dream, sleep, erring) in the sound-version of this same, unchanged condition. The figure is a metaphor of a becoming-sound, not of a becoming-conscious. The title, "At the Borderline of the Night," should not be read as the dawn of a new lucidity but rather as a persistent condition of confusion and dispersion from which there is no escape. The end of the poem confirms this reading: the rising light turns out to be a fall in "the ancient/depth without/end . . ."of the night. The totalization takes place by a return to the emptiness and the lack of identity that resides in the heart of things. The unity affirmed at the beginning of "Am Rande der Nacht" is a negative unity which deprives the self of any illusion of self-insight. By becoming a musical string, the self partakes forever in the erring of things. Yet, it gives voice to this errancy.

This reversal of the figural order, itself the figure of chiasmus that crosses the attributes of inside and outside and leads to the annihilation of the conscious subject, bends the themes and the rhetoric from their apparently traditional mode towards a specifically Rilkean one. It is difficult to comprehend this reversal on the level of the themes. The notion of objects as containers of a subjectivity which is not that of the self that considers them is incomprehensible as long as one tries to understand it from the perspective of the subject. Instead of conceiving of the poem's rhetoric as the instrument of the subject, of the object, or of the relationship between them, it is preferable to reverse the perspective and to conceive of these categories as standing in the service of the language that has produced them. The metaphor of the violin fits the dramatic action of the text so perfectly and the image seems so flawlessly right because its external structure (box, string, cleft that produces and liberates the sound) triggers and orders the entire figural play that articulates the poem. The metaphorical entity is not selected because it corresponds analogically to the inner experience of a subject but because its structure corresponds to that of a linguistic figure: the violin is *like* a metaphor because it transforms an interior content into an outward, sonorous "thing." The openings in the box (so fittingly shaped like the algorithm of the integral calculus of totalization) correspond precisely to the outside-directed turn that occurs in all metaphorical representations. The musical instrument does not represent the subjectivity of a consciousness but a potential inherent in language; it is the metaphor of a metaphor. What appears to be the inwardness of things, the hollow inside of the box, is not a substantial analogy between the self and world of things but a formal and structural analogy between these things and the figural resources of words. The coming into being of metaphor corresponds point by point to the apparent description of the object. But it is not surprising that, in evoking the details of the metaphorical instrument or vehicle (the perfect fit of the string to the box, the openings in the sounding-board, etc.), the metaphor comes into being before our eyes, since the object has been chosen exactly for this purpose. The correspondence does not confirm a hidden unity that exists in the nature of things and of entities; it is rather like the seamless encasement of the pieces in a puzzle. Perfect adjustment can take place only because the totality was established beforehand and in an entirely formal manner.

The poem "Am Rande der Nacht" still disguises this strategy by simulating the birth of metaphor as the confirmation and the proof of the unity apodictically announced at the beginning of the text. But a careful reading can reveal the stratagem without having recourse to outside information. The poem, which first appeared to be a confrontation between man and nature, is in fact the simulacrum of a description in which the structure of the described object is that of a figural potential of language. Moreover, one should not forget that the metaphor of the metaphor is represented as an acoustical process: the metaphorical object is, literally, a musical instrument. The perfect encasing of the figures makes language sing like a violin. The priority of the phonic element that was stressed with regard to *The Book of Monastic Life* has not been abandoned. Not only is it audible in the parallel between the symbolic action and the euphony of the assonances, but it extends to the play of figuration. *The Book of Images* is not less "phonocentric" than *The Book of Hours*—far from it, since now the imperatives of euphony govern not only the choice of words but the choice of figures as well.

The linguistic strategy of this still relatively early poem (which has several equivalences among the other texts that make up *The Book of Images*) will dominate the work until the end. The determining figure of Rilke's poetry is that of chiasmus, the crossing that reverses the attributes of words and of things. The poems are composed of entities, objects and subjects, who themselves behave like words, which "play" at language according to the rules of rhetoric as one plays ball according to the rules of the game. "Am Rande der Nacht" is particularly revealing because it still makes use of the classical schema of a subject/object dialectic. The linguistic character of one of the poles involved in the inversion is therefore relatively easy to perceive, whereas it will often be hidden in the later work. At the same time, the almost programmatic tonality of the poem, the unity first asserted and then "demonstrated" by the transformations of the figures, will also disappear. In the *New Poems* (*Neue Gedichte*) the same poem would have been constructed differently. It might have been called "The Violin"; the two first lines would in all probability have been replaced by a description that reverses the "real" schema of events: instead of being the result of their union, it might have been music itself that brought the string and the violin in contact with each other. A poem like the following, the entrance text to *The Book of Images* ("Eingang," 1:127), clearly indicates the structure of the reversal. In the evocation of what could be called an abridged landscape, the reversal appears in the fact that the eyes of the person who is being addressed constitute a world of objects, instead of the objects directing their glance:

> Mit deinen Augen . . .
> hebst du ganz langsam einen schwarzen Baum
> und stellst ihn vor den Himmel: schlank, allein.
> Und hast die Welt gemacht.

> (With your eyes . . .
> You slowly lift up a black tree
> and stand it, thin, alone, before the sky.
> You made the world.)

The world which is thus created is then explicitly designated as a verbal world. Contact with this world is comparable to the discovery of meaning in an interpretation, and the interpretation engenders the text by appearing to describe the object:

> Und hast die Welt gemacht. Und sie ist gross
> und wie ein Wort, das noch im Schweigen reift.
> Und wie dein Wille ihren Sinn begreift,
> lassen sie deine Augen zärtlich los . . .

> (You made the world. And it is wide
> and like a word that ripens still in quiet.
> And once you vouch to understand their sense
> They'll gently let your eyes go free . . .)

But this poem is something of an exception. In the vast majority of the *New Poems*, only the structure of reversal is maintained, and its orientation towards the pole of language remains implicit. This remark gives access to the dominant pattern of the mature work, but it also implies the possibility of a misreading which will become an integral part of the poetry till well into its latest developments.

By showing the prevalence, in the *New Poems*, of this reversal, one can also isolate the poles around which the rotation of the chiasma takes place. As is clear from the titles of the individual poems that make up the *New Poems*, they are often centered on natural or man-made objects. When they describe personages or settings, they have often been so caught in a stylized perception that they have become like icons, emblems of a feeling or of a destiny as sharply circumscribed as are the properties of things. It soon appears that all these objects share a similar fundamental structure: they are conceived in such a way as to allow a reversal of their categorical properties, and this reversal enables the reader to conceive of properties that would normally be incompatible (such as inside/outside, before/after, death/life, fiction/reality, silence/sound) as complementary. They engender an entity, like the violin and the string of "Am Rande der Nacht," which is also a closed totality. If we question why such or such an object inscribed in the *New Poems* has compellingly attracted Rilke's attention (or why he deliberately selected it), the answer will always be that it forced itself upon him because its attributes allow for such a reversal and for such an (apparent) totalization.

A particularly clear and concrete instance of such a structural reversal would be, for example, the specular reflection. The poem "Quai du Rosaire" (1:290) is a fine case in point. Taking advantage of a light effect at dusk, Rilke can, without seeming to be fantastic, decree that the upside-down world that is reflected in the still water of the canals is more substantial and more real than the ordinary world of the day:

> das abendklare Wasser . . .
>
> darin . . .
> die eingehängte Welt von Spiegelbildern
> so wirklich wird wie diese Dinge nie.

> (the clear evening water . . .
> in which . . .
> the suspended world of mirrored images
> becomes more real than things ever were.)

The description of the details of this upside-down city, although it maintains the realism of the local color (Estaminets, line 16) one expects in a poem that is also like a postcard, thus acquires a somewhat uncanny and as it were surreal character. The reversal of the attribute of reality (the text stresses indeed reality, "Wirklich[keit]") was prepared from the first part on. In an apparent personification, which is in fact a prosopopoeia based on the language-embedded idiom according to which, in German as in English, streets are said to "go" from here to there, the auxiliary condition for an action (the streets, auxiliary device for the action of going) becomes the agent of this same action. The slight note of absurdity sounded in the first evocation of the walking streets ("Die Gassen haben einen sachten Gang / . . . und die an Plätze kommen, warten lang / auf eine andre, die mit einem Schritt / über das abendklare Wasser tritt . . .") ("The streets go with a gentle walk / . . . and when they reach the squares they wait / forever for another which, in one sole step / crosses the clear evening water . . .") prefigures the reversal of the reflection which might otherwise seem too brusque or artificial.

The surreality is not limited to the reflected world. We saw that the reversal acquires poetic value only when it leads to a new totalization; this is why, after having traversed the surface of the looking glass and entered the reflected world, the poem has to return, in the last stanza, to the real world "above." By the same token, the temporal nature of an event that, up till then, was described in spatial and ocular terms, becomes manifest. The blurring of the outlines, which at first seems to be due entirely to the play of light and shadow, takes on a temporal dimension when one remembers that the poem is about "Brugge," "Bruges la morte" as it is called by the poet Georges Rodenbach, a city that used to be prestigious but has become, by the loss of its natural harbor and medieval glory, an emblem for the transience of human achievement, a figure of mutability. The question that introduced the temporal dimension, "Verging nicht diese Stadt?" ("Did not this city perish?"), a question reiterated in line 17: "Und oben blieb?" ("And what remained above?"), is answered at the end: the real world "above" has not been entirely dissolved in the reflection of things past, since the final perception (the bells of the carillon) reach us from above. But this reality is then no longer solidly anchored on the ground. The reflection has emptied it out; its illusory stability has been replaced by the surreal irreality of the mirror image. The descent in the underworld of the mirror uplifts the real and suspends it in the sky, like a constellation. The final totalization takes place within this constellation, which could not have come about without the passage through the fiction of the specular world.

This new totality is itself temporal in kind: the sound of the carillon, the real totality *that remains*, also has for its function to measure the passage of time. By thinking of Brugge no longer as a stable reality but as the figure of temporal loss and erosion, the reality lost in the everyday world of unreflected surfaces is recovered: the live Brugge is much less "real" than "Bruges la morte." Finally, the temporal constellation that functions as a resolution manifests itself, in the last analysis, as *sound*. Perceived in the truth of its mutability, time becomes an audible reality.

This experience of time is highly paradoxical. It acquiesces to all that ordinarily appears as the opposite of permanence and of duration. The affirmation is retained in the seductive but funereal image of a temporal annihilation which is enjoyed as if it were a sensuous pleasure, "der Süssen Traube/des Glockenspiels" ("The sweetened cluster of grapes/of the carillon"), which actually is the death knell that reduced the city to a ghostly memory. Similarly, the sound of this new temporality will have all the attributes of its opposite: at the end of the poem, a new chiasmus crosses the attributes of silence and of sound and designates the sound of the carillon by the properties of silence:

> Und oben blieb?—Die Stille nur, ich glaube,
> und kostet langsam und von nichts gedrängt
> Beere um Beere aus der süssen Traube
> des Glockenspiels, das in den Himmeln hängt.

> (And what remained above?—Only silence, I believe,
> which tastes slowly and unhurriedly
> grape by grape the sweetened cluster
> of the carillon, suspended in the skies.)

The evocation of Brugge as the image of mutability is in itself banal; if it were to be reduced to this theme alone, the poem would be of minor interest. The recovery of duration by means of the subject's acquiescence to the temporal erosion that threatens it is more challenging: it combines the audacity of a paradox with a promise of beauty or even, in the image of the grapes, of sensuous gratification on the far side of the grave. Yet the true interest of the poem does not stem from these thematic statements, but rather from the intricacy and the wealth of movements triggered by the original chiasmus. The crossing of the categories of reality and of specular reflection articulates a sequence of similarly structured reversals: reversal of agent and instrument, of ascent and descent, of inside and outside, of loss and recuperation, death and life, time and sound, sound and silence. A great deal of rhetorical agitation is contained in a brief poetic text which also has the innocent appearance of a picturesque description, of a picture postcard.

Versions of this same pattern reappear in each of the *New Poems*. Each of these poems is closed off in its own self-sufficiency as the description of a particular object or scene, and each poem states in its own terms the enigma of the chiasmus that constitutes it. "L'ange du méridien," for example (to refer only to the best known of the *New Poems*, 1:253), culminates in the totalization of a temporality which can, in opposition to the lacunary time of everyday experience, be said to be full; this total time is evoked by means of the figure of a sundial which, during the night, registers time that would be as entirely imaginary as might be invisible light. The temporal totalization is brought about by the chiasmic reversal of the categories night/day and light/dark. "Der Ball" (1:395) is a strictly descriptive version of a totalization that includes the contradictory motions of rising and falling (*Flug und Fall*). It is brought about by means of an object which, like the violin in "Am Rande der Nacht," has become the depository of an inwardness which is not simply that of the subject. The moment of reversal is graphically represented when the subject becomes, in its turn, a thing whose motion is determined by another thing at the precise instant when the ball reaches the apogee of its own trajectory:

> [der Ball] . . . und sich neigt
> und einhält und den Spielenden von oben
> auf einmal eine neue Stelle zeigt,
> sie ordnend wie zu einer Tanzfigur, . . .

> ([the ball] . . . bows down
> lingers and suddenly, from above,
> points the player to a new place
> ordering place and player as in a figured dance . . .)

The reversal makes it possible to consider the falling motion as if it were an event that partakes, to some degree, in the joyful upsurge of the ball's first trajectory. And this rising motion, by prospective anticipation, already contains within itself the future decline to which the subject can acquiesce.

A kinetic totality is evoked by a reversal of the subject/object, free/determined polarities within a purely spatial and representational schema.

In "Archaischer Torso Apollos" (1:313) the reversal is ocular. The observer is, in its turn, being observed by the fragmentary statue which has been transformed into a single, large eye: "denn da ist keine Stelle, / die dich nicht sieht." The reversal is possible only because the sculpture is broken and fragmentary; if the statue had actually represented the eye of Apollo, the chiasmus could not have come about. The absent eye allows for an imaginary vision to come into being, and it makes the eyeless sculpture into an Argus eye capable of engendering, by itself, all the dimensions of space. We always re-encounter versions of the same negative moment: the hollow of the violin, the irreality of the mirrored image, the darkness of a sundial at night, the falling ball, the missing eye. The absences create the space and the play needed for the reversals and finally lead to a totalization which they seemed, at first, to make impossible. The broken statue becomes more complete than the intact one, decadent Brugge richer than the prosperous reality of the past, the falling ball "happier" than the rising one, the nocturnal dial a more complete timepiece than the sundial at midday, etc.

The unifying principle of the *New Poems* resides in the homology of their rhetorical structure. Even when they evoke entities which, unlike a ball, a fountain, a cat, or a gazelle, are no longer relatively ordinary but transcendental or even divine, the structure remains the same. As a matter of fact the predicates of ordinariness and transcendence are themselves one of the most striking reversals. Rilke describes the rose window of the Chartres cathedral both as the reabsorption of all existence into the oneness of God and as the eye of a cat ("Die Fensterrose," 1:257). The shock of this juxtaposition does not actually deepen our knowledge and understanding of reality and of God, but it seduces the mind by the surprise of its precision. It captures and fascinates attention by the same skill that allows for the virtuosity of its play. It would therefore be a mistake to follow till the end those commentators who read the *New Poems* as a messianic text, seeing them as a hierarchized network of symbolic relationships that ascend towards the parousia of an omnipresent being. The numerous successful poems that appear in the volume are primarily successes of language and of rhetoric. This is hardly surprising, since it has been clear from the start that the Rilkean totalizations are the outcome of poetic skills directed towards the rhetorical potentialities of the signifier.

This reversal of the traditional priority, which located the depth of meaning in a referent conceived as an object or a consciousness of which the language is a more or less faithful reflection, asserts itself in Rilke's poetry by disguising itself at once into its opposite. Very few of the *New Poems* openly refer to language (as was the case with the "Eingang" poem of *The Book of Images*), but the priority of *lexis* over *logos* is always apparent in their structure. Rilke's vocabulary retains this shift in the emphasis and in the authority of the figural structures when he uses, with considerable precision, the term "figure" (*Figur*) to distinguish his rhetorical strategy from that of classical metaphors. By suggesting the potential identification of tenor and vehicle, the traditional metaphor stresses the possible recuperation of a stable meaning or set of meanings. It allows one to see language as a means towards a recovered presence that transcends language itself. But what Rilke calls figure is, on the thematic level, anything but a recuperation. The allegory of figuration in a text such as "Orpheus. Eurydice. Hermes" (1:298) contributes to the understanding of this distinction.

The poem explicitly describes the poetic vocation by means of a thematized version of chiasmic reversal, source of Rilke's affinity with the myth of Orpheus. The theme appears twice in the text and allows one to distinguish the "right" reversal at the end from the "wrong" reversal described in section 3:

> Und seine Sinne waren wie entzweit:
> indes der Blick ihm wie ein Hund vorauslief,
> umkehrte, kam und immer wieder weit
> und wartend an der nächsten Wendung stand,—
> blieb sein Gehör wie ein Geruch zurück.

> (And his senses were as doubled:
> because his sight, like a dog, ran ahead of him,
> turned around, came back to him and stood
> waiting for him at the next roadbend,—
> his hearing tarried as if it were an odor.)

This mode of reversal, to which Orpheus will finally succumb, indicates the impatience and the desire for a possession within presence. The absence of being—the death of Eurydice—is the origin of a desire which expresses itself in the elegiac tonality of the complaint. In a passage that prefigures the central theme of the Tenth Duino Elegy, the complaint is defined as a language capable of creating and filling an entire poetic universe:

> Die So-Geliebte, dass aus einer Leier
> mehr Klage kam als je aus Klagefrauen;
> dass eine Welt aus Klage ward, in der
> alles noch einmal da war: . . .
>
> (1:300)

> (Beloved, so-beloved, that from one lyre
> Came more woe than ever came from wailing women
> and thus arose a world of woe in which
> all things once more were present . . .)

However, since it stems from a desire for presence, the complaint is almost inevitably transformed into the impatience of a desire. It tends to consider the fictional world it engenders as an absent reality, and it tries to repossess what it lacks as if it were an exterior entity. The confusion can only lead to the loss of language which, in the symbolism of the poem, corresponds to Orpheus's increased inability to perceive sounds to the point of forgetting the existence of his lyre. To the extent that metaphor can be thought of as a language of desire and as a means to recover what is absent, it is essentially anti-poetic. The genuine reversal takes place at the end of the poem, when Hermes turns away from the ascending movement that leads Orpheus back to the world of the living and instead follows Eurydice into a world of privation and nonbeing. On the level of poetic language, this renunciation corresponds to the loss of a primacy of meaning located within the referent and it allows for the new rhetoric of Rilke's "figure." Rilke also calls this loss of referentiality by the ambivalent term of "inwardness" ("*innen* entstehen," "Welt*innen*raum," etc.), which then does not designate the self-presence of a consciousness but the inevitable absence of a reliable referent. It designates the impossibility for the language of poetry to appropriate anything, be it as consciousness, as object, or as a synthesis of both.

From the perspective of the language of figuration, this loss of substance appears as a liberation. It triggers the play of rhetorical reversals and allows them the freedom of their play without being hampered by the referential constraints of meaning: Rilke can assert, for instance, that the reflection is more real than reality, or that the sundial records the hours of the night, because his statement now exists only in and by itself. The same freedom also allows him to prefigure a new totality in which the figures will perfectly complement each other, since the totality does not have to take into account any empirical or transcendental veracity that might conflict with its principle of constitution. And it also allows for a perfect articulation of the semantic with the rhetorical and phonic function of language, thus preserving the initial sound-centered manner as a principle of poetic composition. From *New Poems* on, Rilke's poetry will live off the euphoria of this recovered freedom. A constant refinement, which goes far enough to recover a semblance of simplicity, will reduce the diversity of figuration that appears in *New Poems* to a small number of elective figures that are particularly productive in their internal reversals as well as capable of combining with each other in at times dazzling constellations. But the poetry will be able to achieve this mastery only at the cost of a subterfuge to which it finds itself necessarily condemned.

For this "liberating theory of the Signifier" also implies a complete drying up of thematic possibilities. In order to be a pure poetry of what Rilke calls "figures," it should start on the far side of the renunciation which opens up its access to this new freedom. But could any poetry, including Rilke's, lay claim to the purity of such a semantic askesis? Some of Rilke's allegorizing poems, such as "Orpheus. Eurydice. Hermes" or the Tenth Duino Elegy, programmatically thematize the renunciation in a narrative mode, by telling the story of this renunciation. In a more lyrical vein,

Rilke attempted poems that tend towards the impersonality and the detachment that should characterize a poetics of pure "figure." In those poems, an emblematic object is revealed to be a figure without the need of any discourse, by the very structure of its constitution. Such poems appear in his work from *New Poems* on and will recur till the end, including some of the poems written in the French language. These poems are by necessity brief and enigmatic, often consisting of one single sentence. One might well consider them to be Rilke's most advanced poetic achievement. It is through them that he is related to poets such as Trakl or Celan. The figure stripped of any seduction besides that of its rhetorical elasticity can form, together with other figures, constellations of figures that are inaccessible to meaning and to the senses, located far beyond any concern for life or for death in the hollow space of an unreal sky.

But next to these short and necessarily enigmatic tests, Rilke has also produced works of a wider, at times monumental, scope that are more accessible to understanding. The example of predecessors such as Hölderlin or Baudelaire may well have guided him in this direction. The trend is apparent in some of the longer *New Poems* and it culminates in the *Duino Elegies*, the work that, more than any other, has determined the reading of Rilke as a messianic poet. For rather than being themselves poetic figures, the *Elegies* state a genuine existential philosophy of figuration, presented as if it were a coherent principle of inner behavior, with rules and precepts that could be set up as exemplary. In principle, the imperative tone of the *Elegies* is totally incompatible with the very notion of pure figure, which implies the complete renunciation of any normative pathos or ethical coercion. But there representational and subjective elements openly play a determining part. Although they advocate a conception of language that excludes all subjective or intersubjective dimensions, the *Duino Elegies* constantly appeal to the reader's emotion and participation.

This paradox is not due to bad faith or to deliberate deception on the part of Rilke; it is inherent in the ambivalence of poetic language. The primacy of the signifier, on which Rilke's phonocentric poetics of chiasmus is predicated, is not just one property of language among others that would have remained unnoticed during several centuries until particularly perceptive poets such as Mallarmé or Rilke would have rediscovered it. The notion of a language entirely freed of referential constraints is properly inconceivable. Any utterance can always be read as semantically motivated, and from the moment understanding is involved the positing of a subject or an object is unavoidable. In Rilke's major works, the *Duino Elegies* and, to a lesser extent, the *Sonnets to Orpheus*, the relapse from a rhetoric of figuration into a rhetoric of signification occurs in a way that the structural description of the *New Poems* made predictable.

Chiasmus, the ground-figure of the *New Poems*, can only come into being as the result of a void, of a lack that allows for the rotating motion of the polarities. As long as it is confined to objects, this structural necessity may seem harmless enough: the declining motion of a fountain or of a ball, the reflection of a mirror or the opening of a window casement have, in themselves, nothing of pathos about them. But Rilke's figuration must also involve subject/object polarities, precisely because it has to put in question the irrevocability of this particularly compelling polarity. This implies the necessity of choosing as figures not only things but personal destinies or subjective experiences as well, with the avowed purpose of converting them into impersonal over-things, but without being able (or wanting) to prevent that the subjective moment first function on the level of meaning. However, these experiences, like the figural objects, must contain a void or a lack if they are to be converted into figures. It follows that only negative experiences can be poetically useful. Hence the prevalence of a thematics of negative experiences that will proliferate in Rilke's poetry: the insatiability of desire, the powerlessness of love, death of the unfulfilled or the innocent, the fragility of the earth, the alienation of consciousness—all these themes fit Rilke's rhetoric so well, not because they are the expression of his own lived experience (whether they are or not is irrelevant) but because their structure allows for the unfolding of his patterns of figuration. And just as the kinetic totalization had to encompass rising and falling motions into one single trope, or just as the reflective totalization must include both sides of the mirror, so the totalization of subjective experience must lead to a positive assertion that only chiasmus can reveal. The reversal of a negativity into a promise, the ambivalent thematic strategy of the *Duino Elegies*, allows for a linguistic play that is analogous to that in the most discreet of the *New Poems*. They call, however, for a very different tone, whose pathos, fervor, and exaltation make one forget the formal and fictional nature of the unity they celebrate. It is inevitable that the *Elegies* are being read as messianic poems: all their thematic assertions confirm this claim, and it is borne out by the virtuosity of the figuration. Yet the promise asserted by these texts is grounded in a play of language that can only come about because the poet has renounced any claim to extra-textual authority. In conformity with a paradox that is inherent in all literature, the poetry gains a maximum of convincing power at the very moment that it abdicates any claim to truth. The *Elegies* and the *Sonnets* have been the main source of evidence in trying to prove the adequation of Rilke's rhetoric to the truth of his affirmations, yet his notion of figural language eliminates all truth-claims from his discourse.

It would be a mistake to believe that a demystifying reading of Rilke could reduce this contradiction to a passing aberration. The messianic reading of Rilke is an integral part of a work that could not exist without it. The full complexity of this poetry can only appear in the juxtaposition of two readings in which the first forgets and the second acknowledges the linguistic structure that makes it come into being. The question remains whether Rilke himself considered his work under this double perspective or whether he followed the example of his commentators in systematically stressing the former at the expense of the latter.

Some of the particularly enigmatic poems from Rilke's last period cannot easily be reconciled with the positive tonality that is generally associated, even at this same late date, with the theme of the figure. This is the case of the following poem from the *Sonnets to Orpheus*, a text that has proven to be very resistant to interpretation:

> Sieh den Himmel. Heisst kein Sternbild "Reiter"?
> Denn dies ist uns seltsam eingeprägt:
> dieser Stolz aus Erde. Und ein Zweiter,
> der ihn treibt und hält und den er trägt.
>
> Ist nicht so, gejagt und dann gebändigt,
> diese sehnige Natur des Seins?
> Weg und Wendung. Doch ein Druck verständigt.
> Neue Weite. Und die zwei sind eins.
>
> Aber *sind* sie's? Oder meinen beide
> nicht den Weg, den sie zusammen tun?
> Namenlos schon trennt sie Tisch und Weide.
>
> Auch die sternische Verbindung trügt.
> Doch uns freue eine Weile nun
> der Figur zu glauben. Das genügt.
>
> > (1:493)

> (Behold the sky. Is there no constellation called
>   "Horseman"?
> For we have been taught, singularly, to expect this:
> this pride of earth, and his companion
> who drives and holds him, and whom he carries.
>
> Is he not, thus spurred and then reined in,
> like the nervelike nature of Being?
> Track and turn. But a pressure brings them together.
> New expanse—and the two are one.
>
> But *are* they truly? Or is the track they
> travel together *not* the meaning of their way?
> Table and pasture part them more than names.
>
> Star-patterns may deceive
> but it pleases us, for a while,
> to believe in the figure. That is enough.)

Although it does not have the somewhat doctrinal tone of some texts with a similar theme, the poem is important for an understanding of Rilke's poetics, since it deals with the recurrent and central figure of the constellation. The constellation signifies the most inclusive form of totalization, the recuperation of a language that would be capable of naming the remaining presence of being beyond death and beyond time.

The recovered unity comes into being in the play of polarities in the two quatrains, in which we pass from a movement of constraint and opposition to the condition of acquiescence which we have frequently encountered in our readings. The horseman and his steed are first shown in a relationship of duality in which their wills combat each other. The horse's pride rebels against the will of the rider, despite the fact that he is entirely at the mercy of the natural and earthlike power that carries him. The track (*Weg*), the path freely chosen by the animal, and the turn (*Wende*), which designates the will to direct it in a direction of the rider's choice, are at first in conflict with each other. This way of being in the world is characteristic of man, a creature that exists in constant opposition to the spirit of the earth that inhabits plants, animals, and innocent beings. The theme of this alienation, of a human destiny constantly opposed to the natural motion of things, runs through the entire work:

> Dieses heisst Schicksal: gegenüber sein
> und nicht als das und immer gegenüber.
> (Eighth Elegy, 1:471)

> (This is called destiny: to be opposite things
> and nothing else and always opposite.)

Such a mode of existing is said to conform to the "nervelike" (*sehnig*), tough, and resistant nature of being, which lines 5 and 6 put into question:

> Ist nicht so, gejagt und dann gebändigt,
> diese sehnige Natur des Seins?

The answer to this question has to be negative, for Rilke never conceives of his relationship to the world, nor especially of his relationship, as poet, to words, as a dialectical one. His entire strategy is instead to let the poetic meaning be carried by the rhetorical and the phonic dimensions of language: the seductions of the syntax and of the figuration have to make even the most extreme paradoxes appear natural. The "track" of the meaning and the "turn" of the tropes have to be reconciled by and within the figure. The poem isolates and retains this moment in the paradox of a beneficent constraint: "doch ein Druck verständigt." The phrase seizes the instant where the contrary wills are reconciled by a virtuosity that acquires the graceful ease of an apparent freedom. The contrary wills cross over and change place, following the same shift in point of view that made the player acquiesce to the descending motion of the ball. The freedom at once opens up a new free space and reveals a new totality: "Neue Weite. Und die zwei sind eins." This new totality prefigures the passage from the earthlike couple to the figural constellation of "The Horseman."

Once this point has been reached, most of Rilke's poems would stop and celebrate the new relationship to the world which the figuration has revealed. This is what happens, for instance, in the poem from the *Sonnets to Orpheus* that immediately follows upon this one:

> Heil dem Geist, der uns verbinden mag;
> denn wir leben wahrhaft in Figuren.
>
> (1:494)

(Hail to the spirit that may bring us together
for we live truly among figures.)

The second part of the Horseman sonnet, however, puts in question all that has been achieved and reduces the unified totality to a mere illusion of the senses, as trivial and deceiving as the optical illusion which makes us perceive the chaotic dissemination of the stars in space as if they were genuine figures, genuine designs traced upon the background of the skies. "Auch die sternische Verbindung trügt": the imaginary lines that make up actual as well as fictional constellations (the figural constellations of Rilke's poems) are mere deceit, false surfaces. The final affirmation, "Das genügt," especially when compared to the fervent promises that appear in other poems, seems almost derisive. Far from being, as is the case in the opening lines of the Ninth Elegy, a celebration of the moment, it sounds like a disenchanted concession. One can understand the disappointment of one of Rilke's fervent commentators, a true believer in his poetic annunciation: "What are we to think of this odd complacency, which suddenly seems to satisfy itself, and 'for a moment,' with provisional and deceptive hopes?" [Hermann Mörchen]

What is most important in this unexpected thematic turn is that it comes about at the precise instant when the text states its awareness of its linguistic structure and designates the event it describes as an event of language. Not only is the horseman referred to by the metalinguistic term "figure," but the unity is stated in terms that are borrowed from the semantic function of language: "Oder *meinen* beide / nicht den Weg, den sie zusammen tun?" The lines are difficult to interpret, but the emphasis on signification and on meaning is undeniable.

The failure of figuration thus appears as the undoing of the unity it claimed to establish between the semantic function and the formal structure of language. Again, one of the *New Poems* may be the most economical way to make the figure of the "road," which horseman and steed are said to travel together, more comprehensible. The poem entitled "Der Ball" describes the road, the trajectory of the ball; one could say that it *signifies* this trajectory, that the trajectory is the meaning of the poem as its referent. Moreover, the formal, syntactical structure of the single sentence that makes up the text exactly mimics the meaning: the sentence climbs and falls, slows down, hesitates, and speeds up again in a manner that parallels at all points the signified motion. The manner of enunciation corresponds exactly with what is being said. In other poems, the same convergence will be achieved by way of phonic rather than syntactical elements. The logical meaning and the *lexis* indeed travel along the same road.

But can it be asserted that this parallelism signifies, in the full meaning of the term, the unity that it constitutes? Is it not rather a play of language, an illusion as arbitrary as the shape of the constellations which share a common plane only as the result of an optical appearance? The Horseman sonnet confirms that Rilke knew this to be the case: the figure's truth turns out to be a lie at the very moment when it asserts itself in the plenitude of its promise. The sonnet is not the only instance of such a retreat. In a late text entitled "Gong" (2:186) Rilke attempts the ultimate reversal, not just the visual reversal that takes place in "Archaischer Torso Apollos," but the reversal within the phonic dimension, within the ear, itself: "Klang, / der, / wie ein tieferes Ohr, / uns, scheinbar Hörende, hört . . ." ("Sound, / which, / as a deeper ear, / hears us, who appear to be hearing"). Yet, in this poem, the accumulation of the most extreme paradoxes and of ultimate reversals does not lead to the expected totality, but ends instead in the ignominy of a fall which has nothing in common with the happy descent of the ball. It suggests instead the denunciation of the ultimate figure, the phonocentric Ear-god on which Rilke, from the start, has wagered the outcome of his entire poetic success, as error and betrayal:

> Wanderers Sturz, in den Weg,
> unser, an Alles, Verrat . . . : Gong!

> (Fall of the wanderer, on the roadside
> Our, of everything, betrayal . . . : Gong!)

Among Rilke's French poems which, by their use of a foreign language, correspond to the renunciation of the euphonic seductions of language, one finds the same definition of the figure as the conversion of representational and visual into purely auditive rhetoric:

> Il faut fermer les yeux et renoncer à la bouche,
> rester muet, aveugle, ébloui:
> L'espace tout ébranlé, qui nous touche
> ne veut de notre être que l'ouie.

> (We must close our eyes and renounce our mouths,
> remain mute, blind, dazzled:
> Vibrating space, as it reaches us
> demands from our being only the ear.)

At the moment of its fulfillment, this figure announces itself by its real name:

> Masque? Non. Tu es plus plein,
> mensonge, tu as des yeux sonores.

> (Mask? No. You are fuller
> you lie, you have sonorous eyes.)

More still than the thematic statement, which can always be interpreted as a recuperation of the posited theme beyond its most absolute negation, the shift to French indicates not only the knowledge but the advent of the disruption. The promise contained in Rilke's poetry, which the commentators, in the eagerness of their belief, have described in all its severe complexity, is thus placed, by Rilke himself, within the dissolving perspective of the lie. Rilke can only be understood if one realizes the urgency of this promise together with the equally urgent, and equally poetic, need of retracting it at the very instant he seems to be on the point of offering it to us.

The Expressionist Mode

Michael Hamburger

The poetic revolution of 1912 was not without precedent in German literature; apart from Goethe and Hölderlin—poets remote from it in time—it was strongly supported by a whole generation of experimental poets older than the first Expressionists themselves. Rilke's new style had little influence on the movement, since he published very few poems during his critical years. Stefan George kept even more aloof; but even his *Stern des Bundes*, written at this time and first published in a limited edition in 1913, responded to the stirring of the new *Zeitgeist*, if only by the cryptic warnings against it contained in poems much more didactic than George's earlier work. Two of the outstanding early Expressionists—Georg Heym and Ernst Stadler—were at one time influenced by George. Three other poets of Rilke's generation were close enough to the movement to be included in several anthologies and miscellanies of Expressionist poetry: Alfred Mombert, who was writing his mythological poem "Äon vor Syrakus"; Else Lasker-Schüler, whose "Hebräische Balladen" were published in 1913; and Theodor Däubler, who was writing "Der Sternhelle Weg." Both Däubler and Else Lasker-Schüler were among the most enthusiastic apologists and propagators of Expressionism.

To these must be added the Futurist poet August Stramm (1874–1915), whose experiments in diction, syntax and metre were much more extreme than those of the younger generation, the Expressionists proper. What is most striking about his poems is their complete break with the logic of prose and the total absence in them of those descriptive elements which both Symbolists and Naturalists had found indispensable. I shall quote one of his more conventional pieces, "Schwermut" (Melancholy):

From *Reason and Energy: Studies in German Literature.* © 1957 by Routledge & Kegan Paul Ltd.

Schreiten Streben	Striding striving
Leben sehnt	Living longs
Schauen Stehen	Shuddering standing
Blicke suchen	Glances look for
Sterben wächst	Dying grows
Das Kommen	The coming
Schreit!	Screams!
Tief	Deeply
Stummen	We
Wir.	Dumb.

These lines—one can hardly call them a poem—contain no visual images at all, no adjectives and only a single verb. (The word *stummen* in the last line is used neologistically as a verb: *to dumb*.) The "poem" renders nothing but an inward state; but whereas the Expressionist and Imagist poets rendered inward states by projecting them into external scenes, here there is no reference to any recognizable object, person or symbol.

Stramm reversed the process; he suppressed outward reality so that his "poem" would express nothing but the dynamism of feeling, an inward gesture. His words are an abstract pattern that corresponds to his inward state; and the pattern is a dynamic one. Hence the importance of verbs and participles in these lines and Stramm's neologistic use of an adjective as a verb. In other poems he invented onomatopoeic and pun-like sounds to express emotions which cannot be rendered by existing words.

Jacob van Hoddis and Alfred Lichtenstein, the authors of the first Expressionist poems to appear in print, were conventional in comparison with Stramm. "Weltende," by Hoddis, was the first to appear; and Lichtenstein admitted having used it as a model, though he rightly claimed to have improved on it. Both poems are rhymed and in regular stanza form. What was new about them is that they consisted of nothing more than an arbitrary concatenation of images derived from contemporary life; they presented a picture, but not a realistic one, for the objects described were not such as can be found together in the same place and at the same time. They were a kind of *collage*; but *collage* in poetry is a far less drastic device than *collage* in the graphic arts, since poetry has always been free to assemble its imagery without regard to the unity of space and time. Hoddis could not resist giving the show away in the title of his poem—"End of the World"—an exaggeration all the more blatant because so inappropriate to the ironic understatement of the poem itself. (It says that "most people have a cold," relating this observation to others of a more serious kind—for instance, that "the railway trains are falling off the bridges"). Much of the irony is too crude to be effective as satire; but the poem does express a mood that was soon to become endemic.

In Lichtenstein's poem, on the other hand, the images are allowed to speak for themselves. His title—"Twilight"—is ambiguous, though one assumes that his twilight is dusk.

Ein dicker Junge spielt mit einem Teich.
Der Wind hat sich in einem Baum verfangen.
Der Himmel sieht verbummelt aus und bleich,
Als wäre ihm die Schminke ausgegangen.

Auf lange Krücken schief herabgebückt
Und schwatzend kriechen auf dem Feld zwei Lahme.
Ein blonder Dichter wird vielleicht verrückt.
Ein Pferdchen stolpert über eine Dame.

An einem Fenster klebt ein fetter Mann.
Ein Jüngling will ein weiches Weib besuchen.
Ein grauer Clown zieht sich die Stiefel an.
Ein Kinderwagen schreit und Hunde fluchen.

If Lichtenstein's dusk (or dawn) is a cosmic one, he neither says nor implies that it is. He makes no attempt to explain the presence in his poem of the "fat boy playing with a pond," the two lame men creeping over a field, the clown putting on his boots, the screaming pram or the cursing dogs. His poem is "expressionistic" because its real purpose is to communicate the poet's own sense of the absurd and the ridiculous; yet, by saying that "the sky looks dissolute and pale, as if it had run out of make-up," it relates all the disparate images of modern life to a general sense of vanity, as Mr. Eliot was to do with more subtle skill in *The Waste Land*. Lichtenstein's poem is successful not because it expresses a new mood, but because that mood has found its proper "objective correlative"; for all its humour, it is much more disturbing than Hoddis's prognosis of disaster.

Into some of his other poems Lichtenstein introduced a *persona*, Kuno Kohn, as T. S. Eliot was to introduce Prufrock, Burbank and Bleistein into his early poems. Like Eliot also, Lichtenstein made a point of understatement and of the qualifying "If and Perhaps and But." "A fair-haired poet may be going mad," he says in "Dämmerung." Lichtenstein's irony was a considerable advance on that of earlier poets; though not free from the self-mockery made familiar by Heine and, later, by Laforgue, he used the very same ironic effects to mock a whole civilization, without recourse to direct or didactic statement.

The earliest variety of Expressionism, then, was close to caricature, but a kind of caricature that asserted a new freedom of association. The poems of Lichtenstein and Hoddis are distinguished by an irony which has the dual purpose of satirizing contemporary civilization and of expressing a *malaise*, a premonition of doom, which was one of the common premises of all the early Expressionists. That is why the titles of these two early poems were taken up by those who directed the later, more noisy but less significant, activities of the movement. Lichtenstein's "Dämmerung" reappeared in the title of a famous anthology-cum-manifesto of 1920, *Menschheitsdämmerung*, with the difference that his discreet and ambiguous twilight had now become "the dawn of a new humanity." Hoddis's

"Weltende" initiated that abuse of the cosmic and chiliastic which led to the gradual inflation of the verbal currency of Expressionism. Soon it ceased to matter greatly whether a poet predicted the end of the world or a new humanity; both became the stock-in-trade of every poetaster.

But the movement, as I have said, is only of incidental relevance here. One of the very best of the early Expressionist poets, Georg Heym, died in a skating accident in January 1912, when the movement had scarcely begun. Though he died at the age of 24, he left a large number of faultless poems and some interesting experimental prose. Lichtenstein, whose verse and prose are slighter than Heym's but excellent in their way, died in battle soon after the outbreak of war, at the age of 25. By the end of 1914, Ernst Stadler and Georg Trakl were also dead; and August Stramm fell on the Eastern front in the following year. The premature death of all these gifted poets would seem to be one obvious reason why the later developments of Expressionism did not fulfil the promise of 1912. But it is hardly possible to imagine Heym, Trakl, Lichtenstein or even Stadler as middle-aged men of letters. Expressionism, like the eighteenth-century *Sturm und Drang*, was essentially the product of a crisis; and any poet who survived this crisis was bound to modify his earlier practice or to give up writing poetry.

Georg Heym combined the fastidious elegance of Stefan George with a new range of mood and subject matter; and with that dynamic use of imagery and syntax which is the one stylistic trend common to all the early Expressionists. Many of his poems recall the preoccupations of Baudelaire, rather than those of the Symbolists from whom George largely derived; they are explorations of the modern city, which Heym sees both realistically and apocalyptically, as the scene of material squalor and as the demesne of frightful daemons. Three years before the outbreak of war he wrote a poem, "Der Krieg," which is characteristic both of his vision and his style. I can quote only the opening stanzas.

> Aufgestanden ist er, welcher lange schlief,
> Aufgestanden unten aus Gewölben tief.
> In der Dämmrung steht er, gross und unbekannt,
> Und den Mond zerdrückt er in der schwarzen Hand.
>
> In den Abendlärm der Städte fällt es weit,
> Frost und Schatten einer fremden Dunkelheit.
> Und der Märkte runder Wirbel stockt zu Eis.
> Es wird still. Sie sehn sich um. Und keiner weiss.
>
> In den Gassen fasst es ihre Schulter leicht.
> Eine Frage. Keine Antwort. Ein Gesicht erbleicht.
> In der Ferne zittert ein Geläute dünn,
> Und die Bärte zittern um ihr spitzes Kinn.

In truly apocalyptic fashion, Heym personifies war, but as a nameless avenging spirit, not as a mere abstraction or as a figure taken from some archaic play or picture. The poem begins dynamically, with a verb; and the horror of war is compressed into the image of the last line of the first stanza, that of War "crushing the moon in his black hand." In the second stanza Heym brings this horror home by introducing familiar images of city life; its sudden intrusion into the life of ordinary people is rendered by the three brief sentences of the last line, each a complete action, but with a cumulative effect. The neutral "fasst es" of the third strophe serves to keep the horror nameless; for at first the victims do not know what it is that takes hold of them. Their bewilderment is rendered in the next line by the a-syntactical "Eine Frage. Keine Antwort," a typically Expressionist device. The third line adds a faintly gruesome aural effect to the images and actions presented so far. It is not till the last of the poem's ten stanzas that War receives its full apocalyptic significance, as an agent of divine justice dropping "pitch and fire on Gomorrah." Heym, like Baudelaire and Trakl, was obsessed with evil.

The only basic criticism that could be applied to Heym's poetry was expressed long ago by Ernst Stadler, who complained that Heym made use of traditional verse forms to render a "modern" vision; but more often than not the very tension between his regular metres and the dynamic force behind them gives his poems an unusual tautness. Stadler admitted as much; and remarked on the peculiarly sinister effect produced by Heym's nonchalant treatment of horrifying subjects—his poems like "a dance of death that observes the polite conventions of courtly ceremonial." In several of his last poems Heym came closer to the "personal rhythm" which Stadler had missed in his work. I quote the opening stanzas of a poem from his second posthumous collection:

> Deine Wimpern, die langen,
> Deiner Augen dunkele Wasser,
> Lass mich tauchen darein,
> Lass mich zur Tiefe gehn.

> Steigt der Bergmann zum Schacht
> Und schwankt seine trübe Lampe
> Über der Erze Tor,
> Hoch an der Schattenwand,

> Sieh, ich steige hinab,
> In deinem Schoss zu vergessen,
> Fern was von oben dröhnt,
> Helle und Qual und Tag.

The dynamism here is less violent, mitigated by the mood of melancholy tenderness which the almost elegiac metre conveys; but, though the main weight of the poem is carried by its imagery, this imagery is never a static one—as in much Symbolist and Imagist verse—but an imagery of movement. These three stanzas are dominated by the spatial relation between two symbolic planes and by the downward movement from one to the other. Heym breaks up the syntax of the first stanza, so as to be able to present his images before introducing the verb that governs them; he restrains his usual dynamism, so that the static images of long eye-lashes and "your eyes' dark waters" may have their full emotive effect before being related to the action. This action or motion is in full progress when he reaches the second stanza; he therefore starts this stanza with the verb—again contrary to normal usage; for what is significant about his metaphor of the miner descending the shaft is the motion of descent itself, rather than any other analogy between the "I" of the poem and the miner's function. The third stanza relates this metaphor to its meaning; not by a logical comparison—the linking "like" and "as" which Rilke too discarded when he found his new style—but by an independent action parallel to it. The miner goes down the mine-shaft *and* the lover of the poem descends to a dark, subterranean level where noises from above are damped and he is remote from "brightness, torment and day." The falling cadence of the poem—produced by trochees and dactyls—is exactly the right one.

Heym's affinity with Georg Trakl—suggested by the "dying fall" of this poem—becomes more marked in the autumnal imagery of the succeeding stanzas. Ernst Stadler and Franz Werfel represented a different trend of early Expressionism, but one complementary to the other. Their belief in a better future gave their dynamism an ecstatic quality, as opposed to the gloomy forebodings of Heym and Trakl; but both trends arose from the same sense of an imminent cataclysm. Stadler's best-known poem, "Der Aufbruch," has been interpreted too literally as a prophecy and glorification of war; as his editor, Dr. Karl Ludwig Schneider has recently pointed out, its military imagery has little to do with actual warfare, much more with the poet's own personal and literary situation in 1911 and 1912, when he evolved his new style. As a man attached to England, France and Belgium as well as to Germany, Stadler was bound to loathe the very idea of war; but Stadler was a poet of revolt against prejudice, apathy and stuffiness. The warlike imagery of "Der Aufbruch" is one of liberation from outworn conventions. The irony of Stadler's fate is not that he welcomed the war that killed him and defeated his hopes for a better Europe, but that the images of regeneration in his poetry corresponded so closely to the catastrophic event. Stadler believed that "it is the future which all true art serves"; even his excursions into squalor, in his poems on the East End of London, poverty and prostitution, are affirmations of the joy of living and professions of faith in unrealized potentialities. Yet this vitalism is always ambiguous; for the culmination of ecstasy, in Stadler's poems, coincides with a dissolution of consciousness which he usually associates with death. His vitalism—akin to that of Walt Whitman and D. H. Lawrence—gathers momentum in the long, irregular, surging lines of his verse, only to dash itself to pieces in the last.

Der Schnellzug tastet sich und stösst die Dunkelheit entlang.
Kein Stern will vor. Die ganze Welt ist nur ein enger, nacht
    umschienter Minengang,
Darein zuweilen Förderstellen blauen Lichtes jähe Horizonte
    reissen: Feuerkreis
Von Kugellampen, Dächern, Schloten, dampfend, strömend
    . . . nur sekundenweis . . .
Und wieder alles schwarz. Als führen wir ins Eingeweid der
    Nacht zur Schicht.
Nun taumeln Lichter her . . . verirrt, trostlos vereinsamt . . .
    mehr . . . und sammeln sich . . . und werden dicht.
Gerippe grauer Häuserfronten liegen bloss, im Zwielicht
    bleichend, tot—etwas muss kommen . . . o, ich fühl
    es schwer
Im Hirn. Eine Beklemmung singt im Blut. Dann dröhnt der
    Boden plötzlich wie ein Meer:
Wir fliegen, aufgehoben, königlich durch nachtentrissne
    Luft, hoch überm Strom. O Biegung der Millionen
    Lichter, stumme Wacht,
Vor deren blitzender Parade schwer die Wasser abwärts
    rollen. Endloses Spalier, zum Gruss gestellt bei Nacht!
Wie Fackeln stürmend! Freudiges! Salut von Schiffen über
    blauer See! Bestirntes Fest!
Wimmelnd, mit hellen Augen hingedrängt! Bis wo die Stadt
    mit letzten Häusern ihren Gast entlässt.
Und dann die langen Einsamkeiten. Nackte Ufer. Stille.
    Nacht. Besinnung. Einkehr. Kommunion. Und Glut
    und Drang
Zum Letzten, Segnenden. Zum Zeugungsfest. Zur Wollust.
    Zum Gebet. Zum Meer. Zum Untergang.

I shall not even begin to attempt to elucidate this splendid poem, "Fahrt über die Kölner Rheinbrücke bei Nacht." In spite of its realistic imagery, its organization is a purely subjective one. It renders an actual experience— the crossing of a railway bridge at night—but gives such a vast extension of meaning to the experience that one cannot even be sure that the descriptive details—housefronts, lights and chimneys, for instance—are that and no more. As in Surréaliste poetry and that of Dylan Thomas, one image generates another; but all the disparate images are swept in one direction by the dynamism of feeling. Stadler's poem re-creates an immediate experience; far from being "emotion recollected in tranquillity," it approximates as closely as poetry can to the bewildering moment of sensation. This would be easy enough if the writing of a poem could be synchronized with the experience that occasioned it; but, at its most immediate, poetry is emotion generated in retrospect. Stadler's apparent spontaneity, therefore, was the result of deliberate and skilful application.

In the first few lines of the poem realistic imagery preponderates; one attributes their dynamism to the actual speed of the express train. Yet they prepare the reader for the larger symbolism that emerges more clearly later; for the journey is one into the "entrails of night"; and, as in Heym's poem, there is an allusion to a descent into the sub-conscious, symbolized by the mine gallery. It is only the connection between the river of the poem, the Rhine at Cologne, and the sea that establishes a primarily symbolic significance. When the poet writes of "Salut von Schiffen über blauer See" we are suddenly aware that these ships are not part of the actual setting of the poem; his imagination has travelled with the river to the sea. And it is the extraneous image of the sea that dominates the whole poem; for the whole poem is a glorification of the flux of life itself; and the sea is the destination of that flux.

On its realistic level, Stadler's poem is comparable to Hart Crane's *The Bridge*; both poems are affirmations of the new age and attempts to mythologize—or at least to generalize—its specific achievements. Symbolically, Stadler's poem affirms only life itself—and death. The poem ends with the word "Untergang," submergence or extinction; it does so because the utmost intensity of feeling burns itself out. Just as the river's motion comes to rest in the sea, Stadler's ecstatic awareness of being alive culminates in the extinction of consciousness. The last line makes the connection, frequent in Stadler's love poems also, between the total fulfilment of individuality and its total dissolution.

Stadler goes further than Heym in the breaking up of regular syntax, for his vitalism was more impatient of conventional restrictions. For the same reason he was much more apt to coin new combinations of words; examples in this poem are *nacht umschient* ("railed round with night") and *nachtentrissene Luft* ("air snatched away from night"). Because of their extreme dynamism, his poems have a rhetorical effect; but it is private rhetoric, as it were, not aimed at the reader in the manner of Werfel and many of the later Expressionists. Only his excellent craftsmanship saved Stadler from other dangers. Few poets would have got away with the long succession of a-syntactic words—most of them abstract and general—in the last two lines; one would expect them to read like a parody of the new style, quite apart from the inclusion of prayer in the list, between the ecstasy of procreation and self-extinction in the sea. Stadler brings off these verbal and mental leaps, just as he manages to keep his long line from spilling over into prose, and makes his rhymes all the more effective for being delayed.

These varieties of Expressionist poetry—and there are many others—will have to suffice here. All of them go back to before the first World War—a fact that must be stressed only because Expressionism was long regarded as a phenomenon of the interwar years. Even so acute an observer of contemporary life and literature as Robert Musil noted in his diary that when he returned to civilian life "there was Expressionism," contrasting it with the poetry of "intellectual intuition" that had existed before the war. He also noted that "the nature of Expressionism is that of a synthetic method as opposed to the analytical. Expressionism refrains from analysis. . . . That is why it tends towards dogmatism. That is why it tries to discover a new cosmic sense as a chemist tries to discover synthetic rubber. Its limitation: that there is no such thing as a purely synthetic process." Both of Musil's observations are perfectly just if we remember that Expressionism was a style before it was a movement; and Musil was writing about the movement rather than the style. Musil's own novel *Die Verwirrungen des Zöglings Törless*, published in 1912, has been treated as an example of early Expressionist prose! It was the movement that tended towards dogmatism, a political dogmatism which Musil rightly deplored; but most of the pre-war Expressionists were so far from being dogmatic about either religion or politics that one has the greatest difficulty in deducing their beliefs and opinions from their poetry. Musil's observation that Expressionism was a synthetic method, on the other hand, applies to the style as well as to the movement. The Expressionist style, from the very start, was synthetic; and this is where the danger lay.

"Scepticism," Stadler wrote in a book review, "can only lead to the end of all creative power, to decadence. The truly creative man, on the other hand, is he who can create the world anew, who opposes his new and different idea of the world to the created world as it is; the man with a teleological direction, not the one who merely counts up (existing phenomena) on his fingers." Musil's antinomy between the synthetic and analytical processes in literature is the old quarrel—already touched upon frequently [elsewhere]—between head and heart, Reason and Energy, Logos and Imagination; but the quarrel had become more violent and more extreme. Stadler was aware of the extreme implications of his statement; for he proceeded to qualify it by writing that "this was not to justify the blind destructive impulses, as certain radical revolutionaries do"; and that "the new artist should rely on his intellect in the first place, no blind creature of instincts, not a person orientated only by feeling." In theory, this is unobjectionable; and Stadler himself, as it happened, was well balanced, being a critic and a scholar as well as a poet; but I have already observed that the vitalism of the poetry was essentially self-destructive. Musil's analytical subtlety, on the other hand, proved no less dangerous to himself; his extreme scepticism, directed against his own impulses, prevented him from finishing most of the imaginative works which he planned or began in later life, including his masterpiece. Musil's difficulty was that he could not arrive at a synthesis; the more he knew, the more difficult he found it to reduce the complexity of his knowledge to its bare, imaginative essence. Because extremes meet, his scepticism finally turned a somersault and became a kind of mysticism; but a kind of mysticism no less difficult to reconcile with the novelist's primary task.

After 1914, then, Reason and Energy tended to go their separate ways. The finest critical minds of the age, those of Hofmannsthal and Musil, for instance, refused all contact with the dominant generation; and the dominant generation accepted no critical guidance. Hofmannsthal was despised as an "uncreative" traditionalist—because he did not believe that it is the writer's business "to create the world anew"; and, like Musil, Hofmannsthal was indeed inhibited from writing all he might have written by his horror of what was happening in his time. A peculiar melancholy attaches to those writers of the German-speaking nations—both Hofmannsthal and Musil, of course, were Austrians—who were conscious of working within a humanistic tradition; it is the melancholy of Grillparzer, who prophesied that modern civilization would move "from humanity through nationalism to bestiality"—a prophecy not unlike that which emerges from Hofmannsthal's tragedy *Der Turm*. It is the melancholy of Jakob Burckhardt, who refused Ranke's chair of History in Berlin and left it to Treitschke—the most anti-traditional of nationalists. And the melancholy of Hofmannsthal himself, a liberal conservative living at a time when all spontaneous energy tends towards revolt, violence and anarchy.

"Expressionism was dead at the moment when it became a deliberate style," an excellent critic [Dr. K. L. Schneider] of the style has recently written; and it is certainly true that—judged by their poetry alone—the initiators of this style seem less conscious of their innovations than their numerous successors and imitators. Yet, in a different sense, the art of Heym and Trakl was more deliberate than that of the later Expressionists, whose manner strikes us as self-conscious only because it had become a mannerism. In Stadler too intellect and energy were at war; but he was skilful enough to adjust the balance in his poetry. Much of the verse of the later Expressionists is not more, but less, vitalistic than Stadler's; it is the incongruity between their dynamic style and their flabbiness of feeling that makes their rhetoric more offensive than Stadler's.

As for the death of Expressionism, Dr. Schneider's remark is apt enough; but one must add that no corpse has ever raised such a hullabaloo. By 1918 Expressionism was the most influential and the most prolific movement in German, if not in European, literature. (In 1922, 35,859 books were published in Germany—nearly three times as many as in Great Britain; it would be interesting to know just how many of these would have qualified as Expressionist.) Many of the Expressionist poets thought nothing of publishing three collections of verse in a year; and each of these volumes would be highly "original"—if one did not analyze it or compare its "originality" with that of dozens of others—highly topical and bursting with vitality. Those of the innovators who had died before or during the war were posthumously recruited into the movement; to march with it willy-nilly in the columns of such anthologies as *Menschheitsdämmerung*. Gradually the style turned into a weapon of revolutionary dogmatism, pacifist at first, but pugnaciously so.

The hysterical note characteristic of later Expressionism was first sounded by Franz Werfel before the war; but Werfel was not primarily a political poet. He wrote out of the sincere conviction that "we must love one another or die"; and even his rhetoric had the charm of ingenuity, an elegance reminiscent of the Baroque. For a time, Werfel became the spiritual leader of the movement; but after 1920 his poetry ceased to develop. He was succeeded by Herr Johannes R. Becher, the most prolific and the most widely read of the political Expressionist poets. Here is the opening of his "Hymne auf Rosa Luxemburg," written in 1919:

> Auffüllend dich rings mit Strophen aus Oliven.
> Tränen Mäander umwandere dich!
> Stern-Genächte dir schlagend als Mantel um,
> Durchwachsen von Astbahnen hymnischen Scharlachbluts . . .
> O Würze du der paradiesischen Auen:
> Du Einzige! Du Heilige! O Weib!—
>
> Durch die Welten rase ich—:
> Einmal noch deine Hand, diese Hand zu fassen:
> Zauberisches Gezweig an Gottes Rosen-Öl-Baum . . .

The dynamism, the a-syntactic, exclamatory phrases, the unexpected images and new combinations of words—all the ingredients of early Expressionism are there; but they have degenerated into rhetorical devices, determined neither by inward nor outward necessity. The revolutionary heroine of the poem is addressed as a saint—a confusion of terms typical of the diction as a whole, its imprecision and impurity; and after the false sublimity of "Saint!" there follows the bathos of "Woman!" All the imagery is arbitrary; one cannot even call it decorative, for there is nothing to decorate. It is a rank growth that covers up a void; a booby-trap for the reader foolish enough to be drawn to these "strophes of olives," only to be caught and bludgeoned into admiration for the unfortunate subject of the poem. The poem goes on for another sixty lines at this pace; and there is no reason why it shouldn't go on for six hundred, or end with the sixth line. Becher creates an illusion of energy by starting the poem with the present participle of a verb; but whereas the early Expressionists used such devices to render the logic of feeling or of imagination, Becher uses it to wind up the mechanism of his rhetoric. Yet the effect of such verse was to undermine the judgment and coarsen the sensibility of its readers.

This was not a purely German phenomenon; but no public was less critical of it than the German. Hence, in part, the events of 1933, possible only in a country that had been systematically demoralized and brutalized. The later developments of Expressionism are inseparable from politics; for the new style, as I have said, had been turned into a political weapon. A poet of complete integrity, Oskar Loerke, entered the following note in his diary on February 19th, 1933: "I stand between the terrorists of the Right and the Left. Perhaps I shall be destroyed. My nerves won't stand any more. The anguish of being confronted with terrible consequences, without having done, or even known the least thing."

Since my subject here is the Expressionist style, not the movement or the events that led to its suppression, I shall end the survey at this point. Gottfried Benn has divided the Expressionist era into two periods, which he calls Phase 1 and Phase 2: Phase 1 being the period before 1933, Phase 2 the period after 1933, represented almost exclusively by Dr. Benn himself. A better division ould be that into three phases: Phase 1, then, would cover the years between 1911 and 1914, Phase 2 the years between 1914 and 1933, Phase 3 from 1933 to the present time. Of the few Expressionist poets who survived both wars and continued to write, only Gottfried Benn and Ivan Goll can be said to have even attempted to develop the style. Herr Becher, another survivor, has changed his style beyond recognition; his rhetoric now is not *avant-garde*, but sub-literary. Unlike such French Communist poets as M. Aragon, whose pre-war poetry resembled Becher's in combining political propaganda with an "advanced" technique, Herr Becher is no longer obliged to write for an unconverted bourgeoisie or to compete with "bourgeois" writers. M. Aragon's verse of the war years is considerably better than Herr Becher's verse of the same period, though both are deliberate reversions to popular modes.

Ivan Goll, a bi-lingual poet who had been active both in France and in Germany, lived to write a worthy epilogue to his German verse of the inter-war years. During the long illness of which he died in 1950, he wrote a series of poems on the traditional themes of love and death, posthumously collected and published as *Traumkraut*. Unlike the rhetorical verse of his earlier years, they are concentrated and astonishingly lucid; but their simplicity is that of reduction. They are the essence left in the retort after all the diverse experiments that began before the first World War. They neither break with Goll's past—as Becher's recent poetry does with his—nor initiate a new style; they make use of everything that Goll had learnt in his association with the modernist movements in Germany, France and America, but in a curiously chastened and transmuted form. These poems are imagistic, but their imagery is clearly symbolic; their syntax is the dynamic syntax of Expressionism and Surréalisme, but the dynamism is controlled by an obvious logic. In a short poem called "Morgue," Goll could combine such modernist metaphors as "the ice of sleep" with another that recalls the conventional imagery of mediaeval verse, "the inn of Earth." This juxtaposition could be called eclectic or naive; and it is the difficulty of distinguishing between true and false naivety that laid the new style open to abuse. The style was fashioned by the "innocent eye" of true poets; but it was exploited by those who deliberately violated reason, so as to release energy. Innocence can be renewed, and does, in fact, continually renew itself; but in its own good time. To force the process is to fall into crudity and barbarism.

Gottfried Benn

Michael Hamburger

Benn's writings are highly exhilarating and abysmally depressing in turn, as befits an intoxicant. They can induce a euphoria of infinite possibilities, which results from the total release of energy from the bonds of reason; and a corresponding hangover, when Benn returns to himself and reminds us that despair is the mother of all his inventions. Self-pity is the chink in Benn's armour, as in Nietzsche's, who also dramatized his solitude, though with more justification than Benn; for in spite of his claim to the contrary, Benn's solitude was less extreme than Nietzsche's, if only because Nietzsche had already charted the place. Benn himself has summed up his dilemma; but for "we" read "I": "We lived something different from what we were, we wrote something different from what we thought, we thought something different from what we expected; and what remains is something different from what we intended."

It is probably too early to say what will remain of Benn's work; generally, one is inclined to agree with him, that which was farthest from his intentions, farthest from the tedious dialectic of nihilism. In view of his professed aestheticism, one might expect his poetry to have the consistent quality of—say—Valéry's, Stefan George's or, of his own generation, Trakl's; but even Benn's aesthetic standards are curiously unreliable. Almost every one of his collections contain pieces that are not only grossly inferior to his best work, but simply unformed—cerebral jottings in loose free verse or mechanical rhyme that all too clearly communicate something—Benn's concern with his own ego or with ideas not realized poetically. Again it is Benn who has indicated the reason, in one of the few passages of a late work that qualify his earlier views: "Nihilism as the

From *A Proliferation of Prophets*. © 1983 by Michael Hamburger. St. Martin's Press, 1983.

73

negation of history, actuality, affirmation of life, is a great quality; but as the negation of reality itself, it means a diminution of the ego."

But, as his last collections show, Benn continued to diminish his ego by perpetuating the quarrel between subject and object which—however fruitful a field for metaphysicians—is full of dangers for modern poetry. I have already said that all poetry, whatever its theme, affirms life; it does so because form itself is the progeny of the marriage of mind and matter. Only the unformed poem, the bad poem, can be negative. That is why Benn's "subjectivity" is depressing; subjectivity did not become odious until the first ego asserted its independence from the external world; Pascal's *moi haïssable* was the direct consequence of the *cogito ergo sum* of Descartes. The ego has been growing more and more odious since, because more and more interested in its own reflection in the mirror. Benn's nihilism and Winckler's "affliction of thinking" are the recoil of consciousness from a mirror that has lost its mercury and become a blank prison wall.

Very little of Benn's work breaks down this prison wall; but what little of it does so derives a special importance from the point where this breach is made. *Ex nihilo nihil fit*; if Benn's best poems seem to contradict this maxim, it is because they affirm life despite their author's intention. (And of course it is nonsense to affirm "reality" without affirming life, as Benn claims to have done, unless by life he means only some particular mode or manifestation of life, an environment he dislikes.) The poems of Benn's best period, the early 1920s, are almost consistently remarkable; but only two or three of them are faultless. The difference has to do with truth as much as with style; for the fault is always due to the intrusion of irrelevant ideas and inessential phenomena into a poem that ought to have been purely imaginative; and these ideas and phenomena always appertain to Benn's immediate environment. The most blatant of these faults is the introduction of abstract neologisms and scientific terms—witty, and there-fore self-conscious—where they have no business to occur. I refer to such new compound words as *Bewusstseinsträger* (consciousness-bearer), *Satz-bordell* (sentence brothel) and *Tierschutzmäzene* (Maecenases of the RSPCA) and of scientific terms like *Selbsterreger* (auto-exciter), used in the manner of clever journalism. These words—and many more of the same kind—appear in Benn's most outstanding collection of poems, his *Spaltung* of 1925. Of the twenty-eight poems in this book, only one is wholly free from such satirical irrelevances; and one or two more are successful in spite of them, because the tension between myth and modernity is essential to them.

These poems, unfortunately, are the least translatable, precisely be-cause they are the nearest possible approximation to Benn's ideal of "ab-solute poetry." As an example of the fruitful tension between myth and modernity—and of a single line that is "absolute" in the sense of being pure music—I shall quote the opening stanza of "Die Dänin":

> Charon oder die Hermen
> oder der Daimlerflug

was aus den Weltenschwärmen
tief dich im Atem trug,
war deine Mutter im Haine
südlich, Thalassa, o lau—
trug deine Mutter alleine
dich, den nördlichen Tau—

Benn has never written with greater mastery than at this time and in this medium—poems in trochaic or sprung rhythms, in short lines with alternating feminine and masculine rhymes. The poem quoted, as it happens, is one positive even in theme, a poem in praise of a Danish girl, which affirms the present as well as the mythical past, Greece and Scandinavia; because of this affirmation, there is no incongruity in the "Daimlerflug" of the second line. The line of "absolute poetry" to which I alluded—"südlich, Thalassa, o lau"—is an elliptical rendering of the whole Mediterranean and tropical complex so rich in associations for Benn; he is particularly addicted to the "au" sound and therefore evokes a vision of blue skies and seas. And indeed the colour itself presents itself without fail in the next stanza:

meerisch lagernde Stunde,
Bläue, mythischer Flor . . .

In the later stanzas, unfortunately, the tension between past and present is heightened almost to breaking point, again out of a self-conscious ingenuity, a virtuosity bordering on the specious:

Philosophia perennis
Hegels schauender Akt:—
Biologie und Tennis
über Verrat geflaggt.

Benn's tendency to be distracted into the merely topical or into abstract slogans would not matter so much if it were confined to separate poems like the jazzy, polyglot, and obscene "Banane-," though even this poem detracts from the others by parodying them. Benn summed up his purpose at the time in the phrase *trunken cerebral* (drunkenly cerebral); his poems break down where they become cerebral without being drunken.

This is always due to his basic self-division, which assumes the guise of a conflict between inward and outward reality. When this conflict becomes too acute, the mind cries out for its own dissolution or for the destruction of the world. Most of his poems of this period dwell on the second possibility; but where they do so with sufficient intensity, the conflict itself is reconciled and Benn's very nihilism becomes an affirmation of life. So in "Namenlos," "Spuk," and—most flawlessly of all—in "Palau." True, what "Palau" affirms is a biological life force, "bestial" and indestructible; but its philosophical implications are suspended, because it never lapses into cerebral abstractions:

"Rot ist der Abend auf der Insel von Palau
und die Schatten sinken—"
singe, auch aus den Kelchen der Frau
lässt es sich trinken,
Totenvögel schrein
und die Totenuhren
pochen, bald wird es sein
Nacht und Lemuren.

Heisse Riffe. Aus Eukalypten geht
Tropik und Palmung,
was sich noch hält und steht,
will auch Zermalmung
bis in das Gliederlos,
bis in die Leere,
tief in den Schöpfungsschoss
dämmernder Meere.

Rot is der Abend auf der Insel von Palau
und im Schattenschimmer
hebt sich steigend aus Dämmer und Tau:
"niemals und immer"
alle Tode der Welt
sind Fähren und Furten,
und von Fremdem umstellt
auch deine Geburten—

einmal mit Opferfett
auf dem Piniengerüste
trägt sich dein Flammenbett
wie Wein zur Küste,
Megalithen zuhauf
und die Gräber und Hallen,
Hammer des Thor im Lauf
zu den Asen zerfallen—

wie die Götter vergehn
und die grossen Cäsaren,
von der Wange des Zeus
emporgefahren—
singe, wandert die Welt
schon in fremdestem Schwunge
schmeckt uns das Charonsgeld
längst unter der Zunge—

Paarung. Dein Meer belebt
Sepien, Korallen,

was sich noch hält und schwebt,
will auch zerfallen,
rot ist der Abend auf der Insel von Palau,
Eukalyptenschimmer
hebt in Runen aus Dämmer und Tau:
niemals und immer.

("Evening is red on the island of Palau
and the shadows sink—"
sing, from woman's chalices too
it is good to drink,
deathly the little owls cry
and the death-watch ticks out
very soon it will be
Lemures and night.

Hot these reefs. From eucalypti there flows
a tropical palm concoction,
all that still holds and stays
also longs for destruction
down to the limbless stage,
down to the vacuum,
back to the primal age,
dark ocean's womb.

Evening is red on the island of Palau
in the gleam of these shadows
there issues rising from twilight and dew:
"never and always";
all the deaths of the earth
are fords and ferries,
what to you owes its birth
surrounded with strangeness—

once with sacrificial
fat on the pine-wood floor
your bed of flames would travel
like wine to the shore,
megaliths heaped around
and the graves and the halls,
hammer of Thor that's bound
for the Aesir, crumbled, falls—

as the gods surcease,
the great Caesars decline,
from the cheek of Zeus
once raised up to reign—

sing, already the world
to the strangest rhythm is swung,
Charon's coin if not curled
long tasted under the tongue—

Coupling. Sepias your seas
and coral animate,
all that still holds and sways
also longs to disintegrate,
evening is red on the island of Palau,
eucalyptus glaze
raises in runes from twilight and dew:
never and always.)

"Palau" transcends nihilism not because it is "absolute" in any sense invented by Benn, but rather because in it Benn has found the precise "objective correlative" for his state of mind. The poem, therefore, is positive, even if the state of mind is not; it is a poem of tragic affirmation and, as such, requires no reference to the author's intentions or beliefs. Benn's best poems succeed in spite of his theories, because he could not keep reality out of them. He could be indifferent to the meaning of his poetry and to its effect on others; he could disclaim responsibility for it on the grounds that he had no other purpose than to express or please himself; but he could not prevent the isolated fact and the autonomous fantasy from returning to the indivisible reality of which they are parts. He could banish his mind to an island, but he could not make that island disappear from the universe.

Gottfried Benn is one of the very few Expressionist poets who did their best work during Phase 2, the inter-war years. It was not till his incantatory poems of the 1920s that he learned to avail himself of the new freedoms and to combine them with a discipline peculiar to his work. "Palau" makes good use of the dynamic syntax of Expressionism, but its form is much closer to that of the choric poems in Goethe's *Faust* than to any verse form cultivated by the other Expressionists.

With Benn's later work—that of the period which he called Phase 2 and I have called Phase 3 of Expressionism—I can deal only very briefly here. Already his *Statische Gedichte*, a collection of poems written mainly between 1937 and 1947, contains poems in at least three distinct styles: the incantatory style of "Palau," a more sober neoclassical style—sometimes clearly derivative from Goethe's later lyrics, as in the poem "Ach, der Erhabene"—and a self-consciously "modern" style mainly confined to poems in loose free verse. These three styles recur in Benn's last collections.

But for his prose works of the same period, which remained as provocative as his earlier ones, it would be clear to everyone that what Benn calls "Phase 2" is no more than an "apréslude" to Expressionism. Indeed, even his late prose works are not quite as belligerent as the earlier, though one has to read between the lines—or skip a good many—to arrive at the truth about a development that Benn did his best to resist. His *Drei Alte Männer*, published in 1949, belongs to a genre especially dear to Benn, being a peculiar mixture of fact and fantasy, prose lyricism and polemical journalism. The three old men of the title meet at the house of one of them to reflect on their experiences of the past, discuss their attitude to the present, and prove their superiority to the future—in the shape of a young man whose main function is to prompt the main speakers. These speakers are not sufficiently differentiated to qualify as distinct characters; their dialectic is that of Benn's own mind; and their preoccupations those which we know to be his own. Many of their utterances are mere reiterations of the nihilistic or aesthetic commonplaces familiar enough from the earlier works. "God is a drug," for instance; "the only thing that really belongs to us is what we drink"; or "we only live when we forget." But there is also a new note, a mood of melancholy resignation and hopeless courage. "We were a great generation," one of them says: "sorrow and light, verses and weapons, sorrow and light, and when night comes, we shall endure it." The nihilism is unchanged, but it has lost its dynamism, its ecstasy, and its aggressiveness. These old men too speak of the "occidental finale: to believe that something exists," but instead of mocking this belief—as Benn did a decade earlier, in his *Weinhaus Wolf*—they attribute the greatness of Western man to its recurrence after every possible kind of breakdown. The main trend of *Drei Alte Männer* is toward a stoical acceptance of the worst: "To err, and yet to be compelled to renew his belief in his own inner motives, that is man; and beyond both victory and defeat his fame begins."

Die Stimme hinter dem Vorhang (*The Voice behind the Curtain*), a later work by three years, is also a conversation piece. The voice is that of the Father; and "the programme is: what does the progenitor say to his sons and daughters—nowadays." A number of "examples"—presumably meant to be representative of these sons and daughters—give accounts of themselves. There is a man of sixty whose chief aim in life is to commit adultery with young women; an old-age pensioner who is content to let the government provide for him and hopes that "the others will die" before his turn comes; a woman who keeps a brothel that caters for all tastes; and a landlord who is obsessed with different ways of exploiting and cheating his tenants without infringing the law. When they first appear, these characters profess the belief that "what is holy is manifested in all things." In the second part, various sons and daughters confront the Father with a Sunday paper, which provides them with opportunities to poke fun at such institutions as modern democracy, psychoanalysis, and the PEN Club. Their taunts and complaints culminate in more serious accusations, but mainly that of cruelty and indifference to their well-being. To every charge the Father replies: "Well, what do you expect," but finally loses patience and roars out a string of coarse insults that put an end to the discussion. The third conversation takes place two months later, when the "examples" reappear with a Chorus; they accept the fact that "the Old Man too has left us in the lurch" and decide to make do without him. Once again, resignation is their last resort: "To live in the dark, in the dark to do what we can."

In *Monologische Kunst—?* (1953)—an exchange of letters between Gottfried Benn and the Austrian poet Alexander Lernet-Holenia—Benn answers his correspondent's objections to this unorthodox morality play. He argues that faith is a gift which has not been granted to him; that he does not deny the existence of a Creator, but that a "distant" relationship to Him is preferable to one that "exploits God" by too immediate a dependence. "To gape at Him continually with eyes and lips, in my view, is a great offence, for it presupposes that we mean something to Him, while my veneration assumes that He only passes through us with some force, with very limited force, and that it then passes on to something other than ourselves." Lernet-Holenia also tells Benn that "it is time you began to speak to the Nation," proposing the example of Hofmannsthal and warning Benn that it was solitude that brought about Nietzsche's ruin. Benn defends both Nietzsche's solitude and his own; but after rightly distinguishing between Nietzsche's solitary habits and his mental isolation from the community, he proceeds to confuse the issue by a discussion of his own personal habits. Benn affirms that he will not try to emulate the cultural rôle of Hofmannsthal, a rôle for which he was wholly unfitted; but he does qualify his earlier insistence on the totally isolated ego. He admits a certain invisible link between one ego and another, as he must after professing belief in the Creator. "Express your I," he concludes, "and you will be passing on your life to the Thou, passing on your loneliness to the community and the distance."

Both in *Monologische Kunst—?* and another late prose work, *Altern als Problem für Künstler* (1954), Benn still insisted on the antinomy between truth and style. The last fifty years, he claimed in the essay on Nietzsche appended to the former work, were marked by strange movements, "above all, by those that have done away with truth and laid the foundations of style." In the later work, an interesting investigation of the effect of old age on artistic production, he repeated that "art, of course, isn't concerned with truth at all, only with expression." But "style," one of his old men says, "is exaggeration; expression is arrogance and suppression: by such foul methods the mind proceeds." Literature, to Gottfried Benn, remained a form of self-indulgence, the most effective of the drugs that make life bearable. It is therefore of the same order as any other stimulant or narcotic, such as crime, which one of his characters recommends for similar reasons: "And indeed only crime gets us any farther."

There is something admirable as well as pathetic about these attempts of Benn's to cheer himself up and startle his readers with squibs kept in storage for thirty years or more; but the poem knows better than the poet, and much of Benn's later poetry contradicts this obstinate clinging to his function of *enfant terrible* and *fort esprit*. Of Benn's three styles in his collections of the 1950s the neoclassical was a neutral, impersonal style almost free from the more drastically expressive syntax of his modernist phase. Many of the best poems in *Fragmente, Destillationen,* and *Apréslude* are of this kind, regardless of theories that Benn continued to expound. "Blaue Stunde," for instance, is a love poem, clearly addressed to someone and someone other than Benn himself. All of them communicate something that would be valid even if translated into prose. The lessons of recent history are implicit everywhere behind the stoical despair—tinged with remorse in "Die Gitter" or even with compassion in "Denk der Vergeblichen."

The informal free-verse poems, on the other hand, may look like a reversion to Benn's earliest mode, to the manner of *Morgue, Söhne,* and *Fleisch.* Yet Benn's unacknowledged change of heart is even more striking in these informal pieces than in the best of the neoclassical poems, such as "Der Dunkle," "Jener" and "Eingeengt." The informal, less general and less abstract diction of the free-verse poems admits not only direct personal experience but the historical consciousness that Benn had done his best to oppose and exclude in the inter-war years. Indeed, the deliberate prosiness of his late free verse is at the opposite pole to "absolute poetry," as defined by Benn or by his French predecessors. It is close to the practice of Brecht and to that of younger poets writing after World War II. Part of the poem "Spät" (in *Destillationen*) corresponds word for word with a passage in the prose dialogue *Die Stimme hinter dem Vorhang.* Whereas in the earlier phase Benn's prose had tended to erupt into lyricism, in the later phase quite a number of his poems tended toward the rhythms, diction, and syntax of prose. So in "Ideelles Weiterleben?" ("Ideal Survival?"):

> Bald
> ein abgesägter, überholter
> früh oder auch spät verstorbener Mann,
> von dem man spricht wie von einer Sängerin
> mit ausgesungenem Sopran
> oder vom kleinen Hölty mit seinen paar Versen—
> noch weniger: Durchschnitt,
> nie geflogen,
> keinen Borgward gefahren—
> Zehnpfennigstücke für die Tram,
> im Höchstfall Umsteiger.
>
> Dabei ging täglich soviel bei dir durch
> introvertiert, extrovertiert,
> Nahrungssorgen, Ehewidrigkeit, Steuermoral—
> mit allem musstest du dich befassen,
> ein gerüttelt Mass von Leben in mancherlei Gestalt.

Auf einer Karte aus Antibes,
die ich heute erhielt,
ragt eine Burg in die Méditerranée,
eine fanatische Sache:
südlich, meerisch, schneeig, am Rande hochgebirgig—
Jahrhunderte, dramatisiert,
ragen, ruhen, glänzen, firnen, strotzen
sich in die Aufnahme—
Nichts von alledem bei dir,
keine Ingredienzien zu einer Ansichtskarte—
Zehnpfennigstücke für die Tram,
Umsteiger,
und schnell die obenerwähnte Wortprägung:
überholt.

(Soon
a sawn-off, out-of-date
man who died early or may-be late,
of whom one speaks as of a singer
whose soprano is worn out
or of poor little Todhunter and his handful of verses—
even less: average,
never flew in a plane,
never drove a Borgward—
pennies paid out on the tram
a return fare at the most.

Yet daily so much passed through you
introverted, extroverted,
money troubles, marriage vexations, tax morality—
with all these you had to concern yourself,
a full measure of life in many a shape.

On a postcard from Antibes
which I received today
a castle looms over la Méditerranée,
a fanatical object, that:
southerly, snowy, marine, alpine at the edges—
centuries, dramatized,
loom, rest, gleam, glaze, swell
into the photograph—
Nothing of all this about you,
no ingredients at all for a picture postcard—
pennies paid out on the tram
return fares,
and quickly then the above-named caption:
out of date.)

The person, as well as the subject, of that poem is the man whom Benn had once relegated to a life separate and distinct from that of the "absolute" poet. Although Benn retained his habit of addressing himself in the second person, the autobiographical character of the poem is as unmistakable as its concern with an order of reality, the empirical and worldly, which Benn's ecstatic poem of the 1920s had negated or dissolved in an inward flux. The relaxation of this poem's gesture is carried to the point of slackness, as in the placing of the word "man" (line 4) so close to the "Mann" of line 3 in stanza 1.

Another reversal of Benn's premises and assumptions occurs in the late poem "Menschen Getroffen" ("People Met"), which not only admits but celebrates the "neighbour" so consistently banished from his earlier works. But for those premises and assumptions Benn's belated recognition here that other people exist might seem so naïve or perverse as to make the reader wonder not at those people but at the poet's wonderment:

Ich habe Menschen getroffen, die,
Wenn man sie nach ihrem Namen fragte,
Schüchtern—als ob sie garnicht beanspruchen könnten,
Auch noch eine Benennung zu haben—
"Fräulein Christian" antworteten und dann: "Wie der
            Vorname," sie wollten einem die Erfassung erleichtern
Kein schwieriger Name wie "Popiol" oder "Babendererde"—
"Wie der Vorname"—bitte, belasten Sie Ihr
            Erinnerungsvermögen nicht.

Ich habe Menschen getroffen, die
Mit Eltern und vier Geschwistern in einer Stube
Aufwuchsen, nachts, die Finger in den Ohren,
Am Küchenherde lernten,
Hochkamen, äusserlich schön und ladylike wie Gräfinnen—
Und innerlich sanft und fleissig wie Nausikaa,
Die reine Stirn der Engel trugen.

Ich habe mich oft gefragt und keine Antwort gefunden,
Woher das Sanfte und das Gute kommt,
Weiss es auch heute nicht und muss nun gehn.

(I have met people who, when asked what their names
            were,
Apologetically, as if they had no right to claim one's
            attention
Even with an appellation, would answer,
"Miss Vivian," then add, "Just like the Christian name";
They wanted to make things easier, no complicated names
Like Popkiss or Umpleby-Dunball—

"Just like the Christian name"—so please do not burden your
    memory!

I have met people who grew up in a single room together
    with
Parents and four brothers and sisters; they studied by night,
Their fingers in their ears, beside the kitchen range;
They became eminent,
Outwardly beautiful, veritable *grandes dames,* and
Inwardly gentle and active as Nausicaa,
With brows clear as angels' brows.

Often I have asked myself, but found no answer,
Where gentleness and goodness can possibly come from;
Even today I can't tell, and it's time to be gone.)

What matters is that Benn continued to develop as a poet until his
death at the age of seventy—even while denying the change of heart which
made that development possible. Benn's "Phase 3" of Expressionism may
strike us as a reluctant retreat from a position that history had made untenable, but the retreat did carry his poetry over into the post-war, post-
Expressionist and post-modernist era, as well as enabling others to bridge
the same gap; and as Benn wrote in his *Epilogue* (1949) to his early and late
work:

> Leben ist Brückenschlagen
> über Ströme die vergehn.

> (Life is the building of bridges
> over rivers that seep away.)

In a different and more crucial sense, it is Benn's earlier, exclusively
and frenziedly expressive work that is regressive, because its intensity was
attained at the cost of reason and consciousness, the emotional drive chan-
nelled as narrowly as possible to produce the more energy. Unlike the
singing voice of Benn's more ecstatic poems—those written in the nineteen-
twenties—the speaking voice of the late free-verse poems is that of a civilized man, aware of history, of society, of the little realities that make up
our outward lives. Whether he acknowledged it or not, Benn had seen or
sensed the connection between absolute art and absolute politics, alike in
their total rejection and elimination of all that is not grist to their mill, and
the poet had learned the lesson, even if the essayist and public speaker
had not. Seen as a whole, Benn's poetry has the full range and tension of
those perennial contraries Reason and Energy, realism and imagination,
phenomenon and idea; and he produced rather more than the "six or eight
consummate poems," which he claimed to be all that a poet of his time
could achieve.

More than a quarter of a century after his death, with a large body of critical literature and biographical documents available now to his readers, one would suppose Gottfried Benn to have ceased to be the controversial figure he was throughout his active life. Yet the more his critics try to make sense of his work as a whole—whether strictly on its own terms or in terms of the "phenotype" Benn also claimed to be, with due allowance for his various phases—and the more material they have to draw on for their interpretations, the more puzzling and contradictory his case has become.

That poetry is made out of one's quarrel with oneself, out of tensions, is an insight of Yeats few practitioners could honestly call in question; but in most cases those tensions can be recorded in such a way as to yield a graph whose extreme rises and dips still constitute a pattern of sorts. However variable, the currents show a certain consistency. Benn's contradictions and ambivalences, though, break the recording machine. No critical chart of them can accommodate such violent and erratic fluctuations.

Of all the collections of his letters now published—from the selected letters volume of 1957 to the correspondence with Paul Hindemith issued in 1978—Benn's letters to F. W. Oelze are by far the most substantial and revealing, taken as a whole, though Oelze forbade the publication of his part in the correspondence, not all of which is extant. As far as possible, the editors have made use of Oelze's letters in their helpful notes, though even fuller elucidations would have been desirable in places; and since Benn's letters to Oelze are remarkable for not being monologues, for an exceptionally delicate responsiveness to another person, one does miss Oelze's letters, regardless of whether their literary qualities matched those of Benn. The extracts quoted in the notes suggest that they did. A short introduction by Oelze appears in the first volume; but Oelze died before the third volume appeared, and he was unable to offer much co-operation in his last years. Since most of Benn's personal relationships were no more constant than anything else in his life, the very time-span covered by these letters sets them apart; and if any friend can be said to have influenced Gottfried Benn during that period, the last twenty-four years of his life, F. W. Oelze was that friend.

That in itself could seem astonishing to anyone who still expects Benn to show a modicum of consistency. When Oelze wrote to Benn in 1932 about Benn's essay on Goethe and the natural sciences—one of his outstanding critical works, as distinct from the rhapsodies more characteristic of Benn as a prose writer—Oelze was a businessman from Bremen, with literary interests and connections, it is true, and distinguished by an elegance, an urbanity and a style consonant with his earlier intention to become a diplomat. Oelze's law studies had taken him to England, as his business interests were to do in later years. To Benn he was not only the Hanseatic patrician familiar from the fiction of Thomas Mann, but a gentleman of the British type. Often, indeed, the letters promote him to an aristocracy that Benn despised Rilke for cultivating. The dependence of Oelze's "aristocratic" ways on his commercial enterprises did not bother

Benn, despite his vehement anti-commercialism elsewhere; on the contrary, he was always urging Oelze to live up to his image of him as a man superior in every regard to the general run of humanity, to keep up his life-style, look after himself and his interests. Oelze's gifts of exquisite flowers, wines and other things beyond Benn's means even before the war, let alone the immediate post-war years, are acknowledged throughout the letters; but what was important to Benn was a sympathy and support on which he could rely in the changing circumstances of all those years, just as he came to rely on Oelze's judgement of his own works, of which Oelze made a unique collection, on Oelze's wider knowledge of literature as a whole, his much more catholic taste and a degree of self-detachment of which Benn was rarely capable. It seems to have been partly due to Oelze that Goethe came to replace Nietzsche as Benn's chief model in later years, a development prefigured in the Goethe essay of 1931, but fully effective only in the neo-classicizing trend of Benn's own poems written in the later thirties and early forties—the poems he called "static." Oelze, then, combined several functions in Benn's eyes; and one of them was that of Maecenas—a friend as different as possible from the "petit-bourgeois" Benn repeatedly described himself as being, not as a poet-pariah, but as a poor man's doctor with a precarious, never very lucrative practice. (That the poet-pariah also regarded himself as an "aristocrat," with a title not of this world, is a paradox by no means peculiar to Gottfried Benn.)

In 1932, though, the poet-pariah was in the process of emerging briefly into public life as a newly-elected member of the prestigious Prussian Academy of Arts, critic, broadcaster and man of letters. That emergence, too, was fraught with contradictions, and plunged Benn into ambivalences he was never to resolve. Professor Jürgen Schröder, one of the editors of the Oelze letters, has devoted a searching and thoroughly documented study to what he calls Benn's "socialization" at this period, and one important fact he establishes is that Benn's frenzied acclamations of the Third Reich were part of this process, which had begun well before the events of 1933. Professor Schröder's book is not an apology for Benn's conduct in 1933 and 1934, for his polemic against the literary emigrants or his connivance in the expulsion from the Academy of writers, like Heinrich Mann and Alfred Döblin, whom he admired more than any of his German contemporaries and had only recently eulogized publicly, in the case of Heinrich Mann. (Benn had also positively liked Heinrich Mann's nephew Klaus, to whom he addressed his notorious "Answer to the Literary Emigrants.") Schröder's book, inevitably, is the study not of one contradiction, one ambivalence, but of a whole chain and complex of contradictions and ambivalences, which he traces back not only to Benn's early writings but to attitudes formed in his childhood, as the son of a poor clergyman dependent on the patronage of aristocrats, the rural Prussian Junkers, with whom Benn partly identified, even when he was in revolt against all power structures and had found more congenial company among the bohemia of Berlin.

On this social and political level, too, no consistency of attitude can be claimed for Benn, who was also apt to identify with the underdogs, the proletarians who came to him with their skin and venereal diseases under insurance schemes, or the lower middle classes oppressed, as he was, by bureaucracy and taxation. While clearing Benn's activities in 1933 and 1934 from the imputation of deliberate opportunism, Schröder has to concede that Benn had a social chip on his shoulder, as manifested in his sneers at the wealth of those writers who had prospered under the Weimar Republic, as Benn never did until its last chaotic years. Yet Schröder shows that Benn's allegiances at the time of his "socialization" were to the extreme conservative factions, rather than to the National Socialist Party. A number of the leaders of those factions did find themselves in opposition to the Nazi régime—as Benn was to do by 1935 at the latest—and some paid for it with their lives; but others saw National Socialism as the fulfilment of the "conservative revolution" they had worked for, or were prepared to compromise with the new regime for one reason or another. Here Benn's private ideological muddles run parallel with more general and public ones; and he was not alone in failing to foresee the consequences of a nihilistic conservatism, a conservatism not rooted in values and institutions but in corporate neuroses sublimated into "ideals." Benn's peculiar brand of Nietzschean cataclysmic aestheticism, combined with half-baked pseudo-scientific theories about eugenics, and his unwillingness to apply himself to the minutiae of anything so boring as political programmes, go a long way towards explaining his brief pro-Nazi euphoria. A less rational—but perhaps more searching—interpretation would have to face up to the possibility that what Benn responded to at this juncture was the catastrophic extremism that underlay the "law and order" of the new régime, the promise of a "clean sweep" that would stop at nothing, not even self-annihilation. A great deal in Benn's earlier work points to this interpretation.

Schröder sees Benn's "socialization" as a compensation for his earlier insistence on the necessarily a-social, if not anti-social, function of art, its total separateness from any social structure, and his early characterization of the artist as a Prometheus, Narcissus or pariah figure:

> That is why Gottfried Benn was predestined to cast the basic socio-political experience of the twentieth century, that is, the still largely unfathomed experience of alienation, powerlessness and isolation of the individual, into its most communicable and enjoyable form. The culinary quality of all his work, unmistakable as a glaze even in his most strident verses and sentences, can indeed be defined as the poetic expression of socially compensatory acts, as a kind of social masturbation. What makes his poems so "beautiful" even in the most "terrible" passages is their unfailing capacity to provide this autistic self-comfort.

Here he may be going a little too far both in granting Benn the "phenotypal" status Benn claimed for himself, and in his judgement of Benn's work as a whole, which is far from being all of a piece; but Schröder does put his finger on the powerlessness of the individual in Benn's work. For all his solipsism, Benn's intellectual world was singularly lacking in freedom, choice or responsibility. Self-destructive revolt or resignation are his pervasive gestures.

By April 1934 Benn's position as an apologist both for "degenerate art" and for the biological "regeneration" of Germany had become untenable. That month he wrote to Oelze with a special request. Benn had been accused by a fellow conservative, the ballad writer Börries von Münchhausen, of being a typical Jewish intellectual, on the grounds that "Benn" was not a German name, that Benn looked like a Jew, behaved like a Jew and wrote like a Jew. His request was that Oelze make enquiries in England about families there with that name, including the owners of a publishing house, so that Benn could establish his "Aryan" pedigree. This did not help much, it turned out, because Münchhausen, like all those who were to persecute Benn on similar grounds, were no more interested in facts or realities than Benn was. (In a letter of 1926, to one of a succession of Jewish girl friends, Benn had called himself "a professed opponent of reality.") Münchhausen's attack was a foretaste of events that drove Benn out of public life, out of his medical practice in Berlin, and back into the Army, which he was able to regard as "the aristocratic form of emigration" until the removal of the old high command, von Fritzsch and Blomberg, in 1938. Very soon he was to exchange letters with Oelze about the progress of the war, only thinly veiling his wish for the defeat of the army whose uniform he continued to wear—one more of the ambivalences Benn did his best to accept as other people accept the weather. Even in the Army Benn's position was subordinate and, at one point, subject to threats from the Party, but it did give him security and a kind of independence until the end of the war.

At the height of his pro-Nazi fervour Benn had not fallen in line with the Party's anti-Semitism. His allegiance—as in questions of the arts—was offered on his own terms. In 1935 he wrote to Oelze: "Next to the Jewish, the aristocratic milieu is the most congenial to me. Here, too, there is something superior and you could say, un-Nordic, that is, refinement." This, of course, is a racist, as well as a crassly snobbish, generalization, but one at odds with the Party's racism; and like all Benn's generalizations, it was personal, idiosyncratic and reversible. In 1951, when Benn's second emergence into public life had come up against misgivings and recriminations from some of the emigrants, including Jewish ones, against whom he had inveighed in 1933, he wrote to Oelze: "Other American emigrants, too, came to see me, less agreeable ones, strangely sterile these Semitic intellectuals are, but think themselves very superior and global"—an exact reversal of the earlier statement, and now couched in the very terms of Nazi racism. At other times Benn's racism was directed against his own people, described as "second-rate. With no capacity for differentiation . . . ," or against "the Slavs and Mongols," who threatened "the last strenuous self-assertion of an ancient race," as he wrote to Oelze in 1934 about the same "second-rate" nation. It all depended on how Benn felt at any particular moment; and the clue to all such vagaries lies not only in his own lack of "differentiation" and discrimination but in a relativism which he called "perspectivism" in one of his first letters to Oelze, dated 27 January 1933:

> In place of the concept of *truth* and of reality, once a theological, then a scientific, requisite, we now have the concept of per-spectivism . . . One develops a perspective. If this is existentially credible, convincing as a way of looking, a vision, its purpose has been achieved . . . Genuine thinking is always dangerous and endangered. The idea and the word, after all, did not originate to justify science and socialism and medical insurance, but as the most terrible weapon, the most cruel cutting blade, the bloodiest morning star to help weaponless mankind in the most cruel of all worlds.

The same letter goes on to explain the connection between this "perspectivism" and what Benn called his "nihilism." Both came out of Nietzsche, of course, but Nietzsche was a balanced, discriminating and moderate thinker in comparison! Above all, Nietzsche could stand back from himself, from his obsessions and irrationalities—the one thing Benn consistently refused to do, at least in public. Even more than with Nietzsche, a reader has to translate seemingly objective statements into personal confessions, if he is not to be confused and misled by Benn's prose. One instance must suffice here. "What are they like, these lyrical poets, psychologically, sociologically, as a phenomenon? First of all, contrary to the common view, they are no dreamers. Other people may dream, they are the utilizers of dreams, by dreams, too, they must be carried on to words. Nor, strictly speaking, are they intellectuals, nor aesthetes, for they produce art, that is, they need a hard, massive brain with molars that grind down resistances, including their own. They are petit-bourgeois with a peculiar urge, born half of vulcanism, half of apathy." The definition occurs not in a letter, but in Benn's widely influential lecture "Probleme der Lyrik" of 1951. Yet it is a self-characterization, down to the specifications of class and motive, not a characterization of lyrical poets in general.

With few exceptions, then, even Benn's seemingly critical prose is best read as fiction—as a sort of poetry that juggles with ideas and concepts, takes up this speculation or that from his altogether haphazard reading—whether it be Spengler's historicizing, the anti-democratic cultural prescriptions of Baron Giulio Evola, or the "Yellow Peril" of the gutter press—and uses them for effects that are aesthetic or expressive, not expository or epistemonical. How could it be otherwise, when Benn believed neither in truth nor reality? His impatience with both—despite his scientific training, or because of it, since it was scientific positivism against which he reacted with unprecedented extremism—is attested by the letters, one of which, the letter to Oelze of 13 August 1939, stands out as an example of a poetic prose as peculiar to Benn as the best of his verse. In that letter, quoting a favourite line from a poem by Nietzsche, he writes of his generation, "it was not our hearts that broke, what broke in us was our consciousness."

Relaxed as most of them are, the impatience is apparent even in the letters. In one of them he asks about the flowers he had seen at Oelze's country house: "Is it clematis or wisteria that climbs the wall? A third possibility would be a grape-vine, but I think: clematis the loveliest blue on earth." Blue, for Benn, was a trigger for rhapsodies; and he was always celebrating flowers in his verse and prose. Yet, considering how different those three plants are, "seen" is hardly the word. In the same letter he writes of the "cynicism and irony" of his response to the "world of order," meaning his wartime office work for the Army, whose "efficiency and meticulousness seems loose to me and ready to be blown off like the spumy head of a buttercup," when quite obviously he is thinking of a dandelion. The same lack of simple observation is conspicuous in all but a few of his poems—the very early ones, which came out of disgust with his medical experience, and a handful of very late ones, largely autobiographical and written in a deliberately casual, flat and understated free verse.

Benn was capable enough of observing and judging when he wanted to be. His letter to Oelze about Ludwig Klages is one example of sober critical judgement. At times he could see through both the historical and biological determinism into which he fell again and again despite his rejection of history and his recognition, as a doctor, that "there is no such thing as *organic* causes of illness," that "health" and "life" are concepts "out of zoology." Though his nihilism seems just about the most constant factor in all his public writings, there is evidence in his late poems—not backed up by his critical writings of the same period—that even the nihilism was subject to shifting perspectives; and in a private jotting of 1953 he noted: "Nihilism for me is a word that rings out from a stupid ashen world I may once have caught with one glance, but do not know at all. A muffled, unanswerable world, whereas I have always answered. The answer—that must be it." As long as he wanted his writing to be only emotive and expressive, such insights had to be put away in a separate compartment; and there is good evidence for believing that as a physician Benn was as attentive, conscientious and sympathetic as he was irresponsible as a thinker. Hence his resort to a "double life" in his apology for it, the autobiography *Doppelleben*.

It is because his letters—and those to Oelze especially—come as close as anything he wrote to bridging the gap between his two lives that they should be read not only by those interested in the work or case of Gottfried Benn but by those interested in the cultural history of Germany between the Second Reich and the two post-war Republics. If Gottfried Benn was a "phenotype," it is his contradictions, ambivalences and muddles that made him so, rather than his understanding either of himself or of his age.

"We lived something other than what we were, we wrote something other than what we thought, we thought something other than what we expected, and what remains is something other than what we intended," is how Benn summed up the basic incongruities in his conversation piece *Drei Alte Männer* of 1949, which he dedicated to Oelze. Though even in this late passage a partial substitution of the first person singular is called for, a good many of his older readers must have identified to some extent with that statement, at least as far as it alludes to political errors. Behind the stoical posture with which Benn accepted this state of affairs, the letters reveal intense suffering, intense guilt—not only over his political stance in 1933, but over personal bereavements like the death of two of his wives and of his mistress Lily Breda, for whose suicide he blamed himself. In his determination never to resolve dichotomies, never to "synthesize," never to correct his specific errors publicly but only admit them so generally that the admission became an excuse, fired off in terms of new questionable generalizations about "the white race," the state of the arts, in which "style" had replaced "truth," or of the sciences and the divided, isolated consciousness they had induced, he concealed the changes of mind and heart, the mellowing we can discern in the letters to Oelze.

If Benn's aspiration to what he called "absolute" poetry had not been as ambiguous and questionable as all his theorizing, biographical documents like the letters would be largely irrelevant to his work. Yet even where his poetry is not undisguisedly confessional, it is so self-obsessed, so self-encapsulated that it demands not less but more sympathy with the person behind it than the work of poets with no such aspiration, but a greater openness to the outside world. Since Benn's empirical self, as revealed in his letters, was a great deal more amenable to sympathy than some of the more extreme projections of his poetical selves, his letters to Oelze can be welcomed more unreservedly than some of the letters of poets, like Rilke, who made an art of letter-writing, as Benn did not. When Benn, in a letter to Oelze of 1941, called Rilke "this little runt of a man, concealing his often degenerate existence in delicate, sickly, shameless and at the same time crafty and for ever squinting and cringing subterfuges," he was responding less to Rilke's work than to his person, as known to Benn from photographs and letters. Elsewhere, needless to say, Benn's response to Rilke was wholly positive; and he had much more in common with Rilke than this physiological condemnation suggests. In the same context Benn, the advocate of "absolute" art, wrote: ". . . either art is life-transforming, i.e., life-destroying, or it's dirt (Plastilin)." A reader disinclined to unravel that kind of "thinking" may concentrate with relief on the more trivially biographical accounts these letters also are, happy to find that its perpetrator was likeable enough as a man.

Georg Trakl: Language in the Poem

Martin Heidegger

We use the word "discuss" here to mean, first, to point out the proper place or site of something, to situate it, and second, to heed that place or site. The placing and the heeding are both preliminaries of discussion. And yet it will require all our daring to take no more than these preliminary steps in what follows. Our discussion, as befits a thinking way, ends in a question. That question asks for the location of the site.

Our discussion speaks of Georg Trakl only in that it thinks about the site of his poetic work. To an age whose historical, biographical, psychoanalytical, and sociological interest is focused on bare expression, such a procedure must seem patently one-sided, if not wayward. Discussion gives thought to the site.

Originally the word "site" suggests a place in which everything comes together, is concentrated. The site gathers unto itself, supremely and in the extreme. Its gathering power penetrates and pervades everything. The site, the gathering power, gathers in and preserves all it has gathered, not like an encapsulating shell but rather by penetrating with its light all it has gathered, and only thus releasing it into its own nature.

Our task now is to discuss the site that gathers Georg Trakl's poetic Saying into his poetic work—to situate the site of Trakl's work.

Every great poet creates his poetry out of one single poetic statement only. The measure of his greatness is the extent to which he becomes so committed to that singleness that he is able to keep his poetic Saying wholly within it.

The poet's statement remains unspoken. None of his individual poems, nor their totality, says it all. Nonetheless, every poem speaks from the whole of the one single statement, and in each instance says that statement.

From *On the Way to Language*. © 1971 by Harper & Row Publishers.

From the site of the statement there rises the wave that in each instance moves his Saying as poetic saying. But that wave, far from leaving the site behind, in its rise causes all the movement of Saying to flow back to its ever more hidden source. The site of the poetic statement, source of the movement-giving wave, holds within it the hidden nature of what, from a metaphysical-aesthetic point of view, may at first appear to be rhythm.

Since the poet's sole statement always remains in the realm of the unspoken, we can discuss its site only by trying to point to it by means of what the individual poems speak. But to do so, each poem will itself be in need of clarification. Clarification is what brings to its first appearance that purity which shimmers in everything said poetically.

It is easy to see that any right clarification itself already presupposes discussion. The individual poems derive their light and sound only from the poetic site. Conversely, the discussion of the poetic statement must first pass through the precursory clarification of individual poems.

All thinking dialogue with a poet's poetic statement stays within this reciprocity between discussion and clarification.

Only a poetic dialogue with a poet's poetic statement is a true dialogue—the poetic conversation between poets. But it is also possible, and at times indeed necessary, that there be a dialogue between *thinking* and poetry, for this reason: because a distinctive, though in each case different, relation to language is proper to them both.

The dialogue of thinking with poetry aims to call forth the *nature* of language, so that mortals may learn again to live within language.

The dialogue of thinking with poetry is long. It has barely begun. With respect to Trakl's poetic statement, the dialogue requires particular reserve. A thinking dialogue with poetry can serve the poetic statement only indirectly. Thus it is always in danger of interfering with the saying of the statement, instead of allowing it to sing from within its own inner peace.

The discussion of the poetic statement is a thinking dialogue with poetry. It neither expounds a poet's outlook on the world, nor does it take inventory of his workshop. Above all, the discussion of the poetic statement can never be a substitute for or even guide to our listening to the poem. Thinking discussion can at best make our listening thought-provoking and, under the most favorable circumstances, more reflective.

With these reservations in mind, we shall try first to point to the site of the unspoken statement. To do so we must start with the spoken poems. The question still is: with which poems? The fact that every one of Trakl's poems points, with equal steadiness though not uniformly, to the statement's one site, is evidence of the unique harmony of all his poems in the single key of his statement.

But the attempt we shall now make to point out the site of his statement must make do with just a few selected stanzas, lines, and phrases. Our selection will inevitably seem arbitrary. However, it is prompted by our purpose to bring our consideration at once to the site of the statement, almost as if by a sudden leap of insight.

I

One of Trakl's poems says:

Something strange is the soul on the earth.

Before we know what we are doing, we find ourselves through this sentence involved in a common notion. That notion presents the earth to us as earthly in the sense of transitory. The soul, by contrast, is regarded as imperishable, supraterrestrial. Beginning with Plato's doctrine, the soul is part of the suprasensuous. If it appears within the sensible world, it does so only as a castaway. Here on earth the soul is miscast. It does not belong on earth. Here, the soul is something strange. The body is the soul's prison, if nothing worse. The soul, then, apparently has nothing else to look forward to except to leave as soon as possible the sensuous realm which, seen in Platonic terms, has no true being and is merely decay.

And yet—how remarkable: the sentence

Something strange is the soul on the earth.

speaks from within a poem entitled "Springtime of the Soul." And there is in that poem not one word about a supraterrestrial home of the immortal soul. The matter gives us food for thought; we will do well to pay heed to the poet's language. The soul: "something strange." Trakl frequently uses the same construction in other poems: "something mortal," "something dark," "something solitary," "something spent," "something sick," "something human," "something pale," "something dead," "something silent." Apart from its varying content, this construction does not always carry the same sense. Something "solitary," "something strange" could mean a singular something that in the given case is "solitary," or by chance is in a special and limited sense "strange." "Something strange" of that sort can be classified as belonging to the order of the strange in general, and can thus be disposed of. So understood, the soul would be merely one instance of strangeness among many.

But what does "strange" mean? By strange we usually understand something that is not familiar, does not appeal to us—something that is rather a burden and an unease. But the word we are using—the German *fremd*, the Old High German *fram*—really means: forward to somewhere else, underway toward . . ., onward to the encounter with what is kept in store for it. The strange goes forth, ahead. But it does not roam aimlessly, without any kind of determination. The strange element goes in its search toward the site where it may stay in its wandering. Almost unknown to itself, the "strange" is already following the call that calls it on the way into its own.

The poet calls the soul "something strange on the earth." The earth is that very place which the soul's wandering could not reach so far. The soul only *seeks* the earth; it does not flee from it. This fulfills the soul's being: in her wandering to seek the earth so that she may poetically build and dwell upon it, and thus may be able to save the earth *as* earth. The soul, then, is not by any means first of all soul, and then, besides and for whatever reason, also a stranger who does not belong on earth.

On the contrary, the sentence:

> Something strange is the soul on the earth

gives a name to the essential being of what is called soul. The sentence does not predicate something about the soul whose nature is already known, as though the point were merely to make the supplementary statement that the soul had suffered the unfitting and thus strange accident of finding neither refuge nor response on earth. The soul, on the contrary, *qua* soul is fundamentally, by its nature, "something strange on the earth." Thus it is always underway, and in its wandering follows where its nature draws it. We, meanwhile, are pressed by this question: whither has this "something strange," in the sense just made clear, been called to turn its steps? A stanza from the third part of the poem "Sebastian in Dream" gives the answer:

> O how still is a walk down the blue river's bank
> To ponder forgotten things, when in leafy boughs
> The thrush called to a strange thing to go under.

The soul is called to go under. Then it is so after all: the soul is to end its earthly journey and leave the earth behind! Nothing of the sort is said in the verses just quoted. And yet they speak of "going under." Certainly. But the going under of which these verses speak is neither a catastrophe, nor is it a mere withering away in decay. Whatever goes under, going down the blue river,

> Goes down in peace and silence.
> ("Transfigured Autumn")

Into what peace does it go? The peace of the dead? But of which dead? And into what silence?

> Something strange is the soul on the earth.

The stanza in which this sentence belongs continues:

> . . . Ghostly the twilight dusk
> Bluing above the mishewn forest . . .

Earlier, the sun is mentioned. The stranger's footfall goes away into the dusk. "Dusk" means, first, darkness falling. "Dusk bluing." Is the sunny day's blueness darkening? Does it fade in the evening to give way to night? But dusk is not a mere sinking of the day, the dissolution of its brightness in the gloom of night. Dusk, anyway, does not necessarily mean the twilight of the end. The morning, too, has its twilight. The day rises in twilight.

Twilight, then, is also a rising. Twilight dusk blues over the "mishewn," tangled, withered forest. The night's blueness rises, in the evening.

The twilight dusk blues "ghostly." This "ghostliness" is what marks the dusk. We must give thought to what this oft-named "ghostliness" means. The twilight dusk is the sun's descending course. That implies: twilight dusk is the decline both of the day and of the year. The last stanza of a poem called "Summer's End" sings:

> So quiet has the green summer grown
> And through the silvery night there rings
> The footfall of the stranger.
> Would that the blue wild game were to recall his paths,
> The music of his ghostly years!

These words, "so quiet," recur in Trakl's poetry again and again. One might think that "quiet" means at most a barely audible sound. So understood, what was said refers to our perception. However, "quiet" means slow, slowly fading away. Quiet is what slips away. Summer slips away into autumn, the evening of the year.

> . . . through the silvery night there rings
> The footfall of the stranger.

Who is this stranger? Whose paths are they that a "blue wild game" is to recall? To recall means to "ponder forgotten things,"

> . . . when in leafy boughs
> The thrush called to a strange thing to go under.

In what sense is the "blue wild game" to recall what is going under? Does the wild game receive its blue from the "blueness" of the "ghostly twilight dusk" which rises as night? The night is dark, to be sure. But darkness is not necessarily gloom. In another poem night is apostrophized with these words:

> O gentle corn flower sheaf of night.

Night is a cornflower sheaf, a gentle sheaf. So, too, the blue game is called "shy game," the "gentle animal." The sheaf of blueness gathers the depth of the holy in the depths of its bond. The holy shines out of the blueness, even while veiling itself in the dark of that blueness. The holy withholds in withdrawing. The holy bestows its arrival by reserving itself in its withholding withdrawal. Clarity sheltered in the dark is blueness. "Clear" originally means clear sound, the sound that calls out of the shelter of stillness, and so becomes clear. Blueness resounds in its clarity, ringing. In its resounding clarity shines the blue's darkness.

The stranger's footfalls sound through the silvery gleam and ringing of night. Another poem says:

> And in holy blueness shining footfalls ring forth.

Elsewhere it is said of blueness:

> . . . the holiness of blue flowers . . . moves the beholder.

Another poem says:

> . . . Animal face
> Freezes with blueness, with its holiness.

Blue is not an image to indicate the sense of the holy. Blueness itself is the holy, in virtue of its gathering depth which shines forth only as it veils itself. Face to face with blueness, brought up short by sheer blueness, the animal face freezes and transforms itself into the countenance of the wild game.

The frozen rigor of the animal face is not the rigor of the dead. As it freezes, the startled animal face contracts. Its gaze gathers so that, checking its course, it may look toward the holy, into the "mirror of truth." To look means here to enter into silence.

> Mighty the power of silence in the rock

runs the next line. The rock is the mountain sheltering pain. The stones gather within their stony shelter the soothing power, pain stilling us toward essential being. Pain is still "with blueness." Face to face with blueness, the wild game's face retracts into gentleness. Gentleness transmutes discord by absorbing the wounding and searing wildness into appeased pain.

Who is this blue wild game to whom the poet calls out that it recall the stranger? Is it an animal? No doubt. Is it just an animal? No. For it is called on to recall, to think. Its face is to look out for . . ., and to look on the stranger. The blue game is an animal whose animality presumably does not consist in its animal nature, but in that thoughtfully recalling look for which the poet calls. This animality is still far away, and barely to be seen. The animality of the animal here intended thus vacillates in the indefinite. It has not yet been gathered up into its essential being. This animal—the thinking animal, *animal rationale*, man—is, as Nietzsche said, not yet determined.

This statement does not mean at all that man has not yet been "confirmed" as a *factum*. On the contrary, he is all too firmly confirmed as a *factum*. The word means: this animal's animality has not yet been gathered up onto firm ground, that is to say, has not been gathered "home," into its own, the home of its veiled being. This definition is what Western-European metaphysics has been struggling to achieve ever since Plato. It may be struggling in vain. It may be that its way into the "underway" is still blocked. This animal not yet determined in its nature is modern man.

By the poetic name "blue wild game" Trakl evokes that human nature whose countenance, whose countering glance, is sighted by the night's blueness, as it is thinking of the stranger's footfalls and thus is illumined by the holy. The name "blue game" names mortals who would think of the stranger and wander with him to the native home of human being.

Who are they that begin such a journey? Presumably they are few, and unknown, since what is of the essence comes to pass in quiet, and suddenly, and rarely. The poet speaks of such wanderers in the second stanza of his poem "Winter Evening" which begins:

> Many a man in his wanderings
> Comes to the gate by darksome paths.

The blue game, where and when it is in being, has left the previous form of man's nature behind. Previous man decays in that he loses his being, which is to say, decays.

Trakl calls one of his poems "Seven-Song of Death." Seven is the holy number. The song sings of the holiness of death. Death is not understood here vaguely, broadly, as the conclusion of earthly life. "Death" here means poetically the "going down" to which "something strange" is being called. This is why the "something strange" that is being called is also referred to as "something dead." Its death is not decay, but that it leaves behind the form of man which has decayed. Accordingly, the second stanza from the end of "Seven-Song of Death" says:

> O man's decomposed form: joined of cold metals,
> Night and terror of sunken forests,
> And the animal's searing wildness;
> Windless lull of the soul.

Man's decomposed form is abandoned to searing torture and pricking thorns. Blueness does not irradiate its wildness. The soul of this human form is not fanned by the wind of the holy. And so, it has no course. The wind itself, God's wind, thus remains solitary. A poem speaking of blue wild game—which, however, can as yet barely extricate themselves from the "thicket of thorns"—closes with the lines:

> There always sings
> Upon black walls God's solitary wind.

"Always" means: as long as the year and its solar course remain in the gloom of winter and no one thinks of the path on which the stranger with "ringing footfalls" walks through the night. The night is itself only the sheltering veiling of the sun's course. "Walk," *ienai,* is the Indogermanic *ier,* the year.

> Would that the blue wild game were to recall his paths,

> The music of his ghostly years!

The year's ghostliness is defined by the ghostly twilight of the night.

O how earnest the hyacinthine face of the twilight.
("Wayfaring")

The ghostly twilight is of so essential a nature that the poet gave to one of his poems the specific title "Ghostly Twilight." In that poem, too, wild game is met, but this game is dark. Its wildness, moreover, is drawing toward total darkness, and inclining toward the silent blue. Meanwhile, the poet himself, on "black cloud," travels over "the nighting pond, the starry sky."

The poem goes:

> Still at the forest's edge meets
> Dark wild game;
> On the hill, evening breeze softly expires,
>
> Blackbird's plaint falls silent,
> And the gentle flutes of autumn
> Hush in the rushes.
>
> On black cloud, you
> Drunk with poppy travel
> The nighting pond,
>
> The starry sky.
> Always the sister's lunar voice
> Sounds through the ghostly night.

The starry sky is portrayed in the poetic image of the nighting pond. Such would be our usual notion. But the night sky, in the truth of its nature, is this pond. By contrast, what we otherwise call night remains rather a mere image, the pale and empty counterfeit of night's nature. The pond and the pond's mirror recur often in the poet's work. The waters, which are sometimes black and sometimes blue, show to man his own countenance, his countering glance. But in the nighting pond of the starry sky there appears the twilight blue of the ghostly night. Its glance is cool.

The cool light issues from the shining of Dame Moon (*selanna*). All around her radiance, as the ancient Greek verses tell us, the stars turn pale and even cool. All things become "lunar." The stranger going through the night is called "the lunar one." The sister's lunar voice forever ringing through the night is heard by the brother who, in his boat that is still "black" and barely illumined by the stranger's golden radiance, tries to follow the stranger's nocturnal course upon the pond.

When mortals follow after the "something strange," that is to say, after the stranger who is called to go under, they themselves enter strangeness, they themselves become strangers and solitary.

Only through its course on the night's starry pond—which is the sky above the earth—does the soul experience the earth in its "cool sap." The soul slips away into the evening blue of the ghostly year. It becomes the "autumnal soul" and as such the "blue soul."

The few stanzas and lines noted here point into the ghostly twilight, lead onto the stranger's path, and indicate the kind and the course of those who, recalling him, follow him to go under. At the time of "Summer's Decline," the strangeness in his wandering becomes autumnal and dark.

One of Trakl's poems which he entitled "Autumnal Soul" sings in the second stanza from the end:

> Fish and game soon glide away.
> Soon blue soul and long dark journey
> Parted us from loved ones, others.
> Evening changes image, sense.

The wanderers who follow the stranger soon find themselves parted "from loved ones" who to them are "others." The others—that is the cast of the decomposed form of man.

A human cast, cast in one mold and cast away into this cast, is called a kin, of a kind, a generation. The word refers to mankind as a whole as well as to kinship in the sense of race, tribe, family—all of these in turn cast in the duality of the sexes. The cast of man's "decomposed form" is what the poet calls the "decomposing" kind. It is the generation that has been removed from its kind of essential being, and this is why it is the "unsettled" kind.

What curse has struck this humankind? The curse of the decomposing kind is that the old human kinship has been struck apart by discord among sexes, tribes and races. Each strives to escape from that discord into the unleashed turmoil of the always isolated and sheer wildness of the wild game. Not duality as such, the discord is the curse. Out of the turmoil of blind wildness it carries each kind into an irreconcilable split, and so casts it into unbridled isolation. The "fragmented kind," so cleft in two, can on its own no longer find its proper cast. Its proper cast is only with that kind whose duality leaves discord behind and leads the way, as "something strange," into the gentleness of simple twofoldness following in the stranger's footsteps.

With respect to that stranger, all the progeny of the decomposing kind remain the others. Even so, love and reverence are attached to them. But the dark journey in the stranger's train brings them into the blue of his night. The wandering soul becomes the "blue soul."

But at the same time the soul is also set apart. Where to? To where the stranger walks, who at times is poetically called only "he yonder." "He yonder," the stranger, is the other one to the others, to the decomposing kind. He is the one who has been called away from others. The stranger is he who is apart.

Whither is such a being directed which itself assumes the nature of the strange, that it must wander ahead? In what direction is a strange thing called? It is called to go under—to lose itself in the ghostly twilight of the blue, to incline with the decline toward the ghostly year. While this decline must pass through the destructiveness of approaching winter, through November, to lose itself yet does not mean that it crumbles into a shambles and is annihilated. On the contrary, to lose oneself means literally to loosen one's bonds and slowly slip away. He who loses himself does of course disappear in the November destruction, but he does not slip into it. He slips through it, away into the blue's ghostly twilight "at vespers," toward evening.

> At vespers the stranger loses himself in black November
>   destruction,
> Under rotting branches, along the leprous walls,
> Where the holy brother had gone before,
> Lost in the soft lyre music of his madness.

("Helian")

Evening is the decline of the days of the ghostly year. Evening consummates a change. Evening which inclines to the ghostly gives us other things to contemplate and to ponder.

The luminous appearances of whose aspects (images) the poets have their say appear differently in the light of this evening. The essential reality that thinkers try to grasp in thought speaks other words with the onset of this evening. From another sense and another image, evening transmutes all saying of poetry and thinking, and their dialogue. But evening can do so only because it, too, changes. Day goes through evening into a decline that is not an end, but simply an inclination to make ready that descent by which the stranger goes under into the *beginning* of his wandering. Evening changes its own image and its own sense. This change conceals a departure from the traditional order of days and seasons.

But whither does evening accompany the blue soul's dark wandering? To the place where everything has come together in another way, where everything is sheltered and preserved for an other ascent.

The stanzas and lines quoted so far bring us to a gathering, that is to say, they bring us to a site. Of what kind is this site? What shall we name it? Surely the name must fit the poet's language. All that Georg Trakl's poetry says remains gathered and focused on the wandering stranger. He is, and is called, "he who is apart." Through him and around him Trakl's poetic saying is tuned to one unique song. And since this poet's poems are gathered into the song of him who is apart, we shall call the site of Trakl's poetic work *apartness*.

And now, by a second step, our discussion must try to gain a clearer view of this site which so far has only been pointed out.

II

Is it possible to bring apartness itself before our mind's eye, to contemplate it as the poem's site? If at all, it can be done only if we now follow the stranger's path with clearer eyes, and ask: Who is the departed one? What is the landscape of his paths?

His paths run through the blue of night. The light that gives his steps their radiance is cool. The closing words of a poem devoted specifically to the "departed one" speak of "the lunar paths of the departed." To us, departed also means deceased. But into what kind of death has the stranger died? In his poem "Psalm," Trakl says:

> The madman has died

The next stanza says:

> They bury the stranger.

In the "Seven-Song of Death" he is called the "white stranger."
The last stanza of "Psalm" ends with this line:

> In his grave the white magician plays with his snakes.

The dead one *lives* in his grave. He lives in his chamber, so quietly and lost in thought that he plays with his snakes. They cannot harm him. They have not been strangled, but their malice has been transformed. In the poem "The Accursed," on the other hand, we find:

> A nest of scarlet-colored snakes rears up
> Lazily in her churned-up lap.

The dead one is the madman. Does the word mean someone who is mentally ill? Madness here does not mean a mind filled with senseless delusions. The madman's mind senses—senses in fact as no one else does. Even so, he does not have the sense of the others. He is of another mind. The departed one is a man apart, a madman, because he has taken his way in another direction. From that other direction, his madness may be called "gentle," for his mind pursues a greater stillness. A poem that refers to the stranger simply as "he yonder," the other one, sings:

> But the other descended the stone steps of the Mönchsberg,
> A blue smile on his face and strangely ensheathed
> In his quieter childhood and died.

This poem is called "To One Who Died Young." The departed died away early. That is why he is "the tender corpse," shrouded in that childhood which preserves in greater stillness all the burning and searing of the wilderness. He who died early thus appears as the "dark shape of coolness." This shape also appears in the poem entitled "On the Mönchsberg":

> The dark shape of coolness ever follows the wanderer
> Over the footbridge of bone, and the boy's hyacinth voice,
> Softly reciting the forest's forgotten legend . . .

The "dark shape of coolness" does not follow behind the wanderer. It walks before him, because the boy's blue voice retrieves something forgotten and *fore-tells* it.

Who is this boy that died away early? Who is this boy to whom it is said

> . . . softly your forehead bleeds
> Ancient legends
> And dark augury of the flight of birds?

Who is he who has crossed over the bridge of bone? The poet calls to him with the words:

> O Elis, how long you have been dead.

Elis is the stranger called to go under. He is in no way a figure by which Trakl means to represent himself. Elis is as essentially different from the poet Trakl as Zarathustra's figure is from the thinker Nietzsche. But both figures are alike in that their nature and their journey begins with a descent. Elis goes down into the primeval earliness that is older than the aged, decomposing kind of man, older because it is more mindful, more mindful because it is more still, more still because it has itself a greater power to still.

The boyishness in the figure of the boy Elis does not consist in the opposite of girlishness. His boyishness is the appearance of his stiller childhood. That childhood shelters and stores within it the gentle two-fold of sex, the youth and the "golden figure of the maiden."

Elis is not a dead who decays and ceases to be in the lateness of a spent life. Elis is the dead whose being moves away into earliness. This stranger unfolds human nature forward into the beginning of what is yet to be borne. This unborn element in the nature of mortals, which is quieter and hence more stilling, is what the poet calls the unborn.

The stranger who has died away into earliness is the unborn one. The terms "something unborn" and "something strange" say the same. In the poem "Bright Spring" there is this line:

> And the unborn tends to its own peace.

It guards and watches over the stiller childhood for the coming awakening of mankind. Thus at rest, the early dead *lives*. The departed one is not dead in the sense of being spent. On the contrary. The departed looks forward into the blue of the ghostly night. The white eyelids that protect his vision gleam with the bridal adornment that promises the gentler two-fold of humankind.

> Silent the myrtle blooms over his dead white eyelids.

This line belongs in the same poem that says:

> Something strange is the soul on the earth.

The two sentences stand close to each other. The "dead" is the departed, the stranger, the unborn.

But still the "path of the unborn" leads "past gloomy towns, past lonely summers" ("Song of the Hours"). His way leads past those things that will not receive him as a guest, past but already no longer through them. The departed one's journey is lonely, too, of course—but that comes from the loneliness of "the nighting pond, the starry sky." The madman crosses the pond not on a "black cloud" but in a golden boat. What about the gold? The poem "Corner by the Forest" replies with the line:

> Gentle madness also often sees the golden, the true.

The stranger's path leads through the "ghostly years" whose days are everywhere turned toward the beginning and are ruled, set right, from there. The year of his soul is gathered into rightness.

> O how righteous, Elis, are all your days

sings the poem "Elis." This call is merely the echo of the other call, heard before:

> O Elis, how long you have been dead.

The earliness into which the stranger has expired shelters the essential rightness of the unborn. This earliness is a time of its own kind, the time of the "ghostly years." To one of his poems, Trakl gave the plain title "Year." It begins: "Dark stillness of childhood." The counterpart to that dark stillness is the brighter earliness—brighter because it is an even stiller and therefore other childhood—into which the departed has gone under. The last line of the same poem calls this stiller childhood the beginning:

> Golden eye of the beginning, dark patience of the end.

Here, the end is not the sequel and fading echo of the beginning. The end—being the end of the decaying kind—precedes the beginning of the unborn kind. But the beginning, the earlier earliness, has already overtaken the end.

That earliness preserves the original nature—a nature so far still veiled—of time. This nature will go on being impenetrable to the dominant mode of thinking as long as the Aristotelian concept of time, still standard everywhere, retains its currency. According to this concept, time—whether conceived mechanically or dynamically or in terms of atomic decay—is the dimension of the quantitative or qualitative calculation of duration as a sequential progression.

True time, however, is the arrival of that which has been. This is not what is past, but rather the gathering of essential being, which precedes all arrival in gathering itself into the shelter of what it was earlier, before the given moment. The end and accomplishment has its analogue in "dark patience." Patience bears hidden things toward their truth. Its forbearance bears everything toward its descent down into the blue of the ghostly night. The beginning, on the other hand, corresponds to a seeing and minding

which gleams golden because it is illuminated by "the golden, the true."
This gold and true is reflected in the starry pond of night when Elis on his
journey opens his heart to the night:

> A golden boat
> Sways, Elis, your heart against a lonely sky.

The stranger's boat tosses, playful rather than "timorously," like the
boat of those descendants of earliness who still merely follow the stranger.
Their boat does not yet reach the level of the pond's surface. It sinks. But
where? Does it go under in decay? No. And into what does it sink? Into
empty nothingness? Far from it. One of Trakl's last poems, "Lament," ends
with the lines:

> Sister of stormy sadness,
> Look, a timorous boat goes down
> Under stars,
> The silent face of the night.

What does this nocturnal silence hold that looks down out of the starlight?
Where does this silence itself with its night belong? To apartness. This
apartness is more than merely the state in which the boy Elis lives, the
state of being dead.

The earliness of stiller childhood, the blue night, the stranger's nighting
paths, the soul's nocturnal wing-beat, even the twilight as the gateway to
descent: all these belong to apartness.

All these are gathered up into apartness, not afterward but such that
apartness unfolds within their already established gathering.

Twilight, night, the stranger's years, his paths, all are called "ghostly"
by the poet. The apartness is "ghostly." This word—what does it mean?
Its meaning and its use are very old. "Ghostly" means what is by way of
the spirit, stems from it and follows its nature. "Ghostly" means spiritual,
but not in the narrow sense that ties the word to "spirituality," the priestly
orders or their church. To a superficial reader, even Trakl seems to use the
word in this narrow sense, at least in the poem "In Hellbrunn," where it
says:

> . . . Thus the oaks turn spiritually green,
> Above the dead's forgotten paths.

Earlier, the poet mentions "the shades of princes of the church, of noble
women," "the shades of those long dead" which seem to hover above the
"pond of spring." But the poet, who is here again singing "the blue lament
of evening," does not think of the clergy when he says "the oaks turn
spiritually green." He is thinking of that earliness of the long since dead
which promises the "springtime of the soul." The poem "Song of the
Spirit," composed earlier, strikes the same theme, though in an even more

veiled and searching manner. The spirit referred to in this strangely ambiguous "Song of the Spirit" finds clearer expression in the last stanza:

> Beggar there by ancient stone
> Seems expired in a prayer,
> Shepherd gently leaves the hill,
> In the grove an angel sings,
> Sings a song,
> Sings the children to their sleep.

But, even though the word "spiritual" has no ecclesiastical overtones for the poet himself, he surely could have resorted to the phrase "of the spirit" to refer to what he has in mind, and speak of twilight of the spirit and night of the spirit. Why does he not do so? Because "of the spirit" means the opposite of material. This opposition posits a differentiation of two separate realms and, in Platonic-Western terms, states the gulf between the suprasensuous *noeton* and the sensuous *aistheton*.

"Of the spirit" so understood—it meanwhile has come to mean rational, intellectual, ideological—together with its opposites belongs to the world view of the decaying kind of man. But the "dark journey" of the "blue soul" parts company with this kind. The twilight leading toward the night in which the strangeness goes under deserves as little to be called "of the spirit, intellectual" as does the stranger's path. Apartness is spiritual, determined by the spirit, and ghostly, but it is not "of the spirit" in the sense of the language of metaphysics.

What, then, is the spirit? In his last poem, "Grodek," Trakl speaks of the "hot flame of the spirit." The spirit is flaming, and only in this sense perhaps is it something flickering in the air. Trakl sees spirit not primarily as *pneuma*, something ethereal, but as a flame that inflames, startles, horrifies, and shatters us. Flame is glowing lumination. What flame is the *ek-stasis* which lightens and calls forth radiance, but which may also go on consuming and reduce all to white ashes.

"Flame is the palest pallor's brother" runs a line in the poem "Transformation of Evil." Trakl sees spirit in terms of that being which is indicated in the original meaning of the word "ghost"—a being terrified, beside himself, *ek-static*.

Spirit or ghost understood in this way has its being in the possibility of *both* gentleness *and* destructiveness. Gentleness in no way dampens the ecstasy of the inflammatory, but holds it gathered in the peace of friendship. Destructiveness comes from unbridled license, which consumes itself in its own revolt and thus is active evil. Evil is always the evil of a ghostly spirit. Evil and its malice is not of a sensuous, material nature. Nor is it purely "of the spirit." Evil is ghostly in that it is the revolt of a terror blazing away in blind delusion, which casts all things into unholy fragmentation and threatens to turn the calm, collected blossoming of gentleness to ashes.

But where does the gathering power of gentleness reside? How is it bridled? What spirit holds its reins? In what way is human nature ghostly, and how does it become so?

Inasmuch as the nature of spirit consists in a bursting into flame, it strikes a new course, lights it, and sets man on the way. Being flame, the spirit is the storm that "storms the heavens" and "hunts down God." The spirit chases, drives the soul to get underway to where it leads the way. The spirit carries it over into strangeness. "Something strange is the soul on the earth." The soul is the gift of the spirit—the spirit animates. But the soul in turn guards the spirit, so essentially that without the soul the spirit can presumably never be spirit. The soul "feeds" the spirit. How? How else than by investing the spirit with the flame that is in the soul's very nature? This flame is the glow of melancholy, "the patience of the lonely soul."

Solitude does not separate in the kind of dispersion to which all mere forsakenness is exposed. Solitude carries the soul toward the One and only, gathers it into the One, and so starts its being out on its journey. Solitary, the soul is a wanderer. The ardor of its core is charged to carry on its journey the burden of fate—and so to carry the soul toward the spirit.

> Lend your flame to the spirit, ardent and heavy heart;

so begins the poem "To Lucifer," in other words, the poem to the light-bearer who casts the shadow of evil (posthumous volume, Salzburg edition).

The soul's heavy heart glows only when the wandering soul enters into the farthest reaches of its essential being—its wandering nature. That happens when the soul looks toward the face of the blue and beholds its radiance. In that seeing it is "the great soul."

> O pain, thou flaming vision
> Of the great soul!
> ("Thunderstorm")

The soul's greatness takes its measure from its capacity to achieve the flaming vision by which the soul becomes at home in pain. The nature of pain is in itself converse.

"Flaming" pain tears away. Pain's rending, sweeping force consigns the wandering soul into that conjunction of storm and hunt which would storm heaven and hunt down God. Thus it seems as though the stormy sweep were to overwhelm its goal, instead of letting it prevail within its veiling radiance.

Yet this latter is within the power of the beholding "vision." That vision does not quench the flaming sweep, but rejoins it to the fitting submission of seeing acceptance. It is that backward sweep in pain by which pain achieves its mildness, its power to disclose and convey.

Spirit is flame. It glows and shines. Its shining takes place in the beholding look. To such a vision is given the advent of all that shines, where all that is, is present. This flaming vision is pain. Its nature remains impenetrable to any mind that understands pain in terms of sensitivity. Flaming vision determines the soul's greatness.

The spirit which bears the gift of the "great soul" is pain; pain is the animator. And the soul so gifted is the giver of life. This is why everything that is alive in the sense in which the soul is alive, is imbued with pain, the fundamental trait of the soul's nature. Everything that is alive, is painful.

Only a being that lives soulfully can fulfill the destiny of its nature. By virtue of this power it is fit to join in that harmony of mutual bearing by which all living things belong together. In keeping with this relation of fitness, everything that lives is fit, that is to say, good. But the good is good painfully.

Corresponding to the great soul's fundamental trait, everything that has soul is not merely good painfully, but also it can be truthful only in that way; for, in virtue of the fact that pain is converse, the living can give sheltering concealment to their present fellowbeings and thus reveal them in their given nature, let them truly be what they are.

The last stanza of one poem begins:

> So painful good, so truthful is what lives,

One might think that this line merely touches on what is painful. In truth it introduces the saying of the entire stanza, which remains tuned to the silent conquest of pain. To hear it, we must not overlook the carefully placed punctuation, much less alter it. The stanza goes on:

> And softly touches you an ancient stone:

Again this "softly" is sounded, which always leads us softly to the essential relations. Again the "stone" appears which, if calculation were permitted here, could be counted in more than thirty places in Trakl's poetry. Pain conceals itself in the stone, the petrifying pain that delivers itself into the keeping of the impenetrable rock in whose appearance there shines forth its ancient origin out of the silent glow of the first dawn—the earliest dawn which, as the prior beginning, is coming toward everything that is becoming, and brings to it the advent, never to be overtaken, of its essential being.

The old stones are pain itself, for pain looks earthily upon mortals. The colon after the word "stone" signifies that now *the stone* is speaking. Pain itself has the word. Silent since long ago, it now says to the wanderers who follow the stranger nothing less than its own power and endurance:

> Truly! I shall forever be with you.

The wanderers who listen toward the leafy branches for the early dead, reply to these words of pain with the words of the next line:

O mouth! that trembles through the silvery willow.

The whole stanza here corresponds to the close of another poem's second stanza, addressed "To One Who Died Young":

And the silver face of his friend stayed behind in the garden,
Listening in the leaves or the ancient stones.

The stanza which begins

So painful good, so truthful is what lives,

also resolves the chord struck in the first line of the same poem's third section:

How sick seems all that is becoming!

The troubled, hampered, dismal, and diseased, all the distress of disintegrating, is in truth nothing else than the single semblance in which truth—truly—conceals itself: the all-pervading, everlasting pain. Pain is thus neither repugnant nor profitable. Pain is the benignity in the nature of all essential being. The onefold simplicity of its converse nature determines all becoming out of concealed primal earliness, and attunes it to the bright serenity of the great soul.

So painful good, so truthful is what lives,
And softly touches you an ancient stone:
Truly! I shall forever be with you.
O mouth! that trembles through the silvery willow.

The stanza is the pure song of pain, sung to complete the three-part poem called "Bright Spring." The primal early brightness of all dawning being trembles out of the stillness of concealed pain.

To our customary way of thinking, the converse nature of pain—that its sweep carries us truly onward only as it sweeps us back—may easily seem self-contradictory. But beneath this semblance is concealed the essential onefold simplicity of pain. Flaming, it carries farthest when it holds to itself most intimately in contemplating vision.

Thus pain, the great soul's fundamental trait, remains pure harmony with the holiness of the blue. For the blue shines upon the soul's face by withdrawing into its own depth. Whenever it is present, the holy endures only by keeping within this withdrawal, and by turning vision toward the fitting.

The nature of pain, its concealed relation to the blue, is put into words in the last stanza of a poem called "Transfiguration":

Blue flower,
That softly sounds in withered stone.

The "blue flower" is the "gentle cornflower sheaf" of the ghostly night. The words sing of the wellspring from which Trakl's poetry wells up. They conclude, and also carry, the "transfiguration." The song is lyric, tragedy, and epic all in one. This poem is unique among them all, because in it the breadth of vision, the depth of thought, and the simplicity of saying shine intimate and everlasting, ineffably.

Pain is truly pain only when it serves the flame of the spirit. Trakl's last poem is called "Grodek." It has been much praised as a war poem. But it is infinitely more, because it is something other. Its final lines are:

> Today a great pain feeds the hot flame of the spirit,
> The grandsons yet unborn.

These "grandsons" are not the unbegotten sons of the sons killed in battle, the progeny of the decaying generation. If that were all, merely an end to the procreation of earlier generations, our poet would have to rejoice over such an end. But he grieves, though with a "prouder grief" that flamingly contemplates the peace of the unborn.

The unborn are called grandsons because they cannot be sons, that is, they cannot be the immediate descendants of the generation that has gone to ruin. Another generation lives between these two. It is other, for it is of another kind in keeping with its different essential origin in the earliness of what is still unborn. The "mighty pain" is the beholding vision whose flames envelop everything, and which looks ahead into the still-withdrawing earliness of yonder dead one toward whom the "ghosts" of early victims have died.

But who guards this mighty pain, that it may feed the hot flame of the spirit? Whatever is akin to this spirit is of the kind that starts man on the way. Whatever is akin to this spirit is called "ghostly." And thus the poet must call "ghostly" the twilight, the night, and the years—these above all and these alone. The twilight makes the blue of night to rise, inflames it. Night flames as the shining mirror of the starry pond. The year inflames by starting the sun's course on its way, its risings and its settings.

What spirit is it from which this "ghostliness" awakens and which it follows? It is the spirit which in the poem "To One Who Died Young" is specifically called "the spirit of an early dead." It is the spirit which abandons that "beggar" of the "Spiritual Song" to his apartness, so that he, as the poem "In the Village" says, remains "the poor one," "who died lonesome in spirit."

Apartness is active as pure spirit. It is the radiance of the blue reposing in the spirit's depth and flaming in greater stillness, the blue that kindles a stiller childhood into the gold of the first beginning. This is the earliness toward which Elis's golden countenance is turned. In its countering glance, it keeps alive the nocturnal flame of the spirit of apartness.

Apartness, then, is neither merely the state of him who died young, nor the indeterminate realm of his abode. In the way in which it flames, apartness itself is the spirit and thus the gathering power. That power carries mortal nature back to its stiller childhood, and shelters that childhood as the kind, not yet borne to term, whose stamp marks future generations. The gathering power of apartness holds the unborn generation beyond all that is spent, and saves it for a coming rebirth of mankind out of earliness. The gathering power, spirit of gentleness, stills also the spirit of evil. That spirit's revolt rises to its utmost malice when it breaks out even from the discord of the sexes, and invades the realm of brother and sister.

But in the stiller onefold simplicity of childhood is hidden also the kindred twofoldness of mankind. In apartness, the spirit of evil is neither destroyed and denied, nor set free and affirmed. Evil is transformed. To endure such a "transformation," the soul must turn to the greatness of its nature. The spirit of apartness determines how great this greatness is. Apartness is the gathering through which human nature is sheltered once again in its stiller childhood, and that childhood in turn is sheltered in the earliness of another beginning. As a gathering, apartness is in the nature of a site.

But in what way, now, is apartness the site of a poetic work, specifically that poetic statement to which Trakl's poetry gives voice? Is apartness at all and intrinsically related to poetry? Even if such a relation exists, how is apartness to gather poetic saying to itself, to become its site, and to determine it from there?

Is apartness not one single silence of stillness? How can it start a saying and a singing on its way? Yet apartness is not the desolation of the departed dead. In apartness, the stranger measures off the parting from mankind hitherto. He is underway on a path. What sort of a path is it? The poet says it plainly enough, by pointedly setting apart the closing line of the poem "Summer's Decline";

> Would that the blue game were to recall his paths,
>
> The music of his ghostly years!

The stranger's path is the "music of his ghostly years." Elis's footfall rings. The ringing footfall radiates through the night. Does its music die away into a void? He who died into earliness—is he departed in the sense of being cut off, or has he been set apart because he is one of the select—gathered up into an assembly that gathers more gently and calls more quietly?

The second and third stanzas of the poem "To One Who Died Young" hint at an answer:

> But he yonder descended the stone steps of the Mönchsberg,
> A blue smile on his face, and strangely ensheathed
> In his stiller childhood, and died;
> And the silver face of his friend stayed behind in the garden,
> Listening in the leaves or the ancient stones.

Soul sang of death, the green decay of the flesh,
And it was the murmur of the forest,
The fervid lament of the animals.
Always from twilight towers rang the blue evening bells.

A friend listens after the stranger. In listening, he follows the departed and thus becomes himself a wanderer, a stranger. The friend's soul listens after the dead. The friend's face has "died away." It listens by singing of death. This is why the singing voice is "the birdvoice of the deathlike" ("The Wanderer"). It corresponds to the stranger's death, his going under to the blue of night. But as he sings the death of the departed, he also sings the "green decay" of that generation from which his dark journey has "parted" him.

To sing means to praise and to guard the object of praise in song. The listening friend is one of the "praising shepherds." Yet the friend's soul, which "likes to listen to the white magician's fairy tales," can give echo to the song of the departed only when that apartness rings out toward him who follows, when the music of apartness resounds, "when," as it says in "Evensong," "dark music haunts the soul."

If all this comes to pass, the spirit of the early dead appears in the glow of earliness. The ghostly years of earliness are the true time of the stranger and his friend. In their glow the formerly black cloud turns golden. Now it is like that "golden boat" which, Elis's heart, rocks in the solitary sky.

The last stanza of "To One Who Died Young" sings;

Golden cloud and time. In a lonely room
You often ask the dead to visit you,
And walk in trusted converse under elms by the green
      stream.

The friend's invitation to conversation reflects the haunting music of the stranger's steps. The friend's saying is the singing journey down by the stream, following down into the blue of the night that is animated by the spirit of the early dead. In such conversation the singing friend gazes upon the departed. By his gaze, in the converse look, he becomes brother to the stranger. Journeying with the stranger, the brother reaches the stiller abode in earliness. In the "Song of the Departed," he can call out:

O to dwell in the animate blue of night.

Listening after the departed, the friend sings his song and thus becomes his brother; only now, as the stranger's brother, does he also become the brother of the stranger's sister whose "lunar voice rings through the ghostly night," as the last lines of "Ghostly Twilight" say it.

Apartness is the poem's site because the music of the stranger's ringing-radiant footfall inflames his followers' dark wandering into listening song.

The dark wandering, dark because it merely follows after, nevertheless clears their souls toward the blue. Then the whole being of the singing soul is one single concentrated gaze ahead into the blue of night which holds that stiller earliness.

Soul then is purely a blue moment

is what the poem "Childhood" says about it.

Thus the nature of apartness is perfected. It is the perfect site of the poetic work only when, being both the gathering of the stiller childhood and the stranger's grave, it gathers to itself also those who follow him who died early, by listening after him and carrying the music of his path over into the sounds of spoken language, so that they become men apart. Their song is poetry. How so? What is the poet's work?

The poet's work means: to say after—to say again the music of the spirit of apartness that has been spoken to the poet. For the longest time—before it comes to be said, that is, spoken—the poet's work is only a listening. Apartness first gathers the listening into its music, so that this music may ring through the spoken saying in which it will resound. The lunar coolness of the ghostly night's holy blue rings and shines through all such gazing and saying. Its language becomes a saying-after, it becomes: poetry. Poetry's spoken words shelter the poetic statement as that which by its essential nature remains unspoken. In this manner, the saying-after, thus called upon to listen, becomes "more pious," that is to say, more pliable to the promptings of the path on which the stranger walks ahead, out of the dark of childhood into the stiller, brighter earliness. The poet listening after him can thus say to himself:

> More pious now, you know the dark years' meaning,
> Autumn and cool in solitary rooms;
> And in holier blue radiant footfalls ring.
>
> ("Childhood")

The soul that sings of autumn and the year's decline is not sinking in decay. Its piety is kindled by the flame of the spirit of earliness, and therefore is fiery:

> O the soul that softly sang the song of the withered reeds;
> flaming piety.

says the poem "Dream and Shroud of Night." This shroud of night is not a mere darkening of the mind, no more than madness is dementedness. The night that shrouds the stranger's singing brother remains the "ghostly night" of that death by which the departed died into the "golden tremor" of earliness. Gazing after him, the listening friend looks out into the coolness of childhood's greater stillness. But such gazing remains a parting from that cast of man, long since born, which has forgot the stiller childhood as the beginning that is still in store, and has never carried the unborn to full term. The poem "Anif," named after a moated castle near Salzburg, says:

> Great is the guilt of the born. Woe, you golden tremor
> Of death,
> When the soul dreams cooler blossoms.

But that "woe" of pain embraces not only the parting *from* the old kinship. This parting is in a hidden and fated way set apart, set to take the departure called for by apartness. The wandering in the night of apartness is "infinite torment." This does not mean unending agony. The infinite is devoid of all finite restriction and stuntedness. The "infinite torment" is consummate, perfect pain, pain that comes to the fullness of its nature. The simple oneness of pain's converse character comes into pure play only during the journey through the ghostly night, a journey that always takes its parting from the unghostly night. The spirit's gentleness is called to hunt down God, its shy reserve called to storm heaven.

In the poem "The Night," it says:

> Infinite torment,
> That you hunted down God
> Gentle spirit,
> Sighing in the cataract,
> In the waving fir trees.

The flaming rapture of this storm and hunt does not tear "the steep-walled fortress" down; it does not lay the quarry low, but lets it arise to behold the sights of heaven whose pure coolness veils the Divine. The singing reflection of such wandering belongs to the brow of a head marked by consummate pain. The poem "The Night" therefore closes with the lines:

> A petrified head
> Storms heaven.

Correspondingly, the end of the poem "The Heart" runs:

> The steep-walled fortress.
> O heart
> Shimmering away into snowy coolness.

In fact, the triadic harmony of the three late poems "The Heart," "The Storm," and "The Night" is so subtly tuned to One and the Same singing of apartness that the discussion of the poetic work here attempted is further prompted simply to leave those three poems to resound in their song without intruding an elucidation.

Wandering in apartness, beholding the sights of the invisible, and consummate pain—they belong together. The patient one submits to pain's sweep. He alone is able to follow the return into the primal earliness of the generation whose fate is preserved in an old album in which the poet inscribes the following stanza called "In an Old Album":

> Humbly the patient one bows to the pain
> Ringing with music and with soft madness.
> Look! the twilight appears.

In such soft and sweet-sounding saying the poet brings to radiance the luminous sights in which God conceals himself from the mad hunt. It is thus only "Whispered into the Afternoon" when, in a poem by that title, the poet sings:

> God's own colors dreams my brow,
> Feels the gentle wings of madness.

The poet becomes poet only as he follows that "madman" who died away into the early dawn and who now from his apartness, by the music of his footfall, calls to the brother who follows him. Thus the friend's face looks into the face of the stranger. The radiance of the glancing moment moves the listener's saying. In the moving radiance that shines from the site of the poem surges the billow which starts the poetic vision on its way to language.

Of what sort, then, is the language of Trakl's poetic work? It speaks by answering to that journey upon which the stranger is leading on ahead. The path he has taken leads away from the old degenerate generation. It escorts him to go under in the earliness of the unborn generation that is kept in store. The language of the poetry whose site is in apartness answers to the home-coming of unborn mankind into the quiet beginning of its stiller nature.

The language that this poetry speaks stems from this transition. Its path leads from the downfall of all that decays over to the descent into the twilit blue of the holy. The language that the work speaks stems from the passage across and through the ghostly night's nocturnal pond. This language sings the song of the home-coming in apartness, the home-coming which from the lateness of decomposition comes to rest in the earliness of the stiller, and still impending, beginning. In this language there speaks the journey whose shining causes the radiant, ringing music of the departed stranger's ghostly years to come forth. According to the words of the poem "Revelation and Descent," the "Song of the Departed" sings of "the beauty of a homecoming generation."

Because the language of this poetry speaks from the journey of apartness, it will always speak also of what it leaves behind in parting, and of that to which the departure submits. This language is essentially ambiguous, in its own fashion. We shall hear nothing of what the poem says so long as we bring to it only this or that dull sense of unambiguous meaning.

Twilight and night, descent and death, madness and wild game, pond and stone, bird's flight and boat, stranger and brother, ghost and God, and also the words of color—blue and green, white and black, red and silver, gold and dark—all say ever and again manifold things.

"Green" is decay *and* bloom, "white" pale *and* pure, "black" is enclosing in gloom *and* darkly sheltering, "red" fleshy purple *and* gentle rose. "Silver" is the pallor of death and the sparkle of the stars. "Gold" is the glow of truth as well as "grisly laughter of gold." These examples of multiple meanings are so far only two-sided. But their ambiguousness, taken as a whole, becomes but one side of a greater issue, whose other side is determined by the poetry's innermost site.

The poetic work speaks out of an ambiguous ambiguousness. Yet this multiple ambiguousness of the poetic saying does not scatter in vague equivocations. The ambiguous tone of Trakl's poetry arises out of a gathering, that is, out of a unison which, meant for itself alone, always remains unsayable. The ambiguity of this poetic saying is not lax imprecision, but rather the rigor of him who leaves what is as it is, who has entered into the "righteous vision" and now submits to it.

It is often hard for us to draw a clear line between the ambiguous saying characteristic of Trakl's poems—which in his work shows complete assurance—and the language of other poets whose equivocations stem from the vagueness of groping poetic uncertainty, because their language lacks authentic poetry and its site. The peerless rigor of Trakl's essentially ambiguous language is in a higher sense so unequivocal that it remains infinitely superior even to all the technical precision of concepts that are merely scientifically univocal.

This same ambiguity of language that is determined by the site of Trakl's poetic work also inspires his frequent use of words from the world of biblical and ecclesiastical ideas. The passage from the old to the unborn generation leads through this region and its language. Whether Trakl's poems speak in a Christian fashion, to what extent and in what sense, in what way Trakl was a "Christian," what is meant here, and indeed generally, by "Christian," "Christianity," "Christendom" and "Christlike": all this involves essential questions. But their discussion hangs in a void so long as the site of his poetic work is not thoughtfully established. Besides, their discussion calls for a kind of thorough thinking to which neither the concept of a metaphysical nor those of a church-based theology are adequate.

To judge the Christianity of Trakl's poetic work, one would have to give thought above all to his last two poems, "Lament" and "Grodek." One would have to ask: If indeed this poet is so resolute a Christian, why does he not, here in the extreme agony of his last saying, call out to God and Christ? Why does he instead name the "sister's swaying shadow" and call her "the greeting one"? Why does the song end with the name of the "unborn grandsons" and not with the confident hope of Christian redemption? Why does the sister appear also in the other late poem, "Lament"? Why is eternity called there "the icy wave"? Is this Christian thinking? It is not even Christian despair.

But what does this "Lament" sing of? In these words, "Sister . . . Look . . . ," does not an intimate ardent simplicity ring out, the simplicity of those who remain on the journey toward the "golden face of man," despite the danger of the utter withdrawal of all wholeness?

The rigorous unison of the many-voiced language in which Trakl's poetry speaks—and this means also: is silent—corresponds to apartness as the site of his work. Merely to keep this site rightly in mind makes demands on our thinking. We hardly dare in closing to ask for the location of this site.

III

When we took the first step in our discussion of Trakl's poetic work, the poem "Autumn Soul," in its second-to-last stanza, gave us the final indication that apartness is the site of his poetry. That stanza speaks of those wanderers who follow the stranger's path through the ghostly night in order that they may "dwell in its animate blue."

> Fish and game soon glide away.
> Soon blue soul and long dark journey
> Parted us from loved ones, others.

An open region that holds the promise of a dwelling, and provides a dwelling, is what we call a "land." The passage into the stranger's land leads through ghostly twilight, in the evening. This is why the last stanza runs:

> Evening changes image, sense.

The land into which the early dead goes down is the land of this evening. The location of the site that gathers Trakl's work into itself is the concealed nature of apartness, and is called "Evening Land," the Occident. This land is older, which is to say, earlier and therefore more promising than the Platonic-Christian land, or indeed than a land conceived in terms of the European West. For apartness is the "first beginning" of a mounting world-year, not the abyss of decay.

The evening land concealed in apartness is not going down; it stays and, as the land of descent into the ghostly night, awaits those who will dwell in it. The land of descent is the transition into the beginning of the dawn concealed within it.

If we keep these thoughts in mind, we surely cannot then dismiss as mere coincidence the fact that two of Trakl's poems speak explicitly of the land of evening. One bears the title "Evening Land" or "Occident" the other is called "Occidental Song": it sings the same as does the "Song of the Departed," and begins with a call that inclines in wonder:

> O the nocturnal wing-beat of the soul:

The line ends with a colon that includes everything that follows, even to the transition from descent into ascent. At that point in the poem, just before the last two lines, there is a second colon. Then follows the simple phrase *"One* generation." The word "One" is stressed. As far as I can see it is the only word so stressed in Trakl's work. This emphatic *"one* generation" contains the key note in which Trakl's poetic work silently sounds the mystery. The unity of the *one* kinship arises from the race which, along "the lunar paths of the departed," gathers together and enfolds the discord of the generations into the gentler two-fold—which does so in virtue of its apartness, the stiller stillness reigning within it, in virtue of its "forest sagas," its "measure and law."

The *"one"* in *"one* generation" does not mean one as opposed to two. Nor does it mean the monotony of dull equality. *"One* generation" here does not refer to a biological fact at all, to a "single" or "identical" gender. In the emphatic *"one* generation" there is hidden that unifying force which unifies in virtue of the ghostly night's gathering blue. The word speaks from the song which sings of evening. Accordingly, the word "generation" here retains the full manifold meaning mentioned earlier. For one thing, it names the historical generation of man, mankind as distinct from all other living beings (plants and animals). Next, the word "generation" names the races, tribes, clans, and families of mankind. At the same time, the word always refers to the twofoldness of the sexes.

The force which marks the tribes of mankind as the simple oneness of *"one* generation," and thus restores them and mankind itself to the stiller childhood, acts by prompting the soul to set out toward the "blue spring." The soul sings of the blue spring by keeping it silent. The poem "In the Dark" begins:

> The soul keeps the blue spring in silence.

"Keep silent" is here used transitively. Trakl's poem sings of the land of evening. It is one single call that the right race may come to be, and to speak the flame of the spirit into gentleness. In the "Kaspar Hauser Song" we read how God addressed Kaspar Hauser:

> God spoke a gentle flame to his heart:
> O man!

The "spoke," too, is used transitively here, just as "keeps" was above, or as "bleeds" in "To the Boy Elis," or "murmurs" in the last line of "On the Mönchsberg."

God's speaking is the speaking which assigns to man a stiller nature, and so calls on him to give that response by which man rises from what is authentic ruin up into earliness. The "evening land" holds the rising of the dawn of the *"one* generation."

How shallow is our thinking if we regard the singer of the "Occidental Song" as the poet of decay. How incomplete and crude is our understanding if we insist on approaching Trakl's other poem, "Evening Land," always only in terms of its final third section, while stubbornly ignoring the center piece of the triptych together with its preparation in the first section. In "Evening Land" the Elis figure appears once again, whereas "Helian" and "Sebastian in Dream" are no longer mentioned in the last poems. The stranger's footfalls resound. They resound in harmony with the "softly sounding spirit" of the ancient forest legend. The final section—where the "mighty cities/stone on stone raised up/in the plain!" are mentioned—is already overcome, absorbed into the middle section of this work. The cities already have their destiny. It is a destiny other than that which is spoken "beside the greening hill" where the "spring storm sings," the hill which has its "just measure" and is also called the "evening hill." It has been said that Trakl's work is "profoundly unhistorical." In this judgment, what is meant by history? If the word means no more than "chronicle," the rehearsal of past events, then Trakl is indeed unhistorical. His poetry has no need of historical "objects." Why not? Because his poetic work is historical in the highest sense. His poetry sings of the destiny which casts mankind in its still withheld nature—that is to say, saves mankind.

Trakl's work sings the song of the soul, "something strange on the earth," which is only just about to gain the earth by its wandering, the earth that is the stiller home of the homecoming generation.

Is this dreamy romanticism, at the fringe of the technically-economically oriented world of modern mass existence? Or—is it the clear knowledge of the "madman" who sees and senses other things than the reporters of the latest news who spend themselves chronicling the current happening, whose future is never more than a prolongation of today's events, a future that is forever without the advent of a destiny which concerns man for once at the source of his being?

The poet sees the soul, "something strange," destined to follow a path that leads not to decay, but on the contrary to a going under. This going under yields and submits to the mighty death in which he who died early leads the way. The brother, singing, follows him in death. Following the stranger, the dying friend passes through the ghostly night of the years of apartness. His singing is the "Song of a Captured Blackbird," a poem dedicated to L. v. Ficker. The blackbird is the bird that called Elis to go under. It is the birdvoice of the deathlike one. The bird is captured in the solitude of the golden footfalls that correspond to the ride of the golden boat on which Elis's heart crosses the blue night's starry pond, and thus shows to the soul the course of its essential being.

Something strange is the soul on the earth.

The soul journeys toward the land of evening, which is pervaded by the spirit of apartness and is, in keeping with that spirit, "ghostly."

All formulas are dangerous. They force whatever is said into the superficiality of instant opinion and are apt to corrupt our thinking. But they may also be of help, at least as a prompting and a starting point for sustained reflection. With these reservations, we may venture this formulation:

A discussion of the site of Georg Trakl's poetic work shows him to be the poet of the yet concealed evening land.

> Something strange is the soul on the earth.

The sentence occurs in the poem "Springtime of the Soul." The verse that leads over into that final stanza where the sentence belongs, runs:

> Mighty dying and the singing flame in the heart.

There follows the rising of the song into the pure echo of the music of the ghostly years, through which the stranger wanders, the years which the brother follows who begins dwelling in the land of evening:

> Darker the waters flowed round the lovely games of the
> fishes.
> Hour of mourning and silent sight of the sun;
> Something strange is the soul on the earth. Ghostly the
> twilight
> Bluing over the mishewn forest, and a dark bell
> Long tolls in the village; they lead him to rest.
> Silent the myrtle blooms over his dead white eyelids.
>
> Softly murmur the waters in the declining afternoon,
> On the banks the green wilderness darkens, joy in the rosy
> wind;
> The gentle song of the brother by the evening hill.

Georg Trakl: The Revisionary Language of Descent

Brigitte Peucker

Hölderlin's translations from Sophocles were his last work; in them meaning plunges from abyss to abyss until it threatens to become lost in the bottomless depths of language.
　　　　　—WALTER BENJAMIN, "The Task of the Translator"

The myth we need as interpreters, and do not have, is that the stars fell into language.
　　　　　—GEOFFREY HARTMAN, "From the Sublime to the Hermeneutic"

The theme of descent looms large among the poets of the German Romantic tradition because of their common intimation that the origin of their voice is not celestial but deep beneath the surface of the earth or water, locations that prove to be figures for death, the unconscious, the living but estranged mother, the dead but still vital patriarch, and, in the case of Rilke, "writing," an inscribed code of which voice is the expression. In discussing . . . [these poets I would add] to these figures still another, one that merges the awful visage of the patriarch with the inscribed code above-mentioned, which code understood in its most general sense is simply that priority of language which frustrates the poet's will to originality; the resulting composite figure I have called, following Harold Bloom, the "precursor." In turning now to the poetry of Georg Trakl, I shall focus almost exclusively on this . . . figure, but with a difference. Although there will be more than ever to say about the influence of prior poets in the Romantic tradition, it will become clear that the true precursor for Trakl, the object of his descent, is the revisionary language of descent itself, the language of exhaustion that all these poets together appear to have exhausted, and my theme here will therefore be Trakl's complex effort to make that language his own.

　　The poetry of Trakl is opaque by design, wilfully fragmented and always resistant to closure. In the hope of unlocking his hermeticism, many critics have ransacked his life for a key. But what we know of his life is also fragmentary. It was relatively short (1887–1914), and his letters are few and for the most part uninformative. Certain lurid facts do emerge from

From *Lyric Descent in the German Romantic Tradition*. © 1987 by Yale University. Yale University Press, 1987.

which the image of Trakl is typically formed: his sanity was precarious, he was addicted to drugs and alcohol, and his relationship with his sister Margarete was almost certainly incestuous—and from these facts there emerges, if we wish, a hybrid of Hölderlin, Coleridge, and Byron. The conjunction of Trakl's hermetic poetry with his Romantic life has provoked a number of psychoanalytic studies of varying degrees of competence and interest. There is an essay on Trakl, one of five, in Erich Neumann's *Creative Man*; his Jungian focus on the Great Mother archetype, which appears, he argues, in nearly all the Romantics' experiences of nature and landscape, we recognize certainly to cover an aspect of the descent theme as we have approached it in the present study. In a recent study, *The Poet's Madness: A Reading of Georg Trakl*, Francis Michael Sharp derives his readings from what he calls Trakl's metanoia, "a shift in the ontological center of the self . . . a nodal term where poetry and madness have often met," making the Laingian claim that in order to do justice to Trakl's poetry the reader must enter into his hallucinatory world. Maire Jaanus Kurrik's provocative study of Trakl [*Georg Trakl*] correlates changes in his poetic language with his developing schizophrenia, concluding that Trakl's poetry "leads us ultimately to naked primary process." Kurrik's monograph stresses the peculiar intensity with which Trakl experienced language, and she declares that it was "language, not disease, that made his art," but Trakl's poetry as she reads it remains by and large a pathological rather than a literary object. It is the language, after all, of a certain tradition and of particular poets to which Trakl responds with such unquestionable intensity; and for this reason the biographical approach to Trakl needs the complement of other emphases.

There is certainly no need to question the image of Trakl as a schizophrenic—and as an addict from an early age—but side by side with these signs of disorder we must place the impression the letters give of a meticulous, very possibly obsessive but still reliable craftsman. He repeatedly pestered his editor Kurt Wolff to make minor changes in punctuation, he was wont to submit lists of typographical errors, and he worried incessantly about arranging his poems in the right order for publication in a volume. All of this bespeaks a strong interest in form and in closure of all kinds. He could never stop revising, as is attested by "the famous cafe napkins which are the bedevilment of Trakl's editors: layer upon layer of alternative readings," [as Howard Stern calls them]. Thus far we remain at least arguably in the domain of obsessive madness, but what must supplement the idea that Trakl's poetry is an unstructured transformation of illness and excess into language is the frequent, careful, and systematic borrowing from other poets that has been noticed by a number of his interpreters. Perhaps foremost among these is Bernhard Böschenstein, to whose rich and suggestive essay on Trakl's borrowing from Hölderlin I shall often refer. Although he does not stress the point, Böschenstein makes it clear that Trakl sees himself as an heir to Hölderlin deeply preoccupied with the possibility of founding a poetry of his own.

From another perspective, after listing pages of Trakl's borrowings from Rimbaud, Reinhold Grimm notes that Trakl's manner of incorporating Rimbaud's poetry suggests an unusual attitude toward the literary tradition and toward the value of originality; for Trakl, Grimm argues, poetry is no longer the private possession of the poet but is simply verbal material of which anyone can make use. While it is unlikely that any poet could suppress individualism sufficiently to take such a detached view of the poet's function and of his or her predecessors' priority, Grimm's insight concerning existing poetry as verbal material to be appropriated remains a valuable one to which the ensuing argument is much indebted. If borrowings are taken without regard to context, they are severed from existing poetry and become ciphers or counters of what might be called poeticality. As is yet more obvious in the poetry of Helmut Heissenbüttel, for instance, the accrued meaning of such borrowings is not suppressed but becomes enigmatically immanent and overrich, simultaneously an homage to tradition and a mockery of its will-to-mean.

Trakl's borrowings, whether they repeat single words, whole phrases, or images and situations, point to themselves *as* borrowings, as quotations bordering on cliché. An obvious example is Novalis's "blaue Blume," which appears everywhere in Trakl's poems. In borrowing of this kind there is an element, to be sure, of the Freudian compulsion to repeat, to gain mastery of a procedure; and there is also, in the wearing down of significance by repetition, what Harold Bloom calls the effort to "undo" the achievement of the poet from whom one borrows. But it is not only a matter of borrowing from other poets; Trakl repeats himself, in poem after poem, with the same mystification through loss of context that accompanies his repeated borrowings from others. Resembling Eichendorff most in this, Trakl moves a highly restricted assemblage of images and verbal material in and out of position like pieces in a board game. The result is a finite set of repetitions and variations—worked out on one napkin or scrap of envelope after another—proceeding not only from draft to draft but also from poem to poem. Walther Killy, who has examined the chaos of manuscripts with painstaking care, has pointed out that in Trakl's work individual words mean differently in different places ("silbern" is his main example), that variants of the same poem may at least appear to contradict one another, and that what apparently determines a given poem is a grid-like verbal pattern that remains constant from one revision to another. The deeper principles governing repetitions of this kind, Killy remains convinced, are inaccessible. He concludes, in the tradition of Hugo Friedrich, that Trakl is more interested in *Sprachmagie* than in meaning.

It is with Friedrich and the more recent scholarly writing based on his ideas that Paul de Man takes issue, in his "Lyric and Modernity," for jumping too quickly to the conclusion that the discourse (especially the lyric discourse) of modernity is programmatically non-referential. In this essay de Man skillfully mediates between the commonsensical awareness (ignored by the school of Friedrich) that all poetry retains some mode of reference and the simultaneous understanding that the very plenitude of reference in the "modern lyric," in excess of any possible configural resolution, is what finally undermines univocal meaning. Most importantly, de Man recommends an approach to the reading of poetry that incorporates "semantic plurality . . . even and especially if the ultimate 'message' is held to be a mere play of meanings that cancel each other out." In my view, this is the double awareness that the reader of Trakl must be willing to sustain, if only because there are always at least two apparently conflicting impulses at work in his poetry: on the one hand there is the semantically charged desire at once to preserve and to undermine in revising the language of the past—especially that of Romantic poetry—by placing it in a new setting, and on the other hand there is the desire to empty that same language of all content whatsoever in order to release from its constraint the "pure" language which has preoccupied Romantic theorists, as we shall see further, from Hamann to Walter Benjamin. . . .

> *O die Flöte des Lichts, O die Flöte des Tods.*
> *Was zwang dich still zu stehen auf*
> *Verfallene Stiege, im Haus deiner Väter?*
> —TRAKL, *Verwandlung des Bösen*

Trakl was an avid reader, and in his early career a brazen literary thief: other poets' voices appear everywhere without disguise in the *Sammlung 1909*, as well as in the *Gedichte 1909–1912*. The seemingly simple yet enigmatic religiosity of the Romantic Clemens Brentano dominates "Das tiefe Lied"; Novalis's *Hymnen an die Nacht* plainly inform "Gesang zur Nacht" and "Nachtlied II"; "Auf den Tod einer alten Frau" reflects Trakl's familiarity with the poems and themes of Rilke's *Neue Gedichte*; the posturing of Heine, his surprising appositions and turns of expression, can be found everywhere, as in "Ein Komödiant, der seine Rolle spricht, / Gezwungen, voll Verzweiflung-Langeweile!" ("Confiteor"); "Melusine II" is written in obvious imitation of Goethe's "Erlkönig"; Eichendorff's cankered flowers and Baudelaire's flowers of evil appear variously as "giftige Blumen" ("Das Grauen"), "blutfarbne Blüten," and "pestfarbne Blumen" ("Sabbath"); and Rimbaud's artificial paradise is represented and subjected to decay in poems such as "Ermatten."

In these poems, Trakl experiments with a wide variety of poetic attitudes and a limited number of forms—as one might expect of a young poet who is at once coming to terms with a poetic tradition and intent on developing a personal style. But unlike most apprentice poets, Trakl is not just imitative, he is pointedly imitative: many poems deviate very little from their models, as if with the intention of learning a technique by rote—one which is then used in attenuated, distorted form in the more personal poems of the same period. Other poems reflect a more complex encounter with the tradition, making a theme of their own borrowing, the resulting self-consciousness of which then precipitates the business of poetic revision. In these poems borrowings are easily recognizable, and serve frequently as vehicles for Trakl's interest in voice—in its role in prior poetry and as he supposes it to function in his own work. A poem of this period in which this process works particularly well, the first in the early group I shall be discussing mainly with respect to Trakl's thematic revisionism, is "Ballade I," which is based in part on Heine's *Die Nordsee*, a lyric cycle in itself preoccupied with filiality.

The deceptively simple "Ballade I" has much to say about the possession of voice in the German lyric tradition:

> Ein Narre schrieb drei Zeichen in Sand,
> Eine bleiche Magd da vor ihm stand.
> Laut sang, o sang das Meer.
>
> Sie hielt einen Becher in der Hand,
> Der schimmerte bis auf zum Rand,
> Wie Blut so rot und schwer.
>
> Kein Wort ward gesprochen—die Sonne schwand,
> Da nahm der Narre aus ihrer Hand
> Den Becher und trank ihn leer.
>
> Da löschte sein Licht in ihrer Hand,
> Der Wind verwehte drei Zeichen in Sand—
> Laut sang, o sang das Meer.

In Heine's "Erklärung," a poem in *Die Nordsee*, it is the poet himself, the central figure of the cycle, who writes "Agnes, ich liebe dich" in the sand, only to have the words erased by the waves. And in the darkly ironic "Fragen," a poem in the same cycle, "ein Narr" waits for an indifferent nature to respond to his questions concerning the meaning of life and the nature of the sublime ("Wer wohnt dort oben auf goldenen Sternen?"). In addition, in *Die Nordsee* as in "Ballade I," a beloved, idealized woman holds sway as muse; and a similar figure appears in Heine's *Lyrisches Intermezzo*, of which one is reminded by the simplicity of Trakl's syntax. Heine's presence in the background helps with the interpretation of Trakl's poem; "Erklärung" suggests, for example, that the "drei Zeichen" may be "ich liebe dich," the *Urworte* that all love poetry displaces and elaborates upon.

The seductive pale maiden who lures a lover to death is also in Heine, but she is just as central in Eichendorff and Brentano and is a familiar spirit, indeed, throughout the German tradition. An admirer of Mörike, Trakl would no doubt have been familiar with that poet's enigmatic, strangely decadent rendering of this figure in his "Peregrina," where the maiden similarly hands the speaker "den Tod im Kelch der Sünden." That eroticism and death are always closely linked in Trakl's lyrics can doubtless be referred to his involvement with his sister; but for our purposes it is more important to note that *Liebestode* of the kind we have been enumerating here, in all the poets mentioned but especially given the chosen vocabulary of Trakl, should be referred back to one of Goethe's best-known, if least understood, ballads, "Der König in Thule," sung by Gretchen in *Faust,* part 1. The chalice or "Becher" that is emblematic of the beloved who has given it to the king at her death, at once her sign and the sign of her absence, is fittingly emptied by the king at every meal. But at the same time this chalice represents the king, whose eyes similarly overflow and empty ("Die Augen gingen ihm über"; part 1, line 2765) whenever he drains it. Just before he dies, the cup itself is said to drink ("Trinken, und sinken tief ins Meer"); and at his death his eyes "sink" in imitation of the cup. As understood by his literary descendants, Goethe's poetics renders the "Becher" a "symbol" in which the corporeal presence of the beloved and of the king can be merged across time. The brilliance of the poem is its accomplishment of this burdensome task, a concretely imagined secular communion via the "heilige Becher," without ever calling attention to its symbolic intent. After the golden cup sinks, it becomes a treasure of the depths, for Droste-Hülshoff the vessel of literary inheritance, as we have seen, which only poetic descent can recover. For Trakl too the "Becher" becomes a symbol of literary accomplishment, of Goethe's success in handling symbolism and of his faith in his own power of containment, his control over the evocative compression essential to lyric. "Becher" for Trakl then becomes a verbal talisman, to repeat which is to participate in the genius of Goethe.

In Heine's *Nordsee,* the poet must also come to terms with his literary inheritance. "Die Götter Griechenlands" is clearly as much a confrontation with Goethe and Schiller as with Greek mythology, and it is beautifully staged: at the very moment when Heine arrives at the destruction of the Titans, of fathers by sons—"Doch auch die Götter regieren nicht ewig,/ Die Jungen verdrängen die Alten"—he addresses "Jupiter Parricida," alluding, perhaps, to the "Jupiter Pluvius" of Goethe's "Wanderers Sturmlied." (One is reminded as well of Hölderlin's "Natur und Kunst oder Saturn und Jupiter.") And when in "Fragen" the poet besieges nature with questions that go unanswered, when the stars remain indifferent, cold, and inaccessible to interpretation, Heine is simultaneously conceding the belatedness of the poet, the "Narr" who can no longer read natural signs, and directing toward Goethe the shrewd Humanist admonition that metaphors taken from the natural world evade rather than illuminate the concerns of mankind.

Trakl's "Ballade I" repeats Heine's swerve away from Goethe but then somewhat revises Heine's supposition that voice is the medium of the poet even if it is not to be found in nature. In Trakl too, nature is oblivious to the human drama; but his "Narr" is neither a poet who voices questions nor one who, when he writes, merely transcribes the voiced sigh of a lover. He is, much more emphatically than Heine's fool, a writer, one whose signs are not words, as far as we are told, but only marks, and whose silence is as conspicuous as that of Heine's nature: "Kein Wort ward gesprochen." Trakl's nature, by contrast, is what sings, albeit unintelligibly, and sings last and loudest, with a persistence that Trakl acknowledges by making it the theme of a refrain and placing it twice—in the first and last stanzas— in symmetrical contrast with the persistence of human silence. Thus for Heine human voice and the writing that records it are alienated for better as well as for worse from the silence of nature, whereas for Trakl human silence and the hermetic writing that perpetuates it are cut off from the vocality of nature in a state of solipsism to which the values of better and worse are irrelevant.

The very complexity with which Trakl's poem stages itself within the tradition of the written word, at once sharing Heine's confrontation with Goethe and rewriting Goethe's signs of lyric power with almost superstitious reverence, heightens both the distance and the significance of the singing sea in this poem yet further. As if in defiance of the mighty sea, which is also the choral *voice* of a poetic tradition in which the event narrated here has occurred so many times before, Trakl seems to entertain the idea of a poetry that does not issue from voice. But his heresy is only tentative; as his title with its allusion to the oral tradition indicates, he is unwilling wholly to identify with "der Narr." He is not ready to say, as he will in "Nachtlied," "gewaltig ist das Schweigen im Stein." The vocal sea is after all the place into which Goethe's golden cup has been cast; its depths hold the promise of renewed natural communion, and Trakl's homage to the poet of this promise, absorbed into the *sound* of "Becher," is too great to permit open defiance. The refrain goes on, "Laut sang, o sang das Meer," and in repeating this refrain with its inner repetition and its vocative "o," Trakl acknowledges that he remains within the vocal tradition—perhaps too much so, indeed, to accord with his developing interest in the poetics of the pure sign. Whatever the reason, this poem was not published during his lifetime.

In his two "Melusine" poems, Trakl once again associates the theme of an inspirited, vocal nature with Goethe. In what is commonly assumed to be the earlier "Melusine," there exists a deep empathy between the "Meerfee" of the title and the elements other than the sea. The wind cries over her fate, and her passion, figured forth by her fiery hair, finds its reflection in the storm. The narrator, with whose words the poem concludes, keeps himself at a safe distance from this temptress, however, safely protected from her pagan spirit by his Christian faith: "Da spricht für dich, du arme Magd, / Mein Herz ein stilles Nachtgebet!" All this is conventional enough, and the suggestive confusion of the poem only arises when we attempt to locate voice, the origin of what is spoken, precisely and consistently. Here is the poem:

An meinen Fenstern weint die Nacht—
Die Nacht ist stumm, es weint wohl der Wind,
Der Wind, wie ein verlornes Kind—
Was ist's, das ihn so weinen macht?
O arme Melusine!

Wie Feuer ihr Haar im Sturme weht,
Wie Feuer an Wolken vorüber und klagt—
Da spricht für dich, du arme Magd,
Mein Herz ein stilles Nachtgebet!
O arme Melusine!

The piety of the narrator makes it the more interesting that he would attempt to explain a natural sound by referring it to a nature spirit. There can be no question, apparently, of a natural voice; the night, which is the time Trakl, with Novalis, prefers, is here denied a voice, being mute, "stumm." Like the night, the speaker's prayer is silent, while the poem by contrast ends with a balladic, vocal refrain. The question then is, if it is not part of the speaker's prayer, who speaks this refrain? Is it the anonymous voice of the ballad genre? In the first stanza it might be assigned to the wind, which cries in presumed sympathy with Melusine. But in the second it is plausibly the narrator's voiced, wholly secular and petitionless version of his "stilles Nachtgebet." Or, since Melusine is connected with "klagen," a verb whose antecedent is vague (her hair could stream like tears or bend like a willow, but how could it lament?), perhaps she herself speaks the refrain in self-pity. Finally, and perhaps most convincingly, the closing refrain can be voiced by the wind insofar as it is also Melusine, the "ver-lornes Kind" to which it is linked in simile. The point of all this ambiguity is, in any case, that voice is now here, now there, but seems never to be the possession of the "speaker"; and the poem's tentative evocation of a nature spirit that in some sense speaks the poet's lines, an anomaly rein-forced by the rhyme of "Wind" with "Kind," may have suggested to Trakl the possibility of recasting his poem in the form and rhythms of an earlier ballad about possession, Goethe's "Erlkönig," a poem Geoffrey Hartman has called a "play of voices" ("Wordsworth and Goethe in Literary History").

In this ballad of 1782, Goethe dramatizes a struggle for a child between two "fathers," a contest between exhortations, seemingly without physical violence, carried out between rivals for the possession of charismatic au-thority. The actual father speaks with the voice of enlightened reason and hears nothing but the sound of wind in dry leaves when his rival speaks; and the aspiring father (or lover), the Erlkönig, is at once a nature spirit and the voice of imagination—albeit a regressive, solipsistic imagination. It is easy to view this struggle, whose arena is the mind of the child and whose aim is to shape his view of nature, as a rivalry between literary impulses that were more even than usually at odds in the 1780s, during which the Enlightenment can be said to have lost out, as it does in the poem, to the avatars of the imagination. As Hartman convincingly argues, toward the beginning of the poem the father's voice can still "contain" that of the child; his lines literally frame the child's. But the Erlkönig becomes wholly dominant by the last stanza, with the death of the child—his desertion of the real world for fairytale and dream—signalling the imagination's victory. Goethe himself can be said however to identify with no one; his is yet another voice in this drama, the impersonal voice of the narrator, or more precisely that of a traditional singer. (The ballad was written for Goethe's *Singspiel, Die Fischerin.*) Here as so often in Goethe, Werther's sensibility being a case in point, the struggle between reason and imagination is distanced, made to seem pseudo-intellectual, by the matter-of-fact simplicity of the ballad form. All voices in "Erlkönig" are framed by the narrator, who speaks the first and last stanzas as though to insist on the insufficiency of any one world-view taken by itself, and the impression of superiority achieved by this Olympian perspective is what convinces us that the object of the struggle between mere ideologies is properly a child and not a poet. The object of the *narrator's* seduction is not the child but the reader, a prospective poet who experiences the abrupt end of the narrative, with its implicit indictment of imagination, as a mortal threat to his or her own creative tendencies and rushes into the arms of Goethe himself for continued life.

Why then would Trakl choose a form and a drama of such manifest complexity as a vehicle for his "Melusine" material? In the first version, certainly, being a nature spirit, Melusine does belong to the world of the Erlkönig and his daughters. In the second version, however, she is reduced to natural proportions, attractive but evidently passive and helpless, "mein Kind"; yet it is in this version, the first poem of *Gedichte 1909–1912*, that Trakl faithfully imitates the rhythms of "Erlkönig" and composes a dialogue between two voices, Melusine's and that of another. Trakl has appropriated Goethe's ballad in order to reapportion its roles. The second voice is that of the seducer, an Erlkönig figure, but there are no Olympian perspectives; the role of the father collapses into the repeated banal solicitude of the poet's "mein Kind." There is some confusion of identity in the poem, as Melusine cannot seem to connect the voice she hears with the face she sees, but the second speaker identifies himself definitely with the somewhat jaded sexuality of the burgeoning Springtime: "er blühte wohl allzu reich." In the midst of falling blossoms and vampiristic kisses, this assertion makes it clear that the scene described in the second "Melusine" is a scene of seduction and deflowering.

For this feverish view of nature, with its emphasis not only on sex but on perversions vaguely evocative of incest, Trakl typically chooses the poetic vehicle of others, as if to accomplish the same distancing accomplished by Goethe's traditional ballad voice. In "Melusine II" Trakl borrows the camouflage of "Erlkönig" not only in order to neutralize the troubled sexuality of his theme but also in order to replicate formally the questions his poem raises about vocal authority. For his emphasis on overripeness Trakl has a literary forerunner in Eichendorff, whose sirens, sphinxes, and fallen gardens he takes over in the poem "Blutschuld." But in other poems in addition to the "Melusine" poems, there are indications that the decaying process world is, to be sure, a personal obsession, but also and more interestingly an implicitly pejorative allusion to Goethe's poetics and to the achievement of Goethe's poetry. Goethe's organicism, Trakl implies in recasting the seemingly bodiless seduction scene of "Erlkönig," is really a mask for decay and putrefaction. We can sense a similar critique behind such passages as "Wie scheint doch alles Werdende so krank!" ("Heiterer Frühling") and "Die Apfelbäume sinken kahl und stad/Ins farbige ihrer Frucht, die schwarz verdarb" ("Im Dorf"). In this land of corruption, the fiefdom of Goethe, as Trakl implies, he locates voice and song, with their power of seduction and dissimulation. Music and the sister are recurrently linked in Trakl's poetry (his sister was a musician), and he implicates the musicality of his own lines and the seductive beauty of his language in the "Verfall" of the fallen landscape. Probably, then, the two voices of "Melusine II" are one after all.

It has been suggested that Trakl's compulsion to repeat is related to the experience of incest, both a mastery of guilt and a sequential equivalent of the lack of difference in "unnatural" sexuality, and this is probably true. Once more, however, I have wished rather to stress the way in which poetic worlds are informed and shaped by preexisting poetic worlds. "Ballade I" and the "Melusine" poems exemplify the interaction, I would say the interfusion, of the personal with the literary. At this point of interfusion the theme which emerges is the poet's effort to overgo the literary past by repeating its forms—its tropes, imagery, and rhythms—repetitions which conceal even while they manifest the poet's will to express his personality as an individual. It is in this accumulated context that we can best understand Trakl's peculiar belief that the Olympian Goethe's poetry was too personal, too confessional, and too freely given over to sensuality; only in the hope that he is the first to suppress personality can Trakl secure his originality. Although "Erlkönig" condemns the regressive paradise of the Elf-king, it does not condemn the power of voice as such but rather glories in it. Rather than celebrating his own skillful control in delaying the outcome of his tale, like Goethe's narrator, Trakl concludes "Melusine II" by drawing down a curtain of night and silence over the scene. As he would say (in one of his many allusions to the conclusion of Hölderlin's "Patmos") in *Verwandlung des Bösen*, "Dem folgt unvergängliche Nacht."

Critics enlist Trakl's same few pronouncements about the writing of poetry in order to make a wide variety of arguments. One such pronouncement, with reference to his early poetry, was prompted by what Trakl took to be the egregious theft of his poetic style by an aspiring poet named Ludwig Ullmann. "Nicht nur," Trakl complains in a letter [from July 1910],

dass einzelne Bilder und Redewendungen beinahe wörtlich über-
nommen wurden . . . sind auch die Reime einzelner Strophen und
ihre Wertigkeit den meinigen vollkommen gleich, vollkommen
gleich meine bildhafte Manier, die in vier Strophenzeilen vier einzelne Bildteile zu einem einzigen Eindruck zusammenschmiedet[,]
mit einem Wort bis ins kleinste Detail ist das Gewand, die heiss
errungene Manier meiner Arbeiten nachgebildet worden.

It remains open to question, though, whether Trakl himself has at this
point in his career achieved a unique style, "heiss errungen." There are
Eichendorff poems, such as "Mondnacht," in which quatrains form a single
impression with a series of four images. In Trakl's "Musik im Mirabell,"
which exemplifies this technique, we find Eichendorff's cadences enlisted
to express Eichendorff's images and themes: the singing of the "Brunnen"
in the evening, clouds in relief against a blue sky, ancestral statues, and,
significantly, "der alte Garten." Amid the statuary and the tendency in
general to pose things in the scene one is not surprised to find a "Faun
mit toten Augen," and Trakl's use of color may also be indebted to Eichendorff: whereas later he would use color in conformance with the
Expressionist painters' ideal of representing an "inner reality," here he
defers apparently to nature—falling leaves could easily be red—but more
probably to the sensuality and sense of danger irradiated by red peonies
in Eichendorff. The glowing fire contributes to this mood and, given the
"Angstgespenster," the "weisser Fremdling" can easily be viewed as another apparition, a familiar of the decaying hallways in the deserted house.
In this poem the extinguishing of the lamp denies vision in favor of au-
dition—"Das Ohr hört nachts Sonatenklänge"—and again the manner in
which this preference is expressed (with a certain insincerity, if what we
have said thus far about Trakl's mistrust of voice holds true at all) will be
familiar to readers of German literature, especially of Mörike's *Maler Nolten*.

Reinhold Grimm argues that this setting with its deserted patriarchal
castle is taken from Rimbaud; but as a genre scene it is more persistently
linked in the early poetry to Eichendorff. In Eichendorff as in Trakl,
the deserted house is connected with the theme of the prodigal son's return, most notably for Eichendorff in "Heimkehr," a poem [previously]
. . . discussed as an occasion on which the poet attempts to come to terms
with his poetic fathers. Trakl's assertion in "Musik im Mirabell" that "Der
Ahnen Marmor ist ergraut" suggests defiance of the fathers, but this defiance is governed by an irony with which we have perforce become familiar, ventured as it is in the voice and manner of one of those fathers,
Eichendorff. Similarly, all that remains of the poet's personal self-assertion
at this moment of defiance, the erotic situation in the background of "Ballade I" and "Melusine II," is the lingering, intimately melancholy after-
sound of a sonata. For a more poetically radical appropriation of these
images and themes, the detritus of aristocratic decline nostalgically rendered that is as old as Northern European poetry and still shapes such

works of art as "L'Année dernière à Marienbad" and "L'Avventura," we must turn to "Verfall [I]":

Es weht ein Wind! Hinlöschend singen
Die grünen Lichter—gross und satt
Erfüllt der Mond den hohen Saal,
Den keine Feste mehr durchklingen.

Die Ahnenbilder lächeln leise
Und fern—ihr letzter Schatten fiel,
Der Raum ist von Verwesung schwül,
Den Raben stumm umziehn im Kreise.

Verlorner Sinn vergangner Zeiten
Blickt aus den steinernen Masken her,
Die schmerzverzerrt und daseinsleer
Hintrauern in Verlassenheiten.

Versunkner Gärten kranke Düfte
Umkosen leise den Verfall—
Wie schluchzender Worte Widerhall
Hinzitternd über off'ne Grüfte.

Here again is the situation of Eichendorff's "Heimkehr": the statuary—"Ahnenbilder"—in the moonlight, the abandoned castle. And here also is another familiar Eichendorff image, the sunken garden which the earlier poet typically renders as a "fallen" garden reflecting the loss of childhood innocence, or as the underworld site of beckoning voices ("der Grund"). "Verfall" obviously belittles the influence of ancestral voices: their laughter is soft and distant, and the "Ahnenbilder" no longer even cast shadows. Such is the irrelevance of their presence, indeed, that they have become ciphers yielding only a trace of intelligible meaning, the pain expressed in their stony faces at having been abandoned. Trakl here accentuates Eichendorff's turn against the fathers: whereas the fathers in "Heimkehr" are drained of authority only when the poet's realization turns them to stone, in "Verfall" they are introduced without preamble as powerless statues. But in their easy dethronement there is a personal cost to the doubly belated poet. Trakl does not repeat Eichendorff's confident ritual of taking up the relinquished sword; he can scarcely carry forward a tradition he has thus consigned to irrecoverable obscurity.

With the opening declaration of his poem, "Es weht ein Wind," Trakl appears to be ushering in an inspiring breath; but instead of exhilarating, the wind uncooperatively snuffs out the lights, making way for the moon, "gross und satt," which fills the empty room. This moment of desublimation, which appears time and again in Trakl's poetry, not only lowers the moon but imprisons it in the empty hall of the fathers. It is rank and overstuffed, Trakl implies, because it has consumed the poets for whom it was an obscure object of desire; and its light is contaminated by its overuse in literature. Moon and moonlight being difficult to tell apart, the light itself may by this time be what is rotting, and the ravens may then bear ironic witness to this fading out of a tradition of which Poe had made them a part. Decay first appears in the poem as that which pervades the room, effecting the merger of two topoi, celestial moonlight and earthy putrefaction, which the Romantic tradition had always kept rigorously separate, except when the former in some Gothic instances was permitted to shine down on the latter. Trakl wants to bring these regions together, as indeed he has already brought them together in the green lights that sing as they are extinguished. In this poem he seems to realize that the props of Eichendorff are less important in themselves than as a means to bring him face to face with the two kinds of metaphor against which his poetry must define itself, the organicism of Goethe (negatively revised as we have seen Trakl revise it elsewhere) and the moonlit interiority of Novalis. These of course would be the oversimplifications of a poet struggling for breathing room; Goethe himself had already brought these regions together in countless ways, they are not always stably polar opposites even in Novalis, Hölderlin's poetry is a struggle to work out their relationship, and their synthesis will be the goal of Rilke's *Sonette an Orpheus*.

The lights extinguished by the wind in "Verfall" are green, and sing a kind of swan song in going out. This synaesthesia, recalling Eichendorff, Baudelaire, and Rimbaud, connects the first stanza with the last, where fragrances are compared with sounds. The "sick" fragrances of the sunken gardens are said to caress the decay within them. In this kind of figure we find embodied at once the *fin de siècle*, the poet's personal life, and the self-consuming conclusion of a poetic tradition; and it must always be borne in mind that for Trakl these moments are inextricably related—as the final two lines demonstrate. They form a metaphor by means of which the fallen garden's fragrances, its residual impressions, are compared with the *echo* of the sobbing words that pass over open tombs. This is the echo of elegy, which is the lyric of belatedness. Just beneath the surface of this concluding metaphor is the Romantic figure of the Aeolian harp, connecting the end of the poem with the beginning, "Es weht ein Wind," in yet another way. Hence at the last moment Trakl acknowledges that his poetry is elegiac after all, and therefore inspired by the residual vocality that arises from the still-open tombs of the dead he had earlier repudiated because they themselves had been, as he thought, irrelevantly elegiac poets. But because the Aeolian harp figures forth the responsive imagination, not the merely imitative one, Trakl preserves a measure of independence for himself. In admitting at last the echo of other poets' words, Trakl describes the aspect of his poetry that is of special interest to us, and he does not really concede anything to the past: the sounds he echoes are already echoes, tokens of secondariness and absence no more immediate than his own. Poetry results from the passage of poetic language *over*, not from, the tombs of the ancestors, who were as much its mouthpiece merely as he is himself, conjoining inherited language with inherited forms. Only the full implications of the Aeolian harp image, if it is present, allow the possibility of poetic renovation; or else, if the echoes are understood purely as echoes, acoustic repetitions, then poetic language can be purified of mediation and returned to the condition of pure language, which expresses only itself. Here we anticipate the drift of the later poetry; but perhaps the early conviction that it may have been reserved for him to accomplish the repristination of language was what disturbed Trakl so much when he found that Ullmann seemed content simply to echo his own work. In the meantime we have seen that his dawning indifference to the logic of representation, the logic he could imagine the poetic tradition to have worn threadbare, frees him to bring together the realms of the celestial and the earthly and thus to suspend the normal range of their meanings, not by cancelling them out but by keeping them both in play.

A brief look at another poem, "Rondel," may serve to summarize these points:

> Verflossen ist das Gold der Tage,
> Des Abends braun und blaue Farben:
> Des Hirten sanfte Flöten starben
> Des Abends blau und braune Farben
> Verflossen ist das Gold der Tage.

Although he modifies and simplifies the French rondel form, Trakl retains its essential circularity, which becomes his theme. Trakl here reifies the passage of time as the flow of language that evokes it, subtly shifting our attention thereby from experience to its representation; he effects this shift by insisting on the literariness of his topoi, themselves survivors of the passage of time. The replacement of sunlight by the brown and blue of evening is also the replacement of a Golden Age of poetry by Trakl's usual temporal site, the evening land—except that, in the absence of their own verb, the brown and blue seem also to be "verflossen." The third line announces that the pastoral impulse of lyric has died in some indefinite past, and it occurs to the reader that the burden of this poem is simply, over and over, that poetry is dead.

The colon preparing us for the heart of the rondel proves a feint, as that central line simply inaugurates the turn of the poem back on itself without further punctuation, and the more advanced realization dawns that the point of the poem is *not* this message, which would be pivotally declared by the third line only if that line were set off by decisive punctuation, the period that marks an endpoint. Poetry is dead, yes, but a Nietzschean twilight persists in which poetic language seems capable of declaring its demise indefinitely. And indeed, it is the brown night of Nietzsche's poem "Venedig" to which Trakl's second and fourth lines refer. And if Novalis's "blaue Blume" still faintly blooms in these lines as well, more prominently in the fourth line once the very persistence of the twilight has become a kind of momentum, then not only poetry but the spirit of Romanticism lives on. But no longer as elegy, no longer as the pastoral plangency of the Sentimental Poet's wish to recover meaning. The rote repetition of lines, justified by the rondel form, seems to release the last two lines from the responsibility of meaning into pure self-declaration as language and sound. Far from insisting that poetry has died, then, this gesture suggests that pure poetry has not yet been born; and the belated Trakl arrives at the earliness of magic spells and incantations. It is in this sense, to quote Heidegger out of context, that Trakl's "land of descent is the transition to the beginning of the dawn concealed within it."

For Heidegger, Trakl discloses a language that carries him from belatedness back to a new, as yet unborn priority. From this point of view, the poem "Verfall" announces the decay of poetic language, to be sure; but from this decomposition of its given contours—syntax and meaning—a pure essence emerges. Or, as Trakl says in "Herbst des Einsamen," "Ein reines Blau tritt aus verfallener Hülle." The fact that a pure language was a central preoccupation of Romantic theorists as long-buried as Hamann only makes Trakl's choice of metaphor here the more appropriate. And perhaps in part it was the mortal remains of Trakl, his fragmented counters of language taken from other poets, that encouraged Walter Benjamin's description of the task of the translator: "to release in his own language that pure language which is under the spell of another, to liberate the language imprisoned in a work in his re-creation of that work. For the sake of pure language he breaks through decayed barriers of his own language."

Confessions of a Poet:
Poetry and Politics in Brecht's Lyric

Reinhold Grimm

Ausschließlich wegen der zunehmenden Unordnung
In unseren Städten des Klassenkampfs
Haben etliche von uns in diesen Jahren beschlossen
Nicht mehr zu reden von Hafenstädten, Schnee auf den
        Dächern, Frauen
Geruch reifer Äpfel im Keller, Empfindungen des Fleisches
All dem, was den Menschen rund macht und menschlich
Sondern zu reden nur mehr von der Unordnung
Also einseitig zu werden, dürr, verstrickt in die Geschäfte
Der Politik und das trockene, "unwürdige" Vokabular
Der dialektischen Ökonomie
Damit nicht dieses furchtbare gedrängte Zusammensein
Von Schneefällen (sie sind nicht nur kalt, wir wissen's)
Ausbeutung, verlocktem Fleisch und Klassenjustiz eine
        Billigung
So vielseitiger Welt in uns erzeuge, Lust an
Den Widersprüchen solch blutigen Lebens
Ihr versteht.

Do away with art? Oh no! Bertolt Brecht does not want to do that. He has no intention of nullifying art—despite all such "confessions." It should— *it must*—exist! Never, not even in these verses from his exile—lines which sound so much of dismissal and finality—did Brecht repudiate art. It must

From *From Kafka and Dada to Brecht and Beyond*, edited by Reinhold Grimm, Peter Spycher, and Richard A. Zipser. © 1982 by The Board of Regents of the University of Wisconsin System. University of Wisconsin Press, 1982.

exist, even if it seems to be criminal and wanton to us, a blatant injustice and impossibility! Man still acts like a wolf toward his fellow men; everywhere, as in times past, men, classes, entire peoples and continents are being enslaved, exploited, and ground to dust; today more than ever a brutish humanity, oppressed and oppressor at the same time, threatens to choke on its own bloody swill. And yet, in spite of everything, art must be. Even "pure" art in the midst of our dark era, as none other than the political poet Brecht confided to us.

For precisely Brecht, the poet who, without any reservation, considered his work to be a fight for the liberation of the exploited and oppressed, the disenfranchised and degraded, the demeaned and defamed: he also spoke in behalf of art, even of "pure" art. Precisely he who placed himself totally in the service of the humanization of humanity desired that art exist. Even by denying it he declared himself for it. He who "solely because of the increasing disorder"—what an immoderate moderation—seems once and for all to forswear any kind of aesthetic pleasure, does this through the medium of art, as a poet, in verse and accomplished, masterfully manipulated language. And there is more yet. He who makes such protestations to us, who from now on intends to employ art "only" as a weapon, expressly and unequivocally professed aesthetic pleasure—indeed at approximately the same time! In Brecht's posthumously published *Me-ti*, his collection of dialectical-didactic prose in the style of the ancient Chinese, there is a text which has an almost more muted and restrained effect than our poem but which is, nonetheless, scarcely less striking. For this short piece of prose—allegory or aphoristic parable, yet quite realistic—bears the title "Über reine Kunst."

But let's listen to Brecht's confession! Let's hear what Me-ti, the political philosopher, has to relate about Kin-jeh, the political poet:

Me-ti sagte: Neulich fragte mich der Dichter Kin-jeh, ob er in diesen Zeitläuften Gedichte über Naturstimmungen schreiben dürfe. Ich antwortete ihm: Ja. Als ich ihn wieder traf, fragte ich ihn, ob er Gedichte über Naturstimmungen geschrieben habe. Er antwortete: Nein. Warum, fragte ich. Er sagte: Ich stellte mir die Aufgabe, das Geräusch fallender Regentropfen zu einem genußvollen Erlebnis des Lesers zu machen. Darüber nachdenkend und hie und da eine Zeile skizzierend, erkannte ich es als nötig, dieses Geräusch fallender Regentropfen für alle Menschen, also auch für solche Menschen zu einem genußvollen Erlebnis zu machen, die kein Obdach besitzen und denen die Tropfen zwischen Kragen und Hals fallen, während sie zu schlafen versuchen. Vor dieser Aufgabe schreckte ich zurück.

Die Kunst rechnet nicht nur mit dem heutigen Tag, sagte ich versucherisch. Da es immer solche Regentropfen geben wird, könnte ein Gedicht dieser Art lange dauern. Ja, sagte er traurig,

> wenn es keine solche Menschen mehr geben wird, denen sie
> zwischen Kragen und Hals fallen, kann es geschrieben werden.

Not only a utopian dimension makes this bit of prose stand out, but also a historical one. For, while Kin-jeh is a fictional figure, Me-ti is one from history. He was a dialectician and "socio-moral philosopher" who lived over two and a half millennia ago as a contemporary and ideological rival of Confucius. Once again, as he did so often, Brecht has slipped on a poetical garment in order to "emerge through real sleeves." Just as little as his choice of two figures can their Chinese disguise deceive us about the confessional aspect of his text. The philosophical dialectician Me-ti is just as much Brecht's *alter ego* as the dialectical lyricist Kin-jeh. At the turn in their conversation ("I shrank back"/"I said temptingly") both, in eloquent silence, indiscernibly blend together. That which "On Pure Art" accomplishes is the same topicality which we already encountered in Brecht's verses. Neither the glimmering of a distant future nor the shadows of the past can conceal this burning present.

To be sure, while in the poem an intensely afflicted ego accounts to us and posterity, in the prose text it conducts a dialogue with itself. But the confessions are the same. Once again they are: "Pure" lyric poetry can and may not be written nowadays. Even lines which merely deal with "the sound of falling raindrops" (or, for that matter, the "smell of ripe apples in the cellar," the sight of "snow on roofs"): these, too, are denied the poet. Indeed, with the awareness of destitution and despair, such sensual writing and reading is not simply despised and prohibited—it is, in view of our "bloody world" with its "awful cramped coexistence" of the naturally beautiful with human injustice and misery, absolutely immoral. Ethics and aesthetics appear irreconcilable, the social and artistic conscience agonizingly divided, as long as those daintily splashing raindrops run down the necks of the homeless and that innocent snow ("not only cold" but also an ancient symbol of purity, as "we know") gleams merrily from the rooftops after it has covered up the cadavers of the frozen—mercifully, as many a poet maintains. And who cares about the smell of apples in the cool, roomy cellars of the rich when elsewhere in the stinking pits of poverty children starve and the sick perish? "Before this task"—again what an immoderate moderation—the poet, both times, "shrank back." In Brecht's verse as well as in his prose piece, art—at least as "pure art"—has become impossible; all that remains is "art as weapon" and with it the painful decision of estrangement and renunciation in order, as he says with the utmost objectivity and austerity, "to become one-sided, reduced, enmeshed in the business of politics and the dry 'indecorous' vocabulary of dialectical economics. . . . " Indeed, the lyrical ego and its epic counterparts confess the same thing to us. The only difference between them is apparently that the decision which does not emerge until the end of the parable is clearly and irrevocably pronounced in the poem. Yet had not Kin-jeh in mute conversation with Me-ti already decreed what Brecht's poem bluntly expresses? Just as, on the other hand, Brecht's poem, although it never mentions "art," let alone "pure art," constantly and unmistakably means precisely this?

Impossible to ignore, however, is that which Kin-jeh proclaims, not to say promises, both himself and us, and not merely between the lines but directly, even if somewhat "sadly." For someday, this he knows for sure, someday "it can be written," although not by him as he fears: that poem about the rain, the snow, and the smell of ripe apples in the cellar, that poem about "cities by the sea," "women," and the sensations "of the flesh," and thus about "all that makes a man round and human." One day, Brecht knows, man will no longer act as a wolf toward his fellow men, but will finally be a "helper." One day, sometime in the future, this humane work of art will, indeed must, be created. Even if in "somber eras," before the time is ripe, ethics and aesthetics are completely irreconcilable, they can— they *must*—be reconciled. The promise is more than just a promise: it is an unalterable demand. Brecht's and Kin-jeh's perception, their uneasy insight into the immorality of pure art today, reveals itself as an ethical postulate. For the less any art may now be possible, all the more so will it be then, in days to come—and precisely as "pure" art, seemingly superfluous and ostensibly non-essential though indispensable as a pleasurable, even joyful human experience. Art should and must exist, according to Kin-jeh as well as to Brecht.

And yet—or at least so it seems—there is still a considerable difference between them. Does not Kin-jeh look primarily into the future, whereas Brecht's lyrical ego gazes into the past? Does not the former speak of an art which cannot yet be and the latter of one which can no longer exist? Is not the somber renunciation of art in our inhumane present the only thing both have in common? But should that be the complete and ultimate answer of Brecht? If art is only present by its absence—doesn't this also mean that it either has, or can gain, presence precisely because it *is* absent? Isn't this the actual, the secret "Testament" of the early admirer of Villon, Bertolt Brecht? Not without reason have I frequently quoted from one of Brecht's most famous poems from the thirties, "An die Nachgeborenen." For here too, in this impressive and truly "Great Testament," the poet, in the midst of political strife, is concerned with nature and the "impressions of nature." And again, in addition to the sensations of the flesh and of love, they represent the human as well as artistic realm. To be sure, there is no longer any mention of pleasure, let alone joyful pleasure. On the contrary, Brecht laconically confides to us:

> Der Liebe pflegte ich achtlos
> Und die Natur sah ich ohne Geduld.

But was he completely "careless"? Completely "without patience"? No matter, just as in the bitter lines of his supposed *adieu* from art (lines which themselves are so artistic), the poet of humanity once again—and right in the province of art itself—experiences the essence of humanity with a bad conscience. And just as in his oriental prose dialogue, so here, too, does the nature poem, the lyric of pure feeling, serve him as a decisive paradigm. The most famous lines from that celebrated elegy are, as is well known, those in which Brecht forbids himself as well as us who, alas, are still his contemporaries although "born later," even a "harmless talk about trees" ("Gespräch über Bäume"). Or rather, "almost" forbids or would like to forbid:

> Was sind das für Zeiten, wo
> Ein Gespräch über Bäume fast ein Verbrechen ist
> Weil es ein Schweigen über so viele Untaten einschließt!

Such verses are, with all restraint, one single scream. May one at all, Brecht asks through Kin-jeh, "write poems about the impressions of nature in these times?" In the midst of this "bloody muddle," this "disorder" of a "dehumanized humanity," this "world which is like a slaughterhouse"? Then must one not disavow, proscribe, and banish from the present, at least the indirect experiences of the human, the round, and the beautiful if we cannot affect the direct ones? Must one not renounce, however reluctantly, every artistic creation today, every enhancement and alleviation of life through art? Brecht as well as Kin-jeh drew this conclusion, painful though it must have been for them. In fact, the poet drew it repeatedly: "solely because of the increasing disorder" and the "awful cramped co-existence." He also draws it, no less poignantly, in "To Those Born Later." But are not his words accomplished language, completely flawless poetry? Did he not once again create art, even while agonizingly negating it? Indeed, are we not tempted—"almost" tempted—to say, "pure" art?

Further, let us not forget that Me-ti, that "tempting" ego in Brecht's parable, answered Kin-jeh's question in the affirmative! And his answer, too, has weight. It cannot be flatly dismissed as irony (although I admit that there is some ironic resonance in it). That which Me-ti has decided about art is recanted no more than that which not only Brecht but "some of us," as he says, "have now decided." Art and the turning away from art, enjoyment of art and uncompromising morality, pleasure and asceticism exist side by side in Brecht—indeed, they merge. The poet did not simply find himself *between* two modes or periods of art, the older of which should no longer exist and the newer of which should not yet come into existence; he is not merely languishing in a hell equidistant from Paradise Lost as well as Paradise Regained. (Those are his images, by the way, not mine; in *Der gute Mensch von Sezuan* a character sings. "Am Sankt Nimmerleinstag / Wird die Erde zum Paradies," and in the same play Brecht exclaims, "Die Zeiten sind furchtbar, diese Stadt ist eine Hölle.") Moreover, Brecht is not only concerned with such kinds of insights or decisions and their manifestations in a politically clear as well as poetically masterful manner. Neither is of importance to Me-ti, Brecht's other *alter ego*. In his text we read, "art does not only have to do with the present day"; and analogously, "since such [impressions of nature and pleasurable artistic experiences] will always exist, a poem of this kind could have a long existence." Thus speaks the advocate of "pure art." And is he not right, too? Is not his reply (the reply of the political philosopher) part and parcel of Brecht's ultimate answer? Not one jot of it is recanted by him.

To be sure, Brecht faced the beauty of nature without much devotion or fond lingering. But he did "see" it. His fleeting, nearly grudging—indeed, almost guilty—look did perceive things of nature: some part of their beauty, however little, remained fixed in his gaze and was transferred into some of his poems, even if merely as a negation. They are, in the truest sense of the word, precious lines, as one used to say in days gone by—and who knows, as one may someday say again. Even the "talk about trees" and what it implies, Brecht's "silence about so many horrors"—a silence, I might add, which was never his since he ceaselessly raised his voice against injustice—even such hopelessly gaping contrasts do not confront one another either absolutely or abruptly. After all, the poetical conversation is only "almost a crime"; and from the often forced, but nonetheless consistently broken political silence emanate not only the loathing for the hangmen and the bitterness about the victims, but also "red anger" and dismay about the innumerable atrocities. For like pure art, the Brechtian nature, again acting as a proxy for everything "that makes a man round and human," also achieves presence precisely through its absence. Nothing less than its elimination attests to its permanence. Again one could think of one of the great French writers, namely Stéphane Mallarmé—whom Brecht didn't exactly venerate, but with whose work he was quite familiar. Only by being denied a reality, and removed from a present state into an absent one, so Mallarmé claims, do things become completely real and achieve definitive presence as (pure) speech and (pure) art. *Une élévation ordinaire verse l'absence.* "Absence," but also—as I deliberately translate—"a mere elevation." Or as Hugo Friedrich writes: "These renounced things have a presence solely in language, as art." Mallarmé's is a "poetry of negatives." In it, "that which is objectively eliminated by means of the language which states its absence, receives its spiritual existence in the selfsame language through its naming." The correspondences with Brecht cannot be overlooked. But in his case, that of the political poet, they have as little to do with *poésie pure* as any *littérature engagée* is to be found in the symbolist Mallarmé. Mallarmé's ethics were to the same degree aesthetic as Brecht's aesthetics were ethical.

Nonetheless, art and morality as well as nature and history are also reconcilable "in these times," and not merely in some distant future. In fact, they are already reconciled despite their contradictions—even in Bertolt Brecht. And the more permanently and agonizingly Brecht experienced those contradictions, the more relentlessly he witnessed and absorbed into his poetry those things that make a man evil and inhuman. Yes, this passionate poet of humanity as well as of class struggle knew more than most people of the personal menace growing out of such a struggle. Brecht proclaimed it (think of his play, *Die Maßnahme*) without any reservation:

> Auch der Haß gegen die Niedrigkeit
> Verzerrt die Züge.
> Auch der Zorn über das Unrecht
> Macht die Stimme heiser. Ach, wir
> Die wir den Boden bereiten wollten für Freundlichkeit
> Konnten selber nicht freundlich sein.

The more directly the poet speaks, the more grippingly he stirs us. Brecht's lament from exile when he was "changing countries more often than shoes" and nearly despairing has, therefore, and with good reason, long been one of his most famous poems. But no less gripping, one could say shattering, are the few lines which he wrote "solely because of the increasing disorder." For this most sparse and austere of his confessions—just one sentence— is at the same time the most pitiless and immeasurably open one. If one "understands" it correctly, as the poet pleads, then it surpasses even his "elegy."

That such verses are not only possible, but indispensable, bears over-whelming witness to the power of poetry, the "necessity of art." And precisely that and how the innocently natural, mired in the sorrow, guilt, and entanglements of history, is taken up and thereby preserved in them is what makes them irrefutable affirmations of Brechtian lyric as well as of poetry in general. But as unique as they seem, they are not isolated phe-nomena within the context of Brecht's *œuvre*. For he has a whole series of poems in which the denial of the lyrical is itself transformed into the purest lyrical expression. Their very titles speak eloquently: "In finsteren Zeiten," "Schlechte Zeit für Lyrik," "Die Landschaft des Exils." And there are many more. "In Dark Times" offers perhaps the best example of that "evocation through negation," at least as far as technique and linguistic skill are con-cerned. Three times the poet begins with an express negation; three times he says expressly, "They won't say." What follows, however, are precisely those "impressions of nature," those sensations "of the flesh" about which he no longer wanted to speak, which he really would have preferred to deny himself as well as us. But it is through this very process that they are confirmed: the wind in the trees; the summer day at the shore; the woman who softly enters the room. Just as indicative, of course, is also the sudden shift at the end of the poem:

> Man wird nicht sagen: Als da der Nußbaum sich im Wind
>   schüttelte
> Sondern: Als der Anstreicher die Arbeiter niedertrat.
> Man wird nicht sagen: Als das Kind den flachen Kiesel über
>   die Stromschnelle springen ließ
> Sondern: Als da die großen Kriege vorbereitet wurden.
> Man wird nicht sagen: Als da die Frau ins Zimmer kam

> Sondern: Als da die großen Mächte sich gegen die Arbeiter
>   verbündeten.
> Aber man wird nicht sagen: Die Zeiten waren finster
> Sondern: Warum haben ihre Dichter geschwiegen?

Time and again, right down to the choice of words, we are confronted with the contrast between Brecht's "talk about trees" and his vocal "silence about so many atrocities." The fact that Hitler is not directly named but appears scornfully as the "house painter" (*der Anstreicher*) should not confuse us. Verses of this kind are, as nature poetry, masterpieces of a poetry of silence and yet, even more so, uncompromising political poetry.

Especially in poems from the Danish exile, one encounters such verses. The lyrical trilogy, "Frühling 1938," contains some of the most impressive examples:

> I
> Heute, Ostersonntag früh
> Ging ein plötzlicher Schneesturm über die Insel.
> Zwischen den grünenden Hecken lag Schnee. Mein junger
>   Sohn
> Holte mich zu einem Aprikosenbäumchen an der Hausmauer
> Von einem Vers weg, in dem ich auf diejenigen mit dem
>   Finger deutete
> Die einen Krieg vorbereiteten, der
> Den Kontinent, diese Insel, mein Volk, meine Familie und
>   mich
> Vertilgen mag. Schweigend
> Legten wir einen Sack
> Über den frierenden Baum.
>
> II
> Über dem Sund hängt Regengewölke, aber den Garten
> Vergoldet noch die Sonne. Die Birnbäume
> Haben grüne Blätter und noch keine Blüten, die
>   Kirschbäume hingegen
> Blüten und noch keine Blätter. Die weißen Dolden
> Scheinen aus dürren Ästen zu sprießen.
> Über das gekräuselte Sundwasser
> Läuft ein kleines Boot mit geflicktem Segel.
> In das Gezwitscher der Stare
> Mischt sich der ferne Donner
> Der manövrierenden Schiffsgeschütze
> Des Dritten Reiches.
>
> III
> In den Weiden am Sund
> Ruft in diesen Frühjahrsnächten oft das Käuzlein.

Nach dem Aberglauben der Bauern
Setzt das Käuzlein die Menschen davon in Kenntnis
Daß sie nicht lang leben. Mich
Der ich weiß, daß ich die Wahrheit gesagt habe
Über die Herrschenden, braucht der Totenvogel davon
Nicht erst in Kenntnis zu setzen.

These three poems are revealing in two respects. First, they provided Brecht with the opportunity for a most telling personal testimony—about the purity, indeed the "autarky," of art; secondly, they are filled—again—with extreme poetic splendor, and not *although*, but rather *because* they are so completely identical with their historical moment. Each one of these poems is a pure nature poem and at the same time a great political lyric, a timeless idyll and a historical epigram. They are filled to the brim with this double reality and all the concomitant contradictions, and yet they are also well-balanced. And almost like a *leitmotif*, these contrasts are once again those between the peaceful world of trees and the pitiless, murderous world of persecutions and the ever-threatening war of annihilation; the contrast between the "talk" about the former, which will not be silenced, and the "silence" about the latter, which becomes an admonishing, warning, far-resounding voice. When "the distant thunder of naval gunfire" blends with the twittering of birds, those natural sounds of silence, lyrical mood and political statement are truly inseparable.

Should, after all, Brecht's purity and autarky of art consist of that? But as much as he was of one mind with Me-ti about such poems, he also agreed with Kin-jeh that this was a "Bad Time for Poetry." His like-named and highly lyrical confession also stems from those years "under the Danish thatched roof." And in it, too, are some of the most impressive and famous lines from Brecht's exile:

Ich weiß doch: der Glückliche
Ist beliebt. Seine Stimme
Hört man gern. Sein Gesicht ist schön.

Der verkrüppelte Baum im Hof
Zeigt auf den schlechten Boden, aber
Die Vorübergehenden schimpfen ihn einen Krüppel
Doch mit Recht.

Die grünen Boote und die lustigen Segel des Sundes
Sehe ich nicht. Von allem
Sehe ich nur der Fischer rissiges Garnnetz.
Warum rede ich nur davon
Daß die vierzigjährige Häuslerin gekrümmt geht?
Die Brüste der Mädchen
Sind warm wie ehedem.

In meinem Lied ein Reim
Käme mir fast vor wie Übermut.

In mir streiten sich
Die Begeisterung über den blühenden Apfelbaum
Und das Entsetzen über die Reden des Anstreichers.
Aber nur das zweite
Drängt mich zum Schreibtisch.

Here, again, Kin-jeh's impression of nature along with Brecht's sensations of the flesh are contrasted with the political and socio-historical moment, and thereby incorporated within poetry. Again we encounter that telling word "almost," wherein the voice of Me-ti, the advocate of art, speaks both cautiously and audibly. Quite consistently, the "rhyme," that is artistry, has taken the place of the simple "talk." To be sure, instead of the term "crime" there is now "insolence"—much more innocent, yet at the same time much more revealing. But for all that, Brecht's verses are no less serious and moving. It is no accident that the "dancing sails" are contrasted with the "torn nets," and the "stooped village woman," with the "young girls." All this corresponds exactly with the *leitmotif* of the trees which appears not solely in the image of a "blossoming apple tree" but is complemented by the opposite image of the "crippled tree in the yard." Such opposites are equally characteristic of Brecht—think of "Der Pflaumen-baum," likewise from his *Svendborger Gedichte*, or of the "Morgendliche Rede an den Baum Griehn" from his *Hauspostille*. But there is no need to go into that any more than it would be into his formal, purely technical innovations. Suffice it to say that the poet again makes use of the "evocation through negation," which banishes the naturally beautiful and humanly round into the realm of nothingness and thereby summons them into existence and permanence. For Brecht saw very well and celebrated those things which he claimed not to see or celebrate, such as "the green boats and the dancing sails on the Sound." The battle between poetic "enthusiasm" and political "loathing" (and not merely about the "speeches of the house painter" and the fascist scum) constantly raged in him. And although "only" the latter drove him "to his desk," he did write all the more grippingly about the former.

That this *poésie engagée* (to coin a new Sartrean term) is firmly anchored both in the historical as well as lyrical moment is also evidenced in poems from Brecht's Finnish and American exile. Even their titles are, for the most part, extremely concrete. Thus, for example, two strophes—which actually indulge in the luxury of rhyme—celebrate a "Finnische Gutsspeisekammer 1940." Brecht, who treasured the low as well as the high, who enjoyed the pleasures "of taste and testicles" (as his corpulent *Glücksgott* sings) as much as delights of a more subtle kind, transforms even a rural larder into a political poem:

O schattige Speise! Einer dunklen Tanne
Geruch geht nächtlich brausend in dich ein
Und mischt sich mit dem süßer Milch aus großer Kanne
Und dem des Räucherspecks vom kalten Stein.

Bier, Ziegenkäse, frisches Brot und Beere
Gepflückt im grauen Strauch, wenn Frühtau fällt!
Oh könnt ich laden euch, die überm Meere
Der Krieg der leeren Mägen hält!

Here, too, one could investigate formal details—the so-called "subtleties of expression," which Brecht supposedly ought to have avoided—and their artistic achievement. The opportunity would present itself especially in the phonetic area. But in the intellectual sphere, one could also go into the conceptions—so characteristic of Brecht—of fortune and the state of happiness which do not merely creep up around the central figure of the Chinese god of good fortune: they are of equal importance elsewhere in Brecht's *œuvre*. To every person who has a healthy sense and sensitivity, such "forbidden" artistic fruits are quite evident.

Therefore, let us take a look at a similar poem from the same time! In spite of its poetic title, "Finnische Landschaft," it, too, is very political:

Fischreiche Wässer! Schönbaumige Wälder!
Birken- und Beerenduft!
Vieltöniger Wind, durchschaukelnd eine Luft
So mild, als stünden jene eisernen Milchbehälter
Die dort vom weißen Gute rollen, offen!
Geruch und Ton und Bild und Sinn verschwimmt.
Der Flüchtling sitzt im Erlengrund und nimmt
Sein schwieriges Handwerk wieder auf: das Hoffen.

Er achtet gut der schöngehäuften Ähre
Und starker Kreatur, die sich zum Wasser neigt
Doch derer auch, die Korn und Milch nicht nährt.
Er fragt die Fähre, die mit Stämmen fährt:
Ist dies das Holz, ohn das kein Holzbein wäre?
Und sieht ein Volk, das in zwei Sprachen schweigt.

Brecht could not prevent nature, in all its beauty and majesty, from constantly intruding on him, indeed almost overpowering him. But did he want to prevent this at all? Almost hymnically the poet invokes the "waters" and "forests," the "mild air" and the earth with its "scents of berries and of birches"; it is almost a poem about the elements which he unfolds in these lines (something one of his heirs, Johannes Bobrowski, later did). But not even here does the landscape become an end unto itself. To be sure, the poetic elevation takes place; and it is enchanting enough. But then the political "refugee," seemingly sitting so romantically beneath the trees, "turns again to his laborious job: continued hoping." It is a hoping and an unswerving laboring not only for the end of the war, but also for the end of all "disorder" and "exploitation," in the country as well as "in our cities of class struggle." All natural and sensual impressions, all those so intensively, so hymnically conjured moods and sensations grow pale, become blurred, and vanish. Brecht enumerates them carefully: "Dizzy with sight and sound and thought and smell." For precisely by not being permitted to remain in life, they are preserved in art, even if only to return someday more secure and more tangible, as the refugee and the poet earnestly hoped. But linked to them are the bitter reality and the present: "a people silent in two tongues." This unforgettable line, this eloquent "rhyme" about silence which closes the strophe, crowns the entire poem and rounds it off into a flawless work of art. It is—like each one of these confessions of a poet, these poetic-political dialogues and monologues "about trees"—anything but "insolent" or even "a crime." Quite the contrary, this is the purest humane art striving for the purest humanity.

Perhaps now we understand what it meant for a poet like Brecht to write verses like the following:

> Aber auch ich auf dem letzten Boot
> Sah noch den Frohsinn des Frührots im Takelzeug
> Und der Delphine graulichte Leiber, tauchend
> Aus der Japanischen See.
> Und die Pferdewäglein mit dem Goldbeschlag
> Und die rosa Armschleier der Matronen
> In den Gassen des gezeichneten Manila
> Sah auch der Flüchtling mit Freude.
> Die Öltürme und dürstenden Gärten von Los Angeles
> Und die abendlichen Schluchten Kaliforniens und die
>   Obstmärkte
> Ließen auch den Boten des Unglücks
> Nicht kalt.

Precisely these lines—although again rhymeless, irregular, and almost prose, again composed in "sparse speech," as the poet said of his play, *Die Mutter*—but precisely these poor twelve lines were "already too lavish," too sumptuous for the refugee. Brecht jotted down this remark, literally, in his diary toward the end of 1944. Even "The Landscape of Exile" (as this poem is entitled) was too lush for him: not *although*, but rather *because* he had stated directly—a quality which he otherwise found most praiseworthy—that which he claimed was no longer capable of direct expression. Brecht realized that he had esteemed things and their beauty not just highly, but too highly. For he neither eliminates them, in the sense of Mallarmé, through sheer negation, nor does he confront them with an aggressive affirmation in the sense of his own conception of art as a weapon. The poet of class struggle ventured one single time to speak lyrically without any restraint—something he had always desired, something, however, he could never give in to. This time he "saw"; indeed, he "beheld with joy." And what he saw, he celebrated. If this "refugee," the "messenger of misfortune," finally does negate, then this happens clearly with a reverse assessment. The "oil derricks" and the "thirsty gardens," the "ravines at evening" and the "fruit market" do not leave even him "*un*moved."

Bobrowski, too, that eager disciple of Brecht's, was driven to a celebratory, a laudatory appeal; he, too, longed for incessant naming ("Immer zu benennen," as the title of one of his most confessional poems reads):

> Immer zu benennen:
> den Baum, den Vogel im Flug,
> den rötlichen Fels, wo der Strom
> zieht, grün, und den Fisch
> im weißen Rauch, wenn es dunkelt
> über die Wälder herab.

But even Bobrowski, who abandoned himself to pure nature much more than did Brecht, was aware of the deceptiveness of poetic color and the enticement of lyrical symbols:

> Zeichen, Farben, es ist
> ein Spiel, ich bin bedenklich,
> es möchte nicht enden
> gerecht.

For the sake of such justice Brecht rejected his own twelve gripping lines, which are among the most tender and moving (I am not afraid of that word) in his entire poetry. "Poems like 'The Landscape of Exile' will not be included," he wrote when putting together his collection of *Gedichte im Exil*, "they are simply too lavish." Like Bobrowski, Brecht found the aesthetic "game" to be "dubious." Like Kin-jeh, he shrank back from that which it "implies"—even if only in retrospect. "Solely because of the increasing disorder" did this poet henceforth intend to speak and write—this poet who once cynically, in a Baal-like approval of the richly contradictory world with its "snowfalls" and its "lured flesh," had called himself the "poor B. B."!

But if, within the Brechtian confessions, this poem is exactly as striking as the lines with which we began, then one can hardly classify them as being too "lush." For their author intends to speak only "about the disorder," about "exploitation" and "class justice." Truly, we find in them the most extreme austerity of expression, barrenness and bareness alike, indeed absolute "privation," as Brecht acknowledged in his diary. But from this very privation in "expression" as well as in "rhythm"—a blunt addition of the poet—the text gains its expressive power and rhythmic variety; from this alone derives its force, its almost unbearable plenitude and poetic intensity. If it is true that anything at all in Brecht's lyric is indeed written "in a kind of 'basic German' " (as he himself once asserted), then these verses have to be cited. Yet they form a poem, which can profoundly move us even today, and perhaps nowadays more than ever.

But for what reason does Brecht no longer want to observe that which is aesthetic? Why does he no longer want to enjoy and create—either for himself or his fellow human beings—that which is human, round, and beautiful? Why does this poet now allow only for battle, "barrenness," and the "business of politics"—not for art and the unrestrained poetic variety of the world? "Solely" and exclusively

> Damit nicht dieses furchtbare gedrängte Zusammensein
> Von Schneefällen (sie sind nicht nur kalt, wir wissen's)
> Ausbeutung, verlocktem Fleisch und Klassenjustiz eine
>   Billigung
> So vielseitiger Welt in uns erzeuge, Lust an
> Den Widersprüchen solch blutigen Lebens.

Brecht was artist enough not only to experience and realize the intense inhumanness of art (or the threat to all art from inhumanity) but also expressly to acknowledge it. That he dared to admit this to himself and to us is the ultimate, the truly shocking, confession of this poet.

Is, then, art *not* to be? The answer of Brecht the artist is that actually it shouldn't. *Art should not exist*—precisely because, in spite of its allure to him, it still seems to be a crime, something wanton, a blatant injustice, and barbaric; because man is still like a wolf to his fellow men; because today, as in times past, entire peoples and continents are being enslaved, exploited, and ground to dust; because this brutish "humanity" simply cannot go on lest it choke on its own bloody slime.

And yet, *art should exist*. Its inhumanity *and* its humanity are, for Brecht, both equally real and cannot be dismissed. The immorality, inhumanity, indeed *impossibility* of art exist side by side with the morality, humanity, indeed *necessity* of art; they even are incorporated and blended together. And only thus do they constitute the *reality of art*. Like the world, art is sorrowfully negated by Brecht and joyfully affirmed, rejected and yet accepted. It does exist: but its rending contradictions, its gaping contrasts remain with the poet. Were they reconciled in him, the man and artist and fighter Bertolt Brecht? Are they in his verses? Will they ever really be in the life of mankind, Brecht's faith notwithstanding?

This extraordinary poem ends with a gesture of utter simplicity, indeed almost of helplessness and despondency. "You understand?" O yes, poor and yet so rich Bertolt Brecht, we understand. At least we think we do.

Marxist Emblems:
Bertolt Brecht's *War Primer*

Reinhold Grimm

Bertolt Brecht's *War Primer* is a collection of photos which Brecht "cut out of newspapers and magazines and for each of which he composed a quatrain." First published in 1955, it is still one of Brecht's lesser-known works and is seldom considered by critics. Two reasons may account for the lack of recognition and regard for this work. One is the obviously long delay in reprinting it. The second and more important is the regrettable mutilation of the collection. In the 1964 edition of Brecht's poems and even in the more recent edition of his *Collected Works*, only the text of the *War Primer* was published; the pictures were omitted. Without them, many of these "photograms," as Brecht liked to call them, are difficult, if not impossible, to understand.

It is more than mere coincidence that an early version of the *War Primer* was found among the papers of the Marxist philosopher Karl Korsch, who, as Wolfdietrich Rasch first noted, exerted a great influence on Brecht's life and work. This influence seems to have left its mark on the *War Primer* as well, the form and content of which are deeply rooted in Brecht's philosophical and political thinking. In general, the early manuscript and the printed version show agreement in content. Both versions used most of the same Swedish and American sources; in both, the war years from 1939 to 1945 are the subject, with a few flashbacks and several glimpses into the future. However, some of the pictures or captions were interchanged and some lines or whole quatrains were altered. Moreover, the earlier version contains several items which were later omitted while others were substituted in their place.

From *Comparative Literature Studies* 12, no. 3 (September 1975). © 1975 by the Board of Trustees of the University of Illinois.

Numbers 42, 46, and 55 of the original manuscript, for example, were not printed. The first picture shows the British politician Ernest Bevin giving a campaign speech while standing on a farm wagon under a tree. Brecht recommends quite bluntly that it would be better to hang him rather than vote for him. Even more drastic is Brecht's comment on the second newspaper picture entitled "Jane Wyman shows her medals." Here Brecht uses the not very inspiring image of a Hollywood star to accuse the film industry of war agitation. Finally, in the third picture, we see a black man in Detroit who has been beaten bloody and is being taken to safety by a soldier.

Highly significant for Brecht's ever-growing sharp opposition to the Western Allies, especially the United States, is a photograph of the landing of the Allied Forces in Normandy on June 6, 1944. Somewhat blurred, it depicts landing craft and a soldier in the foreground making his way to the beach. In the picture, it is not clear whether this is a British or an American soldier. The text of the manuscript, however, is unequivocal:

> An jenem Junitag, nah bei Cherbourg
> Sah kommen aus dem Meer im Morgenlicht
> Der Mann vom fernen Essen an der Ruhr
> Den Mann vom fernen Maine und er verstand es nicht.
>
> (no. 39)

Even clearer is the printed version of 1955:

> In jener Juni-Früh nah bei Cherbourg
> Stieg aus dem Meer der Mann aus Maine und trat
> Laut Meldung gen den Mann an von der Ruhr
> Doch war es gen den Mann von Stalingrad.
>
> (no. 53)

The earlier accusation against the madness of Hitler's war which the soldier does not comprehend is now, under the influence of the cold war, turned into overt ideology. Brecht claims that the "man from Maine" did not come to confront the German but the Russian, the "man from Stalingrad," although it was none other than Russia which continuously and emphatically demanded the invasion.

Not all of Brecht's changes are so radical. In some cases, he merely varies the original. For example, he replaces Ebert, the first president of the Weimar Republic (whom Brecht called the "pig" bought by a "pack of Junkers," [no. 25 in the manuscript]), with Noske the "bloodhound" in the later version (no. 24); or he later chooses a different picture (no. 38) for the verses which are intended to brand Churchill a gangster (no. 43 in the manuscript).

Numbers 6 and 11 of the manuscript are more advantageous for our examination. Their texts and pictures, as well as their changes before printing, permit some conclusions as to the manner in which Brecht worked. These two pictures show French helmets which Brecht, in a good example of his "estrangement" effect, calls "hats." In the printed version, the poet omitted number 6 completely whereas in number 11 he left the quatrain unchanged but substituted another picture. Now the words in the printed version refer to German steel helmets from the last months of the war:

> Seht diese Hüte von Besiegten! Und
> Nicht als man sie vom Kopf uns schlug zuletzt
> War unsrer bittern Niederlage Stund.
> Sie war, als wir sie folgsam aufgesetzt.
>
> (no. 57)

Clearly, the message is now much more precise and succinct. It appears obvious that Brecht did not write his text after some time had lapsed, but immediately following the events, as soon as he had found and cut out his materials. This is confirmed by the poet's remarks "On Epigrams" written during the war. As early as 1940 in Finland, Brecht mentioned "quatrains" or "small epigrams." In 1944 in California he explicitly noted:

> I am working on a new series of photo-epigrams. A survey of the older ones which originated in the earlier part of the war shows that there are practically no omissions necessary (none at all in regard to politics). This in itself is good proof of the quality of the point of view taken, considering the continuously changing aspects of the war. As of now, sixty quatrains exist and together with *Fear and Misery of the Third Reich*, the volumes of poetry, and perhaps the essay on "Five Difficulties in Writing the Truth," this particular work constitutes a satisfactory literary report about the exile period.

Both Brecht's son Stefan and Brecht's collaborator Ruth Berlau, the editor of the *War Primer*, emphasize the journalistic character and the spontaneous origin of the work.

It has been noted how much Brecht had to omit or change, even politically, despite his claim to the contrary. It is therefore hardly surprising that there are also formal changes, such as the last line of the epigram about Göring and Goebbels (no. 28 in the manuscript). This epigram could undoubtedly stand on its own without the picture which goes with it. But a comparison shows that only the photogram—the combination of picture and text—(no. 1) achieves the highest satirical effect:

> "Joseph, ich hör, du hast von mir gesagt:
> Ich raube."—"Hermann, warum sollst du rauben?
> Dir was verweigern, wär verdammt gewagt.
> Und hätt ichs schon gesagt, wer würd mir glauben?"
>
> (no. 27)

Brecht has eliminated only one word from the original version. There, the last line reads: "Und hätt ichs schon gesagt, wer würd mir *etwas* glauben?"

The extent to which the success of this epigram depends on this small alteration needs no further comment.

Even more obvious, however, is the artistic difference between the following two texts. The early version seems almost monotonous:

> "Was macht ihr, Brüder?"—"Einen Eisenwagen
> Die Truppe durch die Panzerschlacht zu tragen."
> "Was macht ihr, Brüder, noch?"—"Ach, lass dein Fragen:
> Granaten, die durch Eisenwände schlagen."

The printed version is much more dynamic and ends in an inimitable, masterful climax which reveals the cruel nonsense of war:

> "Was macht ihr, Brüder?"—"Einen Eisenwagen."
> "Und was aus diesen Platten dicht daneben?"
> "Geschosse, die durch Eisenwände schlagen."
> "Und warum all das, Brüder?"—"Um zu leben."
>
> (no. 2)

These lines, too, would unquestionably be effective without a picture but have their strongest impact with the accompanying photo (no. 2). This case in particular illustrates Brecht's efforts to overcome very general concepts— "What are you making?" "What else are you making?"—in favor of more specific ones which add precision to the interpretation of the picture, as "And what about those sheets of metal over there?"

What the poet succeeds in demonstrating with his illustrated primer is the opposite of the accusations he had made in 1931 against the bourgeois press. At the time, the *Arbeiter-Illustrierte-Zeitung aller Länder (A-I-Z—* "Workers Illustrated Paper for All Countries") celebrated its tenth anniversary and Brecht, the communist neophyte, wrote:

> The tremendous development of photojournalism has contributed practically nothing to the revelation of the truth about the conditions in this world. On the contrary, photography, in the hands of the bourgeoisie, has become a terrible weapon *against* the truth. The vast amount of pictured material that is being disgorged daily by the press and that seems to have the character of truth serves in reality only to obscure the facts. The camera is just as capable of lying as is the typewriter. The task of the *A-I-Z*, which is to restore the truth, is of paramount importance under these circumstances and it seems to me that it fulfills this purpose extremely well.

In the same sense, Brecht thought it the task of the *War Primer* to serve the truth and to reconstruct the actual facts. Ruth Berlau's preface makes this unmistakably clear. The purpose of the book, she says, is to teach the art of interpreting pictures. For the untrained eye, it is just as difficult to interpret pictures as to decipher any kind of hieroglyphics:

> The great ignorance concerning social relations, an ignorance nursed carefully and brutally by capitalism, reduces thousands of photos in illustrated journals to hieroglyphs which are undecipherable for the unsuspecting reader.

Berlau maintains that, because of this predicament and because people cannot escape the course of events by ignoring them, it is justifiable and even necessary to show and interpret "at this particular time" such "gloomy pictures from the past."

It would seem, therefore, that the *War Primer* is a blatant form of ideological propaganda. But it is more than that. The idea of hieroglyphs which must be deciphered suggests not merely the interrelations of contemporary social politics but also those of European intellectual history of past ages, as exemplified by emblematics. What comes closest to Brecht's *War Primer* (in the form in which it was first published, with pictures and quatrains) is precisely that didactic art form of the Renaissance and Baroque periods which also served to decipher and elucidate hidden truths.

It is uncertain whether Brecht was familiar with emblem books. But considering how well-read he was, such knowledge is by no means unlikely. And it is he who refers to hieroglyphs, thus arousing our curiosity in the first place. It is certain, at any rate, that one of the paths which led Brecht to his "photograms" was the same which once led Andrea Alciato, the father of the emblematic art in the sixteenth and seventeenth centuries, to his emblems. Like the author of the *Emblematum liber* of 1531, the author of the *War Primer* of 1955 resorted to Greek epigrams. The first of the previously mentioned remarks "On Epigrams" amply testifies to this and leaves no doubt about the social background. All that is missing here, as in later notes, is the direct use of the term "emblem." That Brecht was familiar with this term is indicated, for instance, by his commentary on the production of *Mother Courage and Her Children* when he describes "a fragile and light object, consisting of a trumpet, a drum, a flag and lightballs which are illuminated." Visible and esthetically pleasing to the audience, these objects serve "to switch over to the musical parts of the play, to let the music speak, as it were." These objects and others like them, lowered from the flies at the beginning of each song, Brecht calls "emblems."

If there were no further proof, such similarities and parallels might be a mere coincidence and could be discarded as such. But it is obvious that there is a close relation between the combination of pictures and texts found in Brecht's photograms and the structure of emblems. To take an example from Julius Wilhelm Zincgreff's collection of 1619 and compare it with one from the *War Primer*: Zincgreff's emblem shows the sun mirrored in the waves of a river, accompanied by the motto *Monstratur in undis* and the French quatrain:

> Cest invisible Dieu n'entre dedans nos yeux
> Que par reflexion de ses oeuvres visibles,

C'est par là seulement que sont intelligibles
Ses mystères cachez au plus ingenieux.

In Brecht's work, there is, for example, a picture of two soldiers, both of whom are equipped with helmets and camouflage nets and who are very much alike in posture and facial expression. The corresponding epigram reads:

Ein Brüderpaar, seht, das in Panzern fuhr
Zu kämpfen um des einen Bruders Land!
So grausam ist zum Elefanten nur
Sein Bruder, der gezähmte Elefant.

(no. 55)

In addition, this photo-epigram contains a brief notice on the picture itself: "A German Landser—And His Russian Counterpart."

I have deliberately chosen these two examples which are quite different in theme. The sequence of the various elements, too, is somewhat arbitrary. In Brecht's case, the newspaper clipping with its caption appears on the upper half of the page and the quatrain follows only after a considerable blank space. Zincgreff's example begins with the motto followed by a circular copper engraving with the epigram underneath. But it is precisely because of this reversal of elements and thematic difference that the structure common to both examples becomes apparent. Both *Denkbilder* (as Herder called emblems) exhibit the "double function of representation and interpretation, of depicting and deciphering," characteristic of such "picture-poetry." And there is the division into *inscriptio* or motto, *pictura*, and *subscriptio*, which characterizes the ideal emblem. This is so obvious that Brecht's example needs no further explanation. *Pictura* and *subscriptio* present no difficulties; the English caption naturally functions as *inscriptio*.

The correspondence in structure, however, should not obscure the fact that these three parts are differently interrelated in each case. Zincgreff and all Baroque authors of emblems incorporate, to some degree, the coexistence of the literal meaning of the word and its hidden or spiritual significance. It is an interrelationship in the form of both allegory and conceit. In his *Trattato degli emblemi* the Italian Emanuele Tesauro provides more precise information about emblems. To him, emblems and *imprese* are "metafore simboliche"; they have "vn Significante sensibile, e vn Significato intelligibile, e mostrando vna cosa ne accennano vn'altra." These "Argomenti poetici" also indicate the didactic content because "la simiglianza della proprietà significante, con la proprietà significata ha vna tacita virtù entimematica di persuadere ò dissuadere alcuna cosa." Using a metaphor which had already been used by Harsdörffer and long before him by Paolo Giovio, Tesauro adds that emblems are composed of a "body" and a "soul," "intendendo per *corpo* la Figura visibile; con le Parole, che sono l'Anima materiale della Figura; e per *anima spirituale*, e quasi ragioneuole, il concetto significato." Tesauro is by no means reluctant to conclude: "Quindi è, che riguardando la nuda essenza, cosi l'Emblema come l'Impresa potrebbono sossistere senza le Parole; bastando per Corpo la Figura, e per Anima spirituale il Concetto mentale de chi l'intende."

But for our purposes we need not pursue this idea any further. It suffices to point out the general method of comparison, the "spiritualizing" process, and the elements of conceit in the interrelationship which create the emblem. With Zincgreff, however, these elements manifest themselves rather indirectly. They become more evident only in the German version of his quatrain:

> Die Göttlich Majestät nicht gantz erkent mag werden
> Dann an seinem Geschöpff
> im Himmel und auff Erden
> Zusehen in die Sonn vnser Augen nicht tügen
> Im Wasser wir zum theil den Schatten sehen mügen.

Completely developed, however, is the "metafora simbolica" in the next emblem which originates from Camerarius, depicts two ostriches breathing upon their eggs, and bears the subscript:

> Passer ut ova fovet flatu vegetante marinus:
> Sic animat mentes gratia dia pias.

"Corpo" and "anima" in this distich are not only clearly differentiated but are also arranged in the correct order. Camerarius even names the connecting link between them: "*just as* the ostrich furthers the development of its eggs by breathing on them, *so* the divine grace quickens pious souls." Attitude and interrelationship are clearly defined in the sense of Tesauro's theory of emblems.

But what about Brecht? What kind of attitude and interrelationship are to be found in his *War Primer*?

Before answering this, let us examine several more Brechtian "emblems." There is, for instance, a photograph showing Brecht's lifelong friend Lion Feuchtwanger in a French concentration camp. The subscript and the epigram read: "LION FEUCHTWANGER [. . .] behind the barbed wire in the brickyard concentration camp. This hitherto unpublished picture was smuggled out of France by Mr. Feuchtwanger." Brecht commented:

> Er war zwar ihres Feindes Feind, jedoch
> War etwas an ihm, was man nicht verzeiht
> Denn seht: ihr Feind war seine Obrigkeit.
> So warfen sie ihn als Rebell ins Loch.
>
> (no. 13)

Another picture, from a Swedish newspaper, shows a view of the destruction of London. Brecht adds the following comment, making the city itself speak:

> So seh ich aus. Nur weil gewisse Leute
> Tückisch in andre Richtung flogen als
> Ich plante; so wurd ich statt Hehler Beute
> Und Opfer eines, ach, Berufsunfalls.
>
> (no. 16)

The newspaper text reads: "CITY AV I DAG. De centrala delarna av London ha under luftkrigets förlopp i mycket antagit karaktären av ruinkvarter. Denna vy över City är tagen från St Pauls-katedralen."

The content of the next example is provided in the detailed caption: "German assault troops, here emerging from beneath railroad cars to attack the Albert Canal line, were young, tough and disciplined. In all there were 240 divisions of them. But despite the world's idea that the conquest was merely by planes and tanks, it actually depended on the old-fashioned tactic of superior mass of firepower at the decisive point." Brecht's quatrain, however, by no means refers to these tactical considerations, but rather to the soldiers' strained faces:

> Nach einem Feind seh ich euch Ausschau halten
> Bevor ihr absprangt in die Panzerschlacht:
> Wars der Franzos, dem eure Blicke galten?
> Wars euer Hauptmann nur, der euch bewacht?
>
> (no. 8)

At the end of the volume is an epigram with a similarly surprising punch line, although perfectly logical in the Brechtian sense. It portrays a jubilant group of French prisoners of war in the spring of 1945:

> Heimkehrer, ihr, aus der Unmenschlichkeit
> Erzählt daheim nunmehr mit Schauder, wie's
> Bei einem Volk war, das sich knechten liess
> Und haltet euch nicht selbst schon für befreit.
>
> (no. 66)

One can easily guess the text of this newspaper clipping: "Returning to a changed world—French soldiers, released after five years of captivity, march down a road in Germany on the first leg of their journey home."

It would be easy to continue the series of examples. The overwhelming majority of the photograms in the *War Primer* follow the same pattern. However, the most striking and most brutal examples are those which come closest to emblematic art in form and content. This is particularly true for the shocking picture, which shows the charred head of a Japanese tank gunner, accompanied by the following text: "A Japanese soldier's skull is propped up on a burned-out Jap tank by U.S. troops. Fire destroyed the rest of the corpse." It is well known how important a role death, graves, and decay played in Baroque literature and how they were interpreted at that time. Emblems are no exception. Almost universally, they present skulls, bones, and skeletons as symbols of the transitory nature of human existence and as allusions to the brevity and vanity of that existence. Thus, the Spanish collection of *Emblemas morales* of 1589, referring to a skull crowned by a winged hourglass and a burning candle, and which is likewise "propped up," admonishes

> El tiempo buela como el pensamiento,
> huye la vida sin parar vn punto,
> todo está en vn contino mouimiento,
> el nacer del morir, está tan junto:
> que de vida segura no ay momento,
> y aun el que viue en parte es ya difunto[.]
> Pues como vela ardiendo se deshaze,
> començando a morir desde que nace.

But there is nothing of this mood in Brecht's text. His lines about the charred skull read:

> O armer Yorick aus dem Dschungeltank!
> Hier steckt dein Kopf auf einem Deichselstiel
> Dein Feuertod war für die Domeibank.
> Doch deine Eltern schulden ihr noch viel.
>
> (no. 44)

Although Brecht calls to mind one of the most famous examples of the *memento mori* from the emblematic age (the churchyard scene in Shakespeare's *Hamlet*), he interprets the soldier's death as being exclusively the work of the big capitalist banks which, according to Brecht, have control over all mankind.

The very next example in the *War Primer* (no. 3) shows the motif of fingers pointing towards Heaven. Once again, the resemblance to emblematic forms is apparent; it even remains in the same thematic context. The look towards Heaven and God and the hope for redemption and eternal salvation in the afterlife is, of course, the necessary completion of every *memento mori*. Or, in the words of the previously cited Spanish collection: EN LA MUERTE ESTA LA VIDA. In Brecht's example, the text explains, "A line of crude crosses marks American graves near Buna. A grave registrar's glove accidentally points toward the sky." For this picture, Brecht wrote the following lines:

> Wir hörten auf der Schulbank, dass dort oben
> Ein Rächer allen Unrechts wohnt und trafen
> Den Tod, als wir zum Töten uns erhoben.
> Die uns hinaufgeschickt müsst *ihr* bestrafen.
>
> (no. 45)

Brecht's message is indeed a counterversion of the Baroque text. This becomes even clearer when it is compared to an almost identical picture from

Gabriel Rollenhagen's *Selectorum emblematum centuria secunda*, published in 1613. It shows a hand stretched up towards Heaven as a military symbol. The epigram, a distich, reads:

> Quod petet, omne feret, CHRISTUM, FIDUCIA CONCORS,
>   Nil populo Dominus denegat ille, suo.

Rollenhagen does not talk about an avenger, who is only an "opium for the people" in any case, but about a benign Lord who grants his people everything and who can be experienced only by a "naive faith." The upright hand refers to Him, as do the ears of corn or the steeples, also "upright fingers" in the Baroque period "pointing toward Heaven." They testify either to God's goodness and fatherly providence or to the fact "that we have no permanent place on earth / but must look for a future one in Heaven." But if an emblem portrays a "demand for revenge," such as a lance erected at a gravesite, it is none other than that "which God himself has ordered."

These examples should suffice to clarify Brecht's attitude and method of interrelationship. Brecht, too, is familiar with the characteristic division into *inscriptio, pictura,* and *subscriptio;* the "double function of representation and interpretation, of depicting and deciphering" also applies to his "photograms." Moreover, there is no doubt that they also serve a didactic purpose. But Brecht does not operate on a spiritual level by relying on similarities nor does he employ conceits in his method of interrelationship. Rather, he relies upon the estrangement effect and the critical attitude it provokes.

The main difference lies in the function of the text which accompanies the picture and, in form at least, corresponds to the *inscriptio.* While the *inscriptio* verbally enhances the hidden content of the *pictura,* the captions accompanying the pictures in the *War Primer* present unreflected or even distorted reality. The motto of a Baroque emblem presents its "soul" in the puzzling form of an ingenious conceit which is then interpreted in the *subscriptio.* In Brecht's case, however, the newspaper text which is comparable to the motto is "carefully and brutally" exposed since, according to Brecht, it either ignores the real facts or deliberately helps to obscure or even suppress them. Therefore, the relationship between the *inscriptio* and *subscriptio* in the *War Primer* exhibits that same tension between lies or even ignorance, on the one hand, and "truth" on the other, which Brecht had already formulated in 1931. This kind of solution—or, if viewed in structural terms, kind of interrelationship—is a surprising, confusing, and often plainly shocking exposure manifesting Brecht's well-known theory of estrangement.

The lines of the photograms, therefore, do not interpret but expose. With their criticism and estrangement effects, they penetrate the familiar aspects of life and its social conventions in order to elucidate the economic forces and class antagonisms which dominate mankind, according to Marxism. It almost sounds like a truism to state that Brecht's interpretations are rooted in this theory. But the question arises whether this interpretation is indeed not only quite natural for him but natural in a more dangerous and in a much subtler way. Aren't his interpretations based on both a literal meaning *and* "another" meaning inherent in it—something he abhorred so much in his criticism of Christianity? This is in fact the case and, although this allegorical meaning is a highly materialistic one, the undeniable relationship between the old Christian and the modern Marxist emblematic art becomes apparent, despite all differences, because of the historically conditioned relationship between them.

The works of Tesauro and Zincgreff reveal how deeply rooted sixteenth and seventeenth century emblematic art was in Christian symbolic theology. "The notion that the world in all its manifestations is filled with secret references and hidden meanings, with covert and therefore discoverable relationships, is a necessary prerequisite in the emblematic process." That this idea stems from the universal allegorism of the Middle Ages is well known. It is expressed most clearly in the following strophe of Alanus ab Insulis:

> Omnis mundi creatura
> Quasi liber et pictura
> Nobis est et speculum.
> Nostrae vitae, nostrae mortis,
> Nostri status, nostrae sortis
> Fidele signaculum.

All of Creation is book, picture, and mirror; it points to the Creator and thereby, symbolically, to man. If most emblems succeed in conveying this message in a particularly ingenious way, it is because they draw upon the ancient heritage of hieroglyphics, epigrams, and rhetoric. With medieval allegorism added to this mixture, Tesauro's idea of the concept becomes evident. He, like Alanus, explained: "Whatever ingeniousness the world possesses is either God or of God."

That there is no reason to confine a *Mundus symbolicus* of this type to one historical era alone has been emphatically stressed by those to whom the most recent research in emblematics owes its impetus. D. W. Jöns, for example, even speaks of the "absolute neutrality" of the emblem form. Albrecht Schöne remarks: "The possibility of understanding the world as consisting of a variety of phenomena which point beyond themselves to a hidden meaning, which in turn can be unequivocally expressed and comprehended, remains at man's disposal even after the Age of Emblems." However, it becomes more difficult to seek out concrete examples of the continued existence of such thinking. Schöne tried to do so, but his attempt to classify Eberhard Buchwald's *Symbolische Physik* in terms of emblematics has the undeniable appearance of artificiality. The quotations cited from this author are much too unconvincing and too general to be considered as proof of a genuine experience of the world.

In Brecht's work, however, this possibility seems to have been realized. His *War Primer*, which is perhaps more strictly delimited than the emblem works, not only contains a "preconceived and inalterable meaning" characteristic of the "ideal" emblem type but also presents itself in the moralizing and didactic form of an illustrated book for the people towards whom, more and more, the development of emblematic literature aimed. Brecht sought to illuminate all phenomena in their totality through the interpretation of pictures and to make them intelligible to everyone. "The pious children of God have one praiseworthy practice—that they can penetrate through the temporal to the eternal." This was the belief of the Baroque age. It can in essence be applied to the pious disciple of Marx, Engels, and Lenin as well. Brecht's photograms *ex historia*, which are no longer based on a "potential actuality" but on crude reality and substantiated facts, create a picture of the world and a world view. Brecht proclaimed a new materialistic *Mundus symbolicus* in which, as in the emblem books, the individual fact is made relevant, reality meaningful, and the course of the world intelligible. What is interpreted in the "photograms" becomes "a model of human behaviour" and an "appeal."

I doubt, however, that an absolute neutrality could be the basis of these extensive similarities. Instead, I would presume that both forms of world perception are inextricably connected because the Marxist world view grew out of the Christian view of the world and because no poet was perhaps more deeply and lastingly influenced by this process of secularization than Bertolt Brecht.

We should recall that our comparison has been based on the "ideal" type of the genre, both as found in Brecht's work and in the original emblem books. The latter, too, are not as uniform as they are presented in the handbooks. The existence of four-part emblems in which a prose commentary has been added to the tripartite emblem as well as examples of two-part emblems in which the motto is completely missing have already been discussed. The same pattern is found in Brecht's work. Many of his emblems have additional commentaries gathered at the end of the volume; other emblems—about one-sixth of the total—contain only picture and quatrain, but nothing corresponding to the motto.

The nature of such prose commentaries can be exemplified by the text that refers to the photogram on the Allied invasion of Normandy discussed at the beginning of this article:

Der 6. Juni 1944 war der "D-Day," der Beginn der von den Völkern Westeuropas lange erwarteten Zweiten Front. Immer wieder hinausgezögert, schickten nun doch England und Amerika ihre Soldaten über den Kanal. Die Soldaten, die am Morgen des 6. Juni aus den Landungsbooten sprangen und durch das Wasser wate-ten, meinten, ihr Leben für die Freiheit Europas zu geben. Sie wussten nicht, dass sie erst in den Kampf geschickt wurden, als die sowjetischen Armeen die geschlagenen Hitlerheere nach Deutschland verfolgten.

We have already encountered several examples of photograms without mottos. To this group belongs the picture of the hats of the conquered and that of the metal sheets produced partly for the construction of tanks and partly for ammunition to penetrate their iron sides. One could also take a verse like the following:

> Dass sie da waren, gab ein Rauch zu wissen:
> Des Feuers Söhne, aber nicht des Lichts.
> Und woher kamen sie? Aus Finsternissen.
> Und wohin gingen sie von hier? Ins Nichts.
>
> (no. 21)

In this picture, taken from the air, one sees only a large mushroom cloud that rises from a destroyed harbor area.

Other photograms have a form which corresponds exactly to the "ideal" type of emblem. These are of primary interest in the present discussion. The best example is the picture (no. 4) which bears the *inscriptio* SINGAPORE LAMENT, written in large letters. Underneath, it shows a rickshaw destroyed by bombs, the corpse of a child, and two grieving women. The *subscriptio* of this emblem is:

> O Stimme aus dem Doppeljammerchore
> Der Opfer und der Opferer in Fron!
> Der Sohn des Himmels, Frau, braucht Singapore
> Und niemand als du selbst braucht deinen Sohn.
>
> (no. 39)

No less instructive, even if less characteristic, is a picture (no. 5) which is thematically and chronologically related to the previous one. The cutout has a motto which gives an exact description of the picture: "Woman of Thailand (Siam) peers out of a crude bomb shelter in Sichiengmai at American bomber from French Indo-China come to bomb border hovels." Brecht's quatrain, too, is not particularly impressive in its formal characteristics or poetic quality:

> Dass es entdeckt nicht und getötet werde—
> Denn in den Lüften rauften sich die Herrn—
> Verkroch viel Volk sich angstvoll in die Erde
> Und folgte ihren Kämpfen so von fern.

What makes the emblem so impressive and sheds light on Brecht's emblematic procedure is the fact that the picture is the title page of the magazine *Life*, the word itself functioning as the motto (no. 42). Any word of explanation is superfluous here as one finds a corresponding phenomenon in emblem books: in them, it is not at all unusual to come upon "laconic postulates" of this type.

Emblem books and the *War Primer* resemble each other in thematic as well as in formal aspects. There are, for example, numerous emblems which have satiric, even socially critical, implications. One of them portrays, in a rather vulgar manner, a lawyer "gobbling down presents," indicating his susceptibility to bribes. As he consumes his meal, he is given an enema. The pithy motto translates as "receiving at both ends." The Latin *subscriptio* continues in the same vein and, by ending with the cynical confession of the lawyer, provides a variation on the double meaning of the motto: CAPIO PARTE AB VTRAQUE SIMVL. This remarkable emblem is taken from Barthélemy Aneau's *Picta Poesis* (1552). Even more amazing is the following emblem in the *Morosophie* of Aneau's countryman La Perrière, published in 1553. The picture is quite simple: fallen soldiers and a suit of armor displayed as a trophy. The quatrain explaining this picture is, however, all the more eloquent. La Perrière does not teach "the obvious and that which is clear to everyone"; instead, he "unmasks" what is hidden, concealed, suppressed. He wishes to associate the sacred fame of battle, erroneously attributed to princes and kings, with the actual victims of war:

> Par maint trophée ont acquis grand renom
> Princes et Roys (le fait mal entendu)
> Car de ceux là y deust estre le nom,
> Qui au conflit ont leur sang espandu.

These same verses could have been incorporated four centuries later, almost word for word, into the *War Primer* (cf. no. 5).

And yet Brecht's work—and here again is its relation to the mainstream of emblem books—contains a series of photograms which avoid any type of social criticism. Their texts, which belong to the most successful verses in Brecht's collection, are pure lyricism: they are limited to laments, while the accusation has to be read between the lines.

Two examples should be sufficient to demonstrate this. A picture (no. 6), dating April 1940, shows breakers on a stretch of wide, desolate, northern coastal cliffs. Beneath the picture are the conspicuously irregular verses:

> Achttausend liegen wir im Kattegatt.
> Viehdampfer haben uns hinabgenommen.
> Fischer, wenn dein Netz hier viele Fische gefangen hat:
> Gedenke unser und lass einen entkommen.
>
> (no. 7)

The picture has no motto, which would have been out of place. The observer faces instead the endless emptiness of the elements, out of which arise the ghostly voices of the drowned soldiers and sailors. These lines are almost reminiscent of an incantation, of ritual verses of expiation, of a magical sacrifice for the dead. An aura of irreality surrounds them, yet there is no sign of softening the all too real correspondence between the deadly "net" and the "cattle ship" (a word which echoes all of Brecht's revulsion). Furthermore, the irregularity of the third line is certainly not a fault but the highest realization of formal demands. Its expanded length makes concrete the overflowing mass which is the subject of the quatrain.

In another picture, from the later years of the war, Brecht portrays the voice and image of lamenting mankind. This photo (no. 7) from an American newspaper has the motto: "In Stark General Hospital, Charleston, S.C., a young Japanese-American boy, blinded in Italy at the crossing of the Volturno River, sits patiently in bed." By reporting objectively and with painful accuracy, Brecht's verses successfully suggest the thoughts which the face of the blinded boy so effectively conceal:

> Nicht Städte mehr. Nicht See. Nicht Sternefunkeln.
> Und keine Frau und niemals einen Sohn.
> Und nicht den heitern Himmel, noch den dunkeln.
> Nicht über Japan, noch auch Oregon.
>
> (no. 51)

These unvarying, monotonous lines, consisting only of incomplete negative sentences, seem to have no point. On first sight they arouse, probably intentionally, the appearance of awkwardness. Yet, as one quickly recognizes, they evince in every syllable an acute awareness of form. This epigram appears so flawless because it intentionally thwarts the expectations aroused by our knowledge of the form of the epigram: its point is the total absence of a point. What, after all, could more poignantly express the cessation of time and the finality of the burden of blindness than this absence?

Both examples illustrate Brecht's masterly control of all formal elements in the *War Primer*. Beyond this, they demonstrate once again how inseparably picture and word are interwoven in these modern emblems and how gravely we would underestimate the accomplishments of Brecht the artist and Brecht the man if we tried to separate them from each other, as has been attempted twice.

A few concluding remarks are in order. They refer to certain conclusions made by Albrecht Schöne in his book *Emblematics and Drama* and to an aspect of the *War Primer* not yet mentioned, one very characteristic of Brecht.

It is to Schöne's credit that he directed the attention of German literary scholarship beyond the phenomenon of emblematics to its significance for the world of literary forms. Using Baroque drama, he brilliantly presented the first proof of how such "representational patterns and structural models" were adopted and had their effect. Schöne's basic thesis is this: "The emblematic picture functions as a miniature stage; the theater stage proves to be an emblematic picture enlarged to gigantic size." Drama and emblem in the Baroque are very closely related: the latter is regarded as *Theatrum Vitae Humanae*, the former as "emblematic stage." The degree to which this "structural analogy" applies and the fact that this analogy does indeed determine the fundamental characteristics of the Baroque drama from the smallest poetic unit to the macrostructure of the drama and even to its staging is convincingly demonstrated by Schöne through a wealth of examples.

It is remarkable—although, perhaps, not so surprising—that the completely different kind of drama written by Bertolt Brecht shares the structure of emblematics in important points. Unfortunately, only a rough outline can be provided here; a thorough investigation is definitely needed. But even the most general definition given by Schöne is already startling. Baroque drama was not concerned with "the dynamics of plot and individualizing, motivating characterization" but rather with "the display of exemplary figures, exemplary action and the explanation of its meaning, with the powerful impression made by vivid representation and the rhetorical force of words." This statement about the plays of the seventeenth century, it seems, can be applied almost without reservation to the playwright of the twentieth century whose friendship with Walter Benjamin, the author of *Ursprung des deutschen Trauerspiels*, was certainly not a mere coincidence. One can ascribe to Brecht an "emblematic type of drama" which determines the nature of every aspect of the work from tiny parts of dialogue to the overall structure. This insight neither changes nor counteracts the thorough interpretation of his works by Brecht himself (with the help of the much-discussed concepts of "estrangement," "epic theater," etc.), but rather confirms it.

The correspondence can most easily be found in the instance where Schöne refers to the aphoristic quality of Baroque dialogues and observes: "Such summarizing and interpretative aphorisms are interspersed throughout the Baroque tragedy and bring about a constant interplay of representation with interpretation." "Applied to the behavior of the stage figure, this means that the characters reflect on themselves in emblematic images and state the exemplary nature of their personal situations; thus breaking through the barrier of the individual, they give up their roles, and direct themselves to the spectator or reader." What else does Shen Te do in *The Good Woman of Szechuan*? Ceasing her argument with the carpenter Lin To, who bitterly insists on his wages, she turns to the public with an aphorism: "Ein wenig Nachsicht und die Kräfte verdoppeln sich." Adding two emblematic similes and a rhetorical question which, in turn, climax in another aphorism, she continues ["to the audience"]:

> Sieh, der Karrengaul hält vor einem Grasbüschel:
> Ein Durch-die-Finger-Sehen und der Gaul zieht besser.
> Noch im Juni ein wenig Geduld und der Baum
> Beugt sich im August unter den Pfirsichen. Wie

Sollen wir zusammen leben ohne Geduld?
Mit einem kleinen Aufschub
Werden die weitesten Ziele erreicht.

After that, Shen Te steps back into her role. She "presents herself"—like Baroque figures such as the Catharina of Gryphius or the Sophonisbe of Lohenstein do repeatedly—"as a picture and at the same time proclaims her own *subscriptio.*"

The differences must be recognized, too. What differentiates Shen Te from the Baroque figures, even from a purely formal standpoint, is certainly more than the transition from prose to verse which occurs in *The Good Woman of Szechuan.* Above all, it cannot be ignored that the complete "change in function," which takes place here as in other plays of Brecht, is openly acknowledged by the author, producer, and actor and therefore has to be regarded as a genuine "laying bare of the artistic device" (*obnazhenie prëma*) in the sense of the Russian Formalists. On the other hand, such statements as the one asserting that in Baroque theater, too, "the dramatic figure appears in the double role of the actor and of the interpretor of his own representation," which according to Schöne marks the "beginning of recognition," reveal even deeper emblematic connections between Brechtian and Baroque drama. The fact "that the actor is on the stage as a double figure, as Laughton and as Galilei" and "that Laughton the actor does not merge with the Galilei he plays" but instead portrays "how he imagines Galilei," thereby provoking an act of recognition by the spectator, is one of the basic principles of Bertolt Brecht's epic, non-Aristotelian theory of theater based on estrangement.

Very similar connections between the two forms of drama are found in the larger elements of structure. The Brechtian scene corresponds to the Baroque act, the so-called *Abhandlung;* the Brechtian song to the Baroque chorus or *Reyen;* and their relationship to one another mirrors the *pictura-subscriptio* relationship of emblems. Schöne's remarks about the tragedies of Gryphius, Haugwitz, Lohenstein, and Hallmann apply just as well to the plays of Brecht: "Without the *Reyen* the *pictura* of the action would remain meaningless; without the action the *subscriptio* of the *Reyen* would appear to have no purpose. But when related to each other, the parts acquire their actual meaning: action and *Reyen* of the drama conform to the principle of emblematic form."

Numerous examples can be found in the works of Brecht—and not only in his operas, where such a relationship is self-evident, but even more so in his other plays. Take, for instance, the "Song of Solomon" from *Mother Courage and Her Children* and *The Three Penny Opera.* Or compare the individual acts in the latter, each of which is supplemented by an interpretative generalizing finale *ad spectatores,* to the overall structure of *The Caucasian Chalk Circle* with its tripartite construction consisting of a prologue, an extensively developed "plot" *Abhandlung,* and a concluding moral. This construction seems to correspond quite naturally to the triad of *inscriptio, pictura,* and *subscriptio.* The final *subscriptio* in *The Caucasian Chalk Circle,* which with good reason is directed to the audience as the "opinion of the old people," proclaims "that which exists should belong to those who are good for it":

> Die Kinder den Mütterlichen, damit sie gedeihen
> Die Wagen den guten Fahrern, damit gut gefahren wird
> Und das Tal Bewässerern, damit es Frucht bringt.

It is evident here not only that Brecht's verses are emblematic in content but, as seen in the lines of Shen Te, that they also have their origin in the ideas and concepts of "production," a value which plays a vital role in all the works of Brecht.

Turning again to the structure, the trial scenes, which occur so frequently in Brecht's works, have an especial affinity to emblematics. Almost nowhere else is the interpretation of the preceding action or representation more clearly expressed. The most famous example is *The Good Woman of Szechuan;* other examples are *The Exception and the Rule, The Rise and Fall of the City of Mahagonny, Round Heads and Pointed Heads,* and, with more complicated structure, *The Trial of Lucullus* and *The Measures Taken.* The clearly separated canonization scene in *Saint Joan of the Stockyards,* too, has the function of such interpretation.

But the finest example is the memorable final discussion between Galilei and his former student Andrea. "Academically, his hands folded over his stomach," as the stage directions read, the scholar presents a devastating summary of his life: "In meinen freien Stunden, deren ich viele habe, bin ich meinen *Fall* durchgegangen und habe darüber nachgedacht, wie die Welt der Wissenschaft, zu der ich mich selber nicht mehr zähle, ihn zu *beurteilen* haben wird" (my italics). We know the verdict Galilei reaches: "Ich habe meinen Beruf verraten. Ein Mensch, der das tut, was ich getan habe, kann in den Reihen der Wissenschaft nicht geduldet werden." We also know, however, that Brecht's attitude toward Galileo is almost completely opposite in the first draft. At that time, before the atom bomb was dropped, Galileo was portrayed as the sly, tough dialectician, able to argue against any doctrine and tradition. He does not speak the truth but chooses instead not to show his colors. Avoiding danger in this fashion, he continues to work for the progress of science and enlightenment. Brecht did not view him as a traitor but, like his Herr Keuner, as a model. The conclusion befitting such an attitude is summed up by these words: "Wer das Wissen trägt, der darf nicht kämpfen; noch die Wahrheit sagen; noch einen Dienst erweisen; noch nicht essen; noch die Ehrungen ausschlagen; noch kenntlich sein. Wer das Wissen trägt, hat von allen Tugenden nur eine: dass er das Wissen trägt." No doubt, such a double meaning was possible because the entire play *Galileo* is a gigantic *pictura* for which the poet provided a *subscriptio* appropriate to the circumstances at hand. Only then does it become clear how Brecht was able to revise the play so rapidly and so radically. What was changed was not the picture, which he scarcely needed to touch, but the interpretation.

Therein lies neither a contradiction to emblematics nor a peculiarity of the late, decidedly Marxist Brecht. The emblematic character is, in fact, confirmed anew by such a "re-interpretation." There are dozens of parallel cases: there are emblematic features—and features with multiple meanings in the manner of emblems—not only in the plays around 1930 but even in the earliest ones written shortly after 1918.

A prime example from this early period is the play *In the Jungle of Cities*. Brecht's trusted friend from the twenties, Arnolt Bronnen, sorrowfully related that the playwright "had given different interpretations to the drama at different times." Bronnen's words are credible enough. *In the Jungle of Cities* is a truly confusing work which is given an almost cryptic interpretation, especially in the final discussion between Garga and Shlink. Nevertheless, *pictura* and *subscriptio* are present in emblematic fashion. Again, Arnolt Bronnen testifies to this. He asked Brecht why he had unleashed this chaos and, probing deeper, what he had intended to say in it. The terse answer was: "The last sentence." Actually, Brecht had already alluded to the emblematic conclusion in the prologue of the play: "Zerbrechen Sie sich nicht den Kopf über die Motive dieses Kampfes, sondern beteiligen Sie sich an den menschlichen Einsätzen, beurteilen Sie unparteiisch die Kampfform der Gegner und *lenken Sie Ihr Interesse auf das Finish*" (my italics). The same structure characterizes works like *Drums in the Night*, where Kragler demolishes the stage and the romantic idea of revolution; or *The Life of Edward the Second of England*, in a more complex form.

This great play can and should be analyzed in the context of emblematics. How could it be otherwise, as *The Life of Edward the Second of England*, inspired by Marlowe's work, itself belongs to the age of emblematics? Not only does it represent a turning wheel in its structure, but it is expressly given this sort of interpretation by Mortimer:

> 's ist, Knabe, die schlumpichte Fortuna treibt's
> Ein Rad. 's treibt dich mit nach aufwärts.
> Aufwärts und aufwärts. Du hältst fest. Aufwärts.
> Da kommt ein Punkt, der höchste. Von dem siehst du
> 's ist keine Leiter, 's treibt dich nach unten.
> Weil's eben rund ist. Wer dies gesehn hat, fällt er
> Knabe, oder lässt er sich fallen? Die Frage
> Ist spasshaft. Schmeck Sie!

Of course, the moral judgment, which the "pig" Kragler brushed off and which remained at best encoded in *Jungle*, is even called *childish* in this play: because there is nothing more "dehumanized than cold judgment and justice."

This changed in later works, for example in *Fear and Misery of the Third*

Reich. Judgment continues to be cold, but completely free of doubt: Brecht has learned how dehumanization and justice are to be dispensed. Even the fact that he at times estranges his Marxist truth, as in *The Good Woman of Szechuan*, or only recognizes it gradually, as in *Galileo*, has no bearing on this attitude. In *Fear and Misery of the Third Reich*, Brecht's drama to combat Fascism, the Marxist truth is inexorable and unambiguous from the very beginning.

This play will also bear comparison with emblematics. Each of the twenty-four tableaux is composed of a title or *inscriptio*, a dramatic scene serving as *pictura*, and verses of six lines representing the *subscriptio*. The emblematic relationship between the various elements is exemplary. No wonder Brecht characterized this "montage" as an "array of gestures" which presents the feeling of numbness, the suggestion of looking over one's shoulder, the sense of terror, and the other "gestures" experienced under totalitarian rule, to the audience.

But *Fear and Misery of the Third Reich* is also exemplary in a quite different sense. The term "array of gestures" speaks clearly enough as does Brecht's explanation. Both point to the *Moritat*. It, too, with its "picture board," its pointer, and its tinny minstrel songs determines the structure of this series of scenes, not just emblematics. To an even greater extent, of course, the *Moritat*-structure applies to the *War Primer* as well. That the author is indebted to minstrel songs for many and various stimuli in his drama and in his lyric poetry is nothing new. But in the *War Primer*, it is a matter of the greatest possible degree of correspondence, in the final analysis, of identity. "During the battles for Stalingrad," the composer Paul Dessau reports, Brecht discussed with him the plan for a "German Requiem." "Es wurde daraus das Oratorium 'Deutsches Miserere.' Es besteht aus einem musikalischen Teil und aus Bildern, die Brecht gesammelt und mit Vier-zeilern versehen hatte. Er nannte diese Sammlung . . . *Kriegsfibel*. Bei der Auffährung werden die Bilder mit den Texten auf eine Leinwand proji-ziert." Words, pictures, and music work together to create something which, paradoxically, can only be designated as a new "total work of art" (*Gesamtkunstwerk*). It is rooted in the cosmos of emblematics; but its *telos* is the gigantic *Moritat* from "gloomy times" which Bertolt Brecht sang inces-santly to posterity—happier people, as he hoped.

Laura's Metamorphoses: Eich's "Lauren"

Anselm Haverkamp

Günter Eich's *Moles* are short prose pieces which he allowed, against his will, to be called "prose poems," after his publisher had given them merely the subtitle "prose." Since Baudelaire's "poèmes en prose" the term has become conventional as a terminological expedient. Unlike Baudelaire, who found poetry in prose, Eich finds the prose in poetry without the poetry ever being able to be restored. His moles, suggesting the emergence of blind poetry onto the surface of prose (*Maulwurf*, literally "thrown by the mouth"), are a unique kind of poem that fulfills the genre of the prose poem without being any the less poetic for that. We can see this best by looking at a specimen which itself is concerned with the fate of lyric poetry, recalling the stages of the lyric and proceeding through them to its inevitable end. It is not that poetry is no longer possible (as Adorno said), but rather that it had always been overburdened, always already at the edge of its possibilities, and that the poets have only now noticed and finally come to admit it. What Eich's moles bring to the light of day is the prose from which Eich no longer makes poems, since poets had tried in vain to make poetry of prose for long enough and what was left was prose nevertheless.

Thanks to the recent discussion about "intertextuality" it is now possible to reformulate the aporias that have arisen in coming to terms with the "mixing" of genres (here of poetry and prose) and the specific character of modern genres in particular (here the prose poem). The old rhetorical conception of poetic genres has become obsolete not least because, in rhetorical terms, the novelty of modern texts can only be described as the deviation from a principle of variation whose range is exhausted. The historical specificity of this new difference from the old modes of differentiation is manifested in its break with the continuity of literary forms and its in-

From *Comparative Literature* 36 (Fall 1984). © 1984 by the University of Oregon.

commensurability with their mode of tradition. Intertextuality compensates for the shortcomings of the older rhetorical theory by exchanging the negative deviation from rules and models for the positive relation between texts. In terms of intertextuality, the difference of the new has left its traces within the intertextual relation, a relation which is said to become manifest in an implicit "dialogicity" of the text. What is important is not so much the tracking down of the texts to be found within a text, but the traces they have left in a process of sedimentation. Saussure offers a model for this process when he illustrates the relation of diachrony and synchrony with the metaphor of projection. He speaks of "the relationship between the historical facts and a language-state, which is like a projection of the facts at a particular moment" (*Course in General Linguistics*). For intertextuality, the appropriate root metaphor corresponding to projection is the palimpsest, which plainly expresses the superimposition of texts and suggests the partial readability of an old text under a new one. Because of this transparency, Gérard Genette proposes the term "transtextuality." In transtextuality individual texts are related in a way that the intertextual result as a mediation retains an irresolvable ambiguity.

This is the decisive point that marks the difference between intertextuality and previous investigations into literary influence and *topoi*. In topological research (*Toposforschung*), which overcame the unresolved conflict between the aesthetics of genius and the search for influence by tracing it back to a rhetorical substrate, the intention of the author was reduced and dissolved into the intentionality of a tradition whose *topoi* functioned as clichés or archetypes. To this kind of research the prose poem offers an obvious alternative which manifests itself in the paradoxical identification of prose and poetry. Michael Riffaterre makes this paradox the cornerstone of his theory of intertextuality. The prose poem, like a palimpsest, contains two texts in one, the one replacing the other, a new prose form displacing the conventions of the lyric. Most important here is the conflict between texts that takes place in reading. For Riffaterre, the activity of reading is exhausted in bringing this conflict to a resolution which consists in reducing the given text to its intertext (the hypertext to its hypotext in Genette's terminology), that is, to a pattern which results from its transtextual reference. For Genette such a resolution is not only occasionally impossible (as it also may be in extreme cases for Riffaterre), but essentially so. In his view, the intertextual pattern remains effective behind one's back, even if its operation goes unnoticed. For Genette, explication of this pattern is neither the precondition nor the goal of an appropriate understanding as it is for Riffaterre. The transtextual references result in an irreducible ambiguity which, as a momentum of "differentiation," provides the impetus to the act of reading. Derridean deconstruction comes to terms with this ambiguity of a so-called dissemination by taking the constructive and the destructive together; Riffaterre, on the other hand, neglects the constructive aspect by emphasizing its contrary. Recognizing the dialectic of deconstruction means that the effect of the prose poem cannot be understood merely as the negation of the lyric that it presupposes; it is, in fact, what Adorno called a "determinate negation." The aesthetic significance of deconstruction, therefore, is not yet comprehensible in the self-reflection of poetic codes and in the free play of intertextual "difference," though Derrida himself is quite ambiguous on this point. The same misunderstanding receives apparent support in formalist descriptions of a "poésie formelle," as in the paradigmatic instance of Petrarchism. Consequently, it seems to me, the case of the utterly informal prose poem is well suited to correct the (self-)misunderstanding of deconstruction. The following mole deals with the fate of Petrarchism, the history of "misreadings" inherent in and constitutive of Petrarch's reception. Looking back on this tradition and the history of its misreadings Eich shifts the emphasis from the play of differences to the things played with and thereby shattered: "the 'affection' of things (*res*) by the play of words (*verba*)."

Lauras/Laurels
If there is no Laura, there is still her name. She has small curl-covered ears; this we can state with assurance. Yet even the color of her hair is uncertain, but red would be a surprise. There is less scholarship about Laura than about Wilhelm Tell. It's a pity. I could talk with her better than with Petrarch, who wanted to say everything again, only more beautifully. A mistaken principle of art, but we want to do so, too. What said Eve, what said Bathsheba, what said Noah when he left his friends in the rain. Nobody knows, but we want to say it at last. Nobody knows Laura, but we want to invent her at last. She plays piano. Because the life of her soul demands expression, probably too loud. Her eye is fixed on a point beyond all pianos—now we've got something. I dare say she is a captain's widow. Young, but a woman matured by suffering. Now we've got something further. But more beautiful. Laura becomes ever more beautiful. A beauty-mark, a neck delicate as a flower stem, a waist slender as a wasp's. At once she comes to life and plays piano. Swarmed by suitors, she consumes her meager widow's pension. Francesco and Friedrich are her favorites. Francesco remains, Friedrich later turns to a Caroline and a Charlotte. She endures and survives both. Died 1899 in the institute for the tropics at the University of Tübingen. Once we know her death/their deaths, we know everything. Death, my lord, says Friedrich, omnipotent czar of all flesh.

The significance of Petrarchism appears in the title: Laura in the plural. As the quotation of a name, the title carries two meanings, as does the name itself. The name Laura, in a convention familiar since Petrarch, names an ambivalence which, ever since the love lyric, has become paradigmatic of poetry in general. The ambivalence of the name Laura results from the historical metamorphosis of a myth—the myth, namely, that Ovid relates of Daphne, who escapes the pursuit of Apollo enflamed in his first love only by turning into a laurel tree. The frustrated love of the young god is poetically sublimated by a transformation of the real into an imaginary object. The loss of the beloved is compensated for by the laurel of the poet, the loss of his love by fame. Though Petrarch devoted his love to Laura, he did everything to insure that, however vain his love for Laura, this very vanity would be crowned with the laurel. On April 8, 1341, in the capitol in Rome he was indeed crowned poet laureate. (The irony of the story is that, unknown to Eich, whose name means "oak," the victors of the old Capitolinian games were crowned with oak: "capitolinam quercum," as Juvenal relates.)

Thus Laura is the name of the beloved as well as of the poetically sublimated love. Both, the beloved and the poetic fame that replaces her, answer to the name of Laura. This is already the case for the singular Laura, the one Laura sung by Petrarch, whose plural is Eich's theme. Eich, then, is concerned with the Lauras created after Petrarch's pattern and with the laurels won by following it. What the mole brings to light in the plurality of this pattern is not poetry but the prose of which dreams are made: not another new Laura but the many Lauras, which the history of lyric after Petrarch had multiplied, making the one Laura unrecognizable. Behind this plurality of Lauras there is another significance which is concealed in the title "Lauren." If this were a poem and not prose, the reader would think first neither of the plural of Laura nor the plural of laurel, but rather of the form of apostrophe which addresses the poem to the beloved. "Lauren" in this sense means "To Laura" and is conventionally associated with the ode. That this sense of the title has become unrecognizable means, as a matter of fact, that the form of address, and the convention to which it belonged, have lost their performative force. The title thus contains a completely implicit hypogram for the lyric matrix to which the prose still refers. What had been a pattern for poems is carried over into prose, where it now is no longer applied but objectified. The repression of the poetic matrix, however, results in symptoms of deviation, namely in the incoherence which leaves the critics at a loss. Such inconsistencies function, in Riffaterre's nice metaphor, "as buoys marking the position of a sunken meaning" (*Semiotics of Poetry*). "If there is no Laura, there is still her name": that there is no Laura is the precondition of the plural use of her name which consequently leads to her definitive invention. In what follows I begin with Petrarch's Laura, whose name we know, and proceed to Schiller's Laura, who completed the process of her invention.

The tone of the first section is anything but lyrical; it is not only prose but ironically refers to the prosaic idiom of criticism, including the scholarly observation that in Schiller the theme of the individual (Laura) will be less prominent than that of the historical and political (Tell). The literature in German dealing with Laura is indeed quite limited, so that it is simple to identify the sources of Eich's text. These are primarily two: a slender collection of Petrarch by Hanns Eppelsheimer in 1956 (*Petrarca: Dichtung, Briefe, Schriften*), and Hugo Friedrich's authoritative treatment of Laura in his *Epochs of the Italian Lyric* in 1964. In Eppelsheimer we read, "The example of Dante and Beatrice . . . pales before the new couple, Petrarch and Laura. Love has a new name . . . ; more than this [name] neither his friends nor later literary historians have been able to determine." Friedrich goes into greater detail: "That is all; name, place, and when they first met [1327], place and date of death [1348], the length of their love. In the thirties [the 1330s] the friend and patron of Petrarch, Giacomo di Colonna, came to doubt the real existence of Laura." Borrowing phrases from Petrarch's *Epistolae familiares*, Colonna speaks of *ficta carmina* and *simulata suspiria*, "invented songs" and "artificial sighs." Convinced by the fruitless search for the real Laura, Friedrich argues the other way round: "There exists no compelling reason to deny Laura's existence. But we have reason enough to doubt that she was baptized by this name, though the appearance of this name at that time in Provence can be indubitably ascertained." This brings us back to Eich: "It is too obvious that the name is suited to a symbolic use." Since Petrarch has himself thought of the possibility, it seems clear enough "that it was not Laura's beauty that he fell for but her name." Friedrich argues against the biographical interpretation that tries to read the *Canzoniere* as a concealed love story; on the other hand he does not want to deny the biographical evidence without which Laura would become a merely allegorical figure. The dilemma Friedrich wants to avoid is characteristic not only of the reception of Petrarch but also of modern lyrical poetry in general. Eich illustrates this dilemma in the casual non sequitur of his first two sentences: "If there is no Laura," but "She has small ears."

The logic of this description does not follow from what we know about the real Laura. It is the logic of her name. Friedrich says of this: "The homonyms *l'auro* and *l'oro* appear in the lady's golden hair. . . . She has golden hair blowing in the soft breeze. So purely, picturesquely, and economically does Petrarch write about this golden hair that one could easily forget one of its origins, namely, in the lady's name (*l'auro*), which also fits the blowing breeze (*l'aura*)." The name Laura, mentioned only once in the *Canzoniere*, nevertheless appears in countless paronomasias, phonetic transcriptions which name Laura by describing her appeal and appearance, her aura. If, for example, the first two lines of one sonnet run: "Breezes blow through her golden hair / And turn it into a thousand sweet curls" ("Erano i capei d'oro a l'aura sparsi, / che 'n mille dolci nodi gli avolgea"), then the breezes as well as the golden hair contain the lady's name without expressly naming her. Eich unmistakably cites the curls and hair, and yet alters them: "the color of her hair is uncertain." The golden color is already part of the Ovidian tradition, a literary transference in which Cupid's golden arrow colors its target, so that the question is not really one of Laura's actual hair color. (Red, according to Friedrich, does not appear before the Seicento.)

Furthermore Eich speaks of ears instead of eyes, which play such a prominent role in Petrarch's image of Laura. Eich offers his own metamorphosis,
transposing the sound of the name into German: the association with gold
is cancelled ("the color of her hair is uncertain") and replaced by its phonetic
equivalent in German, the ear (*Ohr*)—covered by curls. In that the ear
finally asserts itself over the eye, the spoken word over the written, the
name triumphs over the described appearance, which vanishes before it.
You may consider this eye-ear business a bad pun, mere playing with
words, which in fact is the typical charge against Eich and his moles. But
just this is the point of the prose, that it unexpectedly leaves the poetic
tradition in the lurch. Allusion to the fragments of tradition, however, is
not the effect that Eich has in mind. Rather he brings to our attention the
pretentiousness of such effects. This reminds us of the "false principle of
art" which Eich cites from Eppelsheimer, who summarizes "Petrarch's definition of poetry" as "saying again what others have said but more beautifully." Eich subverts this paraphrase's classicist bias against the genuine
intention of the paraphrased: Petrarch's version of the so-called "bee-fable"
Eppelsheimer implicitly refers to concerns the transformation into something new and better (*aliud et melius*). In Eich's quotation of the already
quoted the more beautiful remains the same and, as such, doubtful. Like
the humanist Pico della Mirandola who had already remarked, "the *Canzoniere* beautifies a vacuous content with empty words," Eich turns the
Petrarchan lyric against itself: not because of the vacuous content it presents, but because of the self-destructive way it is presented.

   "Nobody knows Laura, but we want to invent her at last." If there
was no Laura and nothing was left but her name, then there was nothing
to find but only to invent. The old art of invention consisted in variations
on a given theme; in this way Petrarchism varied the name of Laura along
with the associated motifs: the breeze-blown hair, the eyes shooting arrows
of love, and so on. Fiction, the new art of invention, now really found at
last—in the terms of German philology after Goethe—"the genuine, immediate, and unmediated Petrarch." The discovery of Petrarch presupposes
a transformation in Petrarchan tradition. The form of the ode, in contrast
to the form of the sonnet and the canzone, brings this process to an end,
and helps to locate its result in the eighteenth century before Schiller. The
high point in the search for the real Laura is a *Report on the Life of Francesco
Petrarch* by the Abbé de Sade who proved on the basis of lost family documents that Laura was, ironically enough, an early de Sade. The book was
published in French in 1764 and translated into German as early as 1774.
The definitive historical invention of Laura, which informs Schiller's conception of her, is parallel to the plurality of Lauras, as documented in pre-
Romantic German poetry. From Johann Peter Uz, the subject of another of
Eich's moles, Schiller borrowed not only a model for his *Ode to Joy* but also
for his *Odes to Laura*. Uz wrote one of the poems in which Laura appears
in the plural, where love becomes possible "because of a Laura," and

possibilities are opened which in the tradition of Petrarchism were impossible and reprehensible. The best known of Schiller's odes to Laura is his "Laura at the Piano," first published in his *Anthology for the Year 1782*. I quote only the passages among its eight strophes to which Eich responds.

> EICH: "She plays piano."
> SCHILLER: Soulful harmonies swarm
>> A lusty storminess
>> From the strings, as from heaven
>> Newborn Seraphim . . .
>> Lovely now as over colored pebbles
>> Trickles a silver flow,—
>> Majestically splendid now
>> Like the thunderous tones of an organ . . .
> EICH: "Because the life of her soul demands expression,
>> probably too loud."
> SCHILLER: Maiden speak! I ask you, tell me:
>> Are you in league with the spirits on high,
>> Is this the language, deceive me not,
>> Which they speak in Elysium?
>> Away all veils from the eye!
>> Rigid bars from the ear! . . .
> EICH: "Her eye is fixed on a point beyond all pianos." ("A
>> tear trembles on her lashes," in an earlier version.)
> SCHILLER: New spirits near the sun
>> Beckon through cracks in the rent heavens—
>> Over the grave, day dawns!
>> Away, you scoffers, with your insect wits,
>> Away, it is a god—
> EICH:"—now we've got something."

It is no longer the sound of her name from which the poet draws poetry. She herself plays the piano and thus becomes the vehicle of theodicy. The rest fits in easily: "I dare say she is a captain's widow. Young but a woman matured by suffering." The tone of these sentences derives from German philology, as it still survives from the nineteenth century in today's Gymnasium. We find this style, for example, in Friedrich Burschell's Schiller book of 1968, published just before Eich wrote "Lauren." At this time (autumn 1968) Eich received the Schiller award and was expected to prepare an acceptance speech on Schiller. So he could have availed himself of the relevant information in Burschell's chapter "The Dramatist in Mannheim" and read about Luise Dorothea Vischer, born Andreae (1751–1816), the captain's widow who was Schiller's landlady in Stuttgart before his move to Mannheim: "How intimate was his relation to her, we can at most suppose. We know for certain only that Schiller enjoyed playing with her three children, that he admired her piano playing, and enjoyed the punch which she could prepare so excellently." Burschell says of the *Odes to Laura* in particular, "concerning Luise Vischer, the widow with the four children, the object of his love [in Burschell's text another child is added right away], nothing remains but the blue eyes and her piano playing. But under the gaze of these eyes he believed himself withdrawn from this world." Eich resumes: "a woman matured by suffering . . . But more beautiful." Petrarch's principle of art in a new application: she who was once described more beautifully becomes herself ever more beautiful, a consequence which in Eich's text appears entirely natural.

So Laura becomes ever more beautiful: "A beauty-mark, a neck delicate as a flower stem, a waist slender as a wasp's. At once she comes to life and plays piano . . ." The more we get now, the more difficult it becomes to follow the mole through the labyrinth of historical allusions which play about the surface of this genre piece. "Francesco and Friedrich"—the role game of fiction: nothing remains for Luise except Francesco, who Schiller was for her, as she was Laura for him. He later turned to the Lengefeld sisters and finally married the one, Charlotte, after he had long sought the other, Caroline. (This Caroline, by the way, played the piano and had her tombstone inscribed with the words, "She erred, suffered, loved.") In fact, there had been another Charlotte in between, Charlotte von Kalb, who should have been his Laura, married as she was and therefore unavailable like the real Laura for Petrarch. To Charlotte von Kalb Schiller later, in the *Thalia* of 1786, addressed his only ode to Laura worth the name. It is entitled "Free-thinking of Passion" and its subtitle associates it with the previous *Odes to Laura*: "When Laura was married in 1782." Charlotte von Kalb was married; Luise was no longer. Think of Laura de Sade as a widow: what would Petrarch have done? The *Canzoniere* would never have been written. *Don Juan* makes fun of this: "Think you, if Laura had been Petrarch's wife, / He would have written sonnets all his life?" Even more obvious: "Had Petrarch's passion led to Petrarch's wedding / How many sonnets had ensued the bedding?" It is the death of Laura on Good Friday in 1348 that makes the *Canzoniere* what it is. In the fame of Petrarch Laura survives as a lyrical figure, a trope. The captain's widow is her last metamorphosis, the last of all transformations to the better which are claimed by Petrarch and denied by Eich. It remains doubtful, however, whether Schiller's Laura was the last of the Lauras. Who is it that "endures and survives both"? None of Schiller's Lauras could have lived that long. "Died 1899 in the institute for the tropics at the University of Tübingen." It is hard to guess whose biography ends with this sentence. As a matter of fact, the foundation of this institute, which still exists, goes back to that year, so that the possibility of referential meaning cannot entirely be dismissed.

The last Laura of a prominent German poet who might fill this blank is Heinrich Heine's last love, though her traces in Eich's text are scattered and almost illegible. This suspicion is nurtured and reinforced by the fact that Heine's best known work, his *Book of Songs*, is a *Canzoniere*. On his deathbed he found his last friend in a woman whom he affectionately called "Mouche," which, besides "fly," means "beauty-mark." Before she became Heine's secretary during his last months, she earned her living by giving piano lessons. Curiously, she had changed her name again and again, changing it once more when, years later, she published her memoir of *Heinrich Heine's Last Days*. Even though she was a Laura she also had many names. Her real name finally remained as obscure as her origins. Heine occasionally called her his "girl from Swabia" ("Schwabenmädchen"), which hints at Tübingen. She died in 1896, not 1899, though older reference books don't agree on this point. In 1899 Heine's beloved sister died, Charlotte Emden, whom he once expressly identified with "his mouche." Charlotte, though, did not die in Tübingen but in Hamburg, location of the other, better-known institute for tropical medicine, which is often confused in reference books with that in Tübingen. The literary traces of the Mouche, if they are indeed of her, consist of only scattered allusions, as I said, and are almost illegible. Their arbitrary and in any event metonymical character is, next to "beauty-mark," most obvious in "a neck delicate as a flower stem" ("ein Blumenhals"). This quotes one of the prominent motifs of Heine's Petrarchism, which—from "lotus flower" up to "passionflower"—abounds in his last poems for the Mouche. One stanza in the long "I had a dream of a summer's night," considered to be his very last poem, runs as follows: "You were the flower, you beloved child /. . . / No lips of flowers are so tender ("Blumenlippen") / No tears of flowers burn so hot ("Blumentränen")." Mouche's portrait as a nameless Laura by Friedrich Hirth, which might be one of Eich's sources, ends with the same flowery lines commencing, "But at the head of my resting place / A flower stood . . ." I have mentioned, so far, only the most obvious traces and should add perhaps that such patchwork conglomeration of references is not the exception in Eich's work but the rule. Anyway, there is still the possibility of reading him figuratively and of being content with the death of Petrarchan tradition in an institute for the tropics at the end of the nineteenth century. (There may be more in this than meets the eye. "The connexion of poetry with laurel is not merely that laurel is an evergreen and thus an emblem of immortality: it is also an intoxicant," we read in Robert Graves who, in his mythological writings, most effectively elaborated the magical "grammar" of all myths. The magical, premedical qualities of the laurel survive in its broad though unspecified use over centuries until they are finally suppressed by the medical institution at the end of the nineteenth century.)

"Once we know of her death/their deaths, we know everything." Hers? Laura's death? The death of the Lauras? Laura's death we know from the *Canzoniere*; the death of the Lauras we hear from Eich. That Laura died a happy death in the plague of 1348 appears nowhere in the *Canzoniere*, which tells only of her heavenly fate. This sententious formula, which Eich adds to the lapidary fact of her death, is the only one I have failed to trace. That it is not a quotation seems highly unlikely because it encapsulates so formulaically what the fate of the Lauras amounts to; that nothing remains but their name. It is easy to recall the contemporary commonplaces associated with this death sentence, though none of them exactly coincides with it. Its tradition goes far back—to the story of King Croesus whom Solon advised that no man can be called happy before his death; to Petrarch's philosophy of fate which made life a permanent *meditatio mortis*; to the stoic maxims of the Baroque, and the more than baroque death motif of the young Schiller.

By far the most difficult task philologically is not to demonstrate the origin of a quotation but to assert that it has none and is rather an invented quotation. Hans Blumenberg maintains (in *Arbeit am Mythos*) that such a demonstration is the apex of all philological endeavour when he says the same of an untraceable motto of Goethe's *Poetry and Truth*. In distinction from Goethe's motto, in Eich's text there are no explicit quotations but only a mime of quotability, which in pointedly casual fashion produces an unquoted sentence that carries the weight of a quotation, as only a quotation could be expected to. The invented quotation puts the theory of intertextuality to a difficult test. The intertextual structure of a text, its dialogicity, does not render superfluous the tracing of quotations but gives it a new function: I do not demonstrate that a sentence is or is not a quotation and afterwards appeal to the principle of intertextuality, but with the presupposition of intertextuality the proof of quotation acquires a special significance. In an extreme case like the one at hand, in which almost all of the sentences are derived (quotations, translations, allusions, paraphrases), perhaps less depends on being able to prove the source than on the discomfort of not being able to do so. So I have accustomed myself to the thought that Eich has "invented" this sentence (which was, of course, his literary profession), and I'll continue to make the best of it (which is, obviously, my critical profession).

So it may well be that Eich introduces himself anonymously into his text in the disguise of the alien words of an invented quotation. This possibility is balanced by a real quotation: "Death, my lord, says Friedrich, omnipotent czar of all flesh," from Schiller's macabre dedication to the *Anthology for 1782*, in which appeared the odes to Laura. It runs as follows: "Inscribed to my lord, Death," prefacing a longer dedication: "Omnipotent czar of all flesh / Omnipresent reducer of the realm / Unfathomable devourer of all nature." This is the author of the *Robbers*, but it is also the author of the *Moles*, who gives the last word to the death of all flesh as he had given the first to the survival of a name. The address to the beloved ("Lauren") is replaced by the dedication to death ("omnipotent czar of all flesh").

I do not here wish to involve myself in the casuistry of intertextuality and its terminological jargon. What makes the present case special is the doubling in which the relation between the quotation and what it quotes (between hypertext and hypotext) is thematized in its mediation through secondary literature. It is presented not as the eternal realm of classical ideas but rather as a history of misreadings, that is, of the distortions that have occurred in the course of historical applications. So it is not just that Eich relates himself in his own way to Petrarch and Schiller, as in the typical cases of what Genette calls hypertextuality—for instance, when Heine's *Book of Songs* quotes Petrarch's *Canzoniere*. Eich neither follows Petrarch's or Schiller's principle of art nor transforms the story of Laura into a new pattern. Indeed, he cites both, the imitations of Petrarch as well as the transformation of their object by Schiller, through the diffraction of tradition. He pushes to absurdity the imitative principle of art in exposing a historical difference which becomes linguistically manifest (between the golden hair and the curl-covered ears). He ironically exposes the transformation of this principle in thematizing the metatextuality of the "relation critique," whether in academic commentary or vulgar popularization. This metatextual function, which relates commentary and criticism as secondary texts to a primary text, consists, according to Michel Foucault (in *L'Ordre du discours*), in "saying *at last* what was *already* silently articulated." That is, in Eich's words, "Nobody knows, but we want to say it at last." As Foucault says, the secondary text must cope with "a paradox that it always postpones but never escapes"; it "must say for the first time what had always been said and must continually repeat what has really never been said." Eich thematizes the process by which metatextual tradition mediates hypertextuality. In whatever terms one would like to describe the way Eich's text reworks others, he does not simply putter with the spoils available in the treasure house of tradition, as Curtius would suggest. His intertext does not consist of free-floating motifs of a cultural code, as even Riffaterre still maintains. What Riffaterre calls intertexts Eich cites in the linguistic forms that reflect their various historical appropriations. Eich thus reflects the process of progressive alienation which occurs as the repetitive force of tradition continually impels new displacements in secondary literature.

Eich speaks the language of secondary literature. What remains of the speaking subject of his text, as grammatical subject, has no chance and yet emerges through anonymous quotation in the guise of the alien word. "It's a pity. *I* could talk better with Laura." It begins in all naiveté; but then it succumbs to the basso of apophantic certainty: "this *one* can state with assurance," "now *we've* got something further," and "*I* dare say." The increasing alienation of a once lyrical *I* through the scholarly *one* and *we* results in an unintended humor. The humorous effect of silliness ("Kalauern" and "Blödeln") does not presuppose knowledge of the tradition quoted; it rather works like the "rediscovery of something known." Eich himself—in a short, angry interview about the "new Eich" of the *Moles*—responded to the question of whether he would describe himself as an educated man, "Not in the slightest. I have at best a moderate education and apply it as best I can. But nobody can prescribe to me." The text of the moles goes beyond catering to the self-satisfaction of the learned. It requires self-irony of those who fall into this trap. But this is not all.

Blumenberg, who first called attention to the "pointed casualness" of the moles, notes (in "Wirklichkeitsbegriff und Wirkungspotential des Mythos") that "from its end the text concentrates its force into an aggressive irony against this end." This concentration of irony against the effect of decomposition turns mere destruction into deconstruction. The quotability of the traditional is driven to absurdity, but the point of this operation is not that tradition is dead but that it always already presupposes the death of its object and lives on in this death: the death of Laura which made it possible to transform Petrarch's love into the composition of the *Canzoniere*. In the plurality of Lauras, she becomes a figure/trope of the vanity of poetry and as such the false pattern of lyrical beautifying ("Schönersagens"). In the alien words of secondary discourse Eich proves the metamorphoses of Laura to be pseudomorphoses of a lyrical intention, which he rehabilitates as the "lost hope" of the lyric. From the end, the "definitive death" of poetry, as announced in the "revolt" of the late sixties, Eich's moles manifest the vanity of modern poetry in order to save and to develop anew in prose what can no longer be maintained in lyrical poetry. Obviously, Eich still is obliged to the tradition of enlightenment, whose dialectic he exemplifies in the *Moles*. The casual manner of his indebtedness should not conceal the aesthetic character of his no longer lyrical texts. Very appropriately, a friend of his, Reinhard Baumgart, speaks (in *Über Günter Eich*) of "the late Eich" as of "the late Beethoven": "As in Opus 111 or 131, so in these moles too something beautiful, great, familiar, a tradition, goes to pieces, this time remarkably brightly." Baumgart, however, still underestimates this brightness, in which one hardly notices the effort and the remaining bitterness; for there is something in it that supersedes the humour and irony needed in overcoming a loss.

Celan and the "Stumbling Block" of Mysticism

Joachim Schulze

May we proceed from the notion (as is now often done) that art is something given, something to be taken for granted . . . ?
                                                        —PAUL CELAN

A few years ago I attempted a mystical commentary on a few poems by Paul Celan based on the observation that we find in them thematic configurations which are related to mystical speech, as well as exact quotes from both Gershom Scholem's presentation of Jewish mysticism and from the sermons of Meister Eckhart. My goal was to make these poems more understandable and to clarify somewhat their obscurity by finding a conceptual framework and by ordering them in a certain universe of discourse in which a particular field of experience is articulated verbally. I would like to illustrate this approach through a short example and then to discuss a problem that has arisen through my commentary on the poems of Paul Celan in a mystical context.

The example is a poem from *Fadensonnen* (1968) which reads:

> Du warst mein Tod:
> dich konnte ich halten,
> während mir alles entfiel.

> (You were my death:
> you I could hold
> when all fell away from me.)

There once was a common universe of discourse describing one's death in or encounter with a "Thou," and this was the poetic and philosophical speech of the Renaissance about love—something one would not like to appropriate for an author like Celan, for whom death is important in a quite different context. What this context is can be seen in the poem "Treckschutenzeit" from *Lichtzwang*, which ends with the lines:

From *Studies in Twentieth Century Literature* 8, no. 1 (Fall 1983). © 1983 by *Studies in Twentieth Century Literature*.

> Todes quitt, Gottes
> quitt.
>
> (Quit of Death, quit
> of God.)

The expression "quit of God" is a citation from the writings of the mystic Meister Eckhart. It comes from the sermon "Beati pauperes spiritu" in which the relevant passage, repeated several times, reads: "Therefore I pray God he may make me quit of God." The main point of Meister Eckhart's thinking in this sermon and elsewhere is that, "to the extent God is conceived of as having his origin with the beginning of all creatures," man's essential being is "above or outside God." But in that essential being, "where God is above all being and all difference," man in his original being was not distinguishable from God. "Therefore," Meister Eckhart continues, "I am my own first cause according to my being, which is eternal, but not according to my becoming, which is temporal. Therefore I am unborn, and after the fashion of unbornness I can never die." It was this last sentence which provided the basis for the subsequent phrase "quit of death" that Celan borrows.

I shall start from the assumption that Celan, who cites Eckhart's mystical teachings in support of a view that his being released or freed from death ("quit of death") also makes him "quit of God," had himself seen death in a similar connection not too long before. Further, I propose the hypothesis that the death in "Du warst mein Tod" is to be understood mystically. The context which presents itself here is not difficult to find. It concerns the different articulations of that religious experience formulated so succinctly in the letters of Paul: "Now if we be dead with Christ, we believe that we shall also live with him" (Rom. 6:8) and "Nevertheless, I live; yet not I, but Christ liveth in me" (Gal. 2:20).

One finds the following commentaries on mystical death by Eckhart:

> Since the love of our Lord is as "strong as death," it kills man in the spiritual sense, and in its own way separates the soul from the body. This happens when man surrenders himself completely, and divests himself of his ego, thus separating him from himself. This, however, happens through the extraordinarily high power of love, which knows to kill so sweetly.

This death is "the death in which the soul dies away in God" to a new life, because

> with this, it completely separates itself from this world and travels to the place it has earned. And where else has it earned to go, if not in Thee, O eternal God, who must be its life because of this dying through love.

The situation which Celan's poem captures seems to me to be comparable to those quoted in Paul and similar texts of mystical speech, for in his poem an "I" dies in an encounter with a "Thou," and it is a death in life which allows it to report about it. Because "everything fell away" from this "I," the poem probably deals with a death in which the "I," in the words of Meister Eckhart, "departs this world," and since the "everything" is apparently meant to be all-inclusive, it would probably also include "giving one's self up completely and divesting one's self of one's ego." What is left to him after this, what he could still "hold," is only this "Thou." There are, however, undeniable differences between Paul and Meister Eckhart. Especially with the former, the "Thou" refers to a specific figure. It has a name and a history, and it had its epiphany in the experience on the road to Damascus. Such concrete details are missing in Celan. With him the "Thou" has neither name nor history. It is simply one's vis-a-vis. In addition, the "Thou" can only be determined by the "I," specifically through its death. It is not clear from the poem whether it has died, or whether its death caused the death of the "I." This, however, plays no significant role in the passages quoted from Eckhart, because at that point Eckhart deals with a passage which does not have reference to Christ's death, viz. Song of Sol. 8:6, according to which "love is strong as death."

A further difference between Celan and mystical speech in regard to the death of the "I" is that Celan speaks of an "I" that can "hold" or retain the "Thou" (which was his death) as the only thing remaining to him—not, however, that this "Thou" is now his life, which is what is essential to Paul and the mystics. The encounter with a "Thou," which causes death and the loss of everything, but through which the "Thou" is won, leads us to assume a certain religious experience. But in an important departure from traditional religious experience, this "Thou" is not interpreted in a traditional manner, but rather remains an indefinite "other."

Precisely this absence of a more exact definition of the "Thou" might lead to the assumption that this is a poem about a deeply disturbing encounter with a beloved that changed the "I" profoundly. In spite of the aforementioned reservations about the "Petrarchian" hypothesis, I wish to explore the question, which is all the more obvious because the poem in *Fadensonnen* which precedes "Du warst mein Tod" speaks explicitly of love in this way:

> Die Liebe, zwangsjackenschön,
> hält auf das Kranichpaar zu.
>
> Wen, da er durchs Nichts fährt,
> holt das Veratmete hier
> in eine der Welten herüber?
>
> (Love, straight-jacket-lovely,
> makes for the pair of cranes.
>
> Whom, since he moves through Nothingness,
> does the expired draw over
> into one of the worlds?)

This poem uses Bertolt Brecht's poem "Die Liebenden" as its point of departure, and, if I'm not mistaken, it calls into question quite literally that poem's statements. From Brecht we have the image of the lovers as a pair of cranes. His poem also speaks of nothingness, albeit somewhat offhandedly:

> Sieh jene Kraniche in grossem Bogen!
>
> . . . .
>
> So mag der Wind sie in das Nichts entführen
> Wenn sie nur nicht vergehen und sich bleiben
> So lange kann sie beide nichts berühren.

(See there two cranes veer by one with another,

. . . .

What though the wind into the void should lead them
While they live and let nothing yet divide them
So for that while no harm can touch their haven.)

In Brecht's poem, love makes the pair of cranes strong enough to withstand even nothingness (translated here as "the void"), if need be. But in Celan, love "makes for" the pair of cranes, which means it has not yet caught hold of them. The main thing that Celan questions is whether it is possible for one who "moves through nothingness" to be drawn over into "one of the worlds." Therefore, the question is not whether love can withstand nothingness, but whether it is able to draw something out of the nothingness. What "one of the worlds" means can be understood by glancing at the poem "Treckschutenzeit," whose final lines I have already cited. In its entirety it reads:

> Treckschutenzeit,
> die Halbverwandelten schleppen
> an einer der Welten,
>
> der Enthöhte, geinnigt,
> spricht unter den Stirnen am Ufer:
>
> Todes quitt, Gottes
> quitt.

> (Barge-time,
> the half-transformed tow
> on one of the worlds,
>
> the dethroned, inwarded,
> speaks under the foreheads on the bank:
>
> Quit of Death, quit
> of God.)

The line "the dethroned, inwarded" refers to passages from Meister Eckhart's sermon "Surge illuminare iherusalem," which says that "God must be dethroned" in order "that we can be raised." It continues: "You should be united from yourself into yourself, so that He may be in you." The background passages to these verses have already been discussed, so that, based on these sources, the poem can be paraphrased in this way: Beneath the foreheads or brows of those on the bank towing the barge, God, "inwarded" in man, promises a state of "single being" in which man is again the cause of his own self. The barge-pullers, however, are only "half-transformed," that is, they have not yet been transformed back into "single beings," but still live in the state of "created being," and it is this that they are towing or hauling. The expression "one of the worlds" means, then, that Celan understands the life of the "born-ness of creatures," (to be distinguished from life in its original state of being "unborn") as the life in *one* possible world, one which is a product of chance as opposed to the primeval "being-ness" which can again be attained.

Therefore, "one of the worlds" in the poem "Die Liebe, zwangsjackenschön" can be taken as an accidental, unessential world whose opposite pole is "nothingness." In another sermon by Meister Eckhart concerned with the soul's becoming "quit of God," he says of nothingness: "The soul suffers total loss—God and all creatures . . . everything must be lost. The soul must subsist in absolute nothingness!" God himself is "one whose nothingness fills the world, and the place of his being is nowhere. . . . He who wishes to come to God, says a master, he comes as a nothing!" He who "moves" through such nothingness, it would seem, is completely lost to the world of "being born" and of creatures. But in the sermon just cited it also says: "Thus these people, in a God-like condition of unselfish openness, are turned outward toward all humankind." Celan's poem could be asking about the possibility of a return through the power of love from a state of nothingness to a relationship with one person. But it stops at the question, and therefore at the position of nothingness from which the question was put. The designation of love as "straightjacket lovely" can perhaps be understood as an exaggeration of the idea of the body as the jail of the soul, as a drastic expression for the sensuality of creation in its "being born."

If the poem "Die Liebe, zwangsjackenschön . . ." is understood in this way, the poem that immediately follows, "Du warst mein Tod," can hardly be taken as a love poem in the usual sense. Even if one is of the opinion that the "Thou" which was the death of the "I" could have been another person, one would have to take into account what Celan wrote in *Der Meridian* about the "other" in his poems. He states there that it had always been one of the hopes of the poem to speak "in the cause of an 'Other'— who knows, perhaps in the cause of a 'wholly Other'." And further: "Perhaps, I must now say to myself—perhaps it is now possible to conceive a meeting of this 'wholly Other,' . . . and an 'other' which is not far removed, which is very near." With this well-known phrase one reflexively thinks of dialectical theology, which calls God the "totally or wholly Other." Thus the "Thou" in a poem of Celan's would not be limited simply to another person, especially since Celan says in the *Meridian*: "Each thing, each person is a form of the Other for the poem, as it makes for this Other."

When my study *Celan and the Mystics*, in which I had attempted a mystical commentary on poems by Celan based on the method I described above, appeared in 1976, I was criticized for not differentiating "between mystical experience and the mystical level of poetry as a possible artistic form of representation." Specifically, I was accused of omitting "Celan's transformation of precisely these [mystical] images." From a book published one year before this review, one can see how such a "transformation" can be conceived and described. In his book *Negativität in der Dichtung Paul Celans* (1977), Georg-Michael Schulz uses a detailed interpretation of the poems "Mandorla" and "Psalm" from *Die Niemandsrose* (1963) in an attempt to answer the question as to what degree the "use of mystical motifs" should lead us to classify the poem "Mandorla" as a "mystical" expression, something I had asserted, and, on the other hand, to what degree there existed a fundamental difference between the poem and the mystical experience.

Schulz believes this "fundamental difference," which separates the poem from the mystical experience, lies in the poem's auto-reference. Though he does not acknowledge it, he is using Roman Jakobson's method. Jakobson's chief maxim of poetic function states: "The set towards the MESSAGE as such, focus on the message for its own sake, is the POETIC function of language."

In reference to the recognizability of the set of the message toward itself and therefore to language in its poetic function, Jakobson explains his second principle of poetics: "The poetic function projects the principle of equivalence from the axis of selection into the axis of combination." Schulz, however, does not use this part of Jakobson's theory. Although a poem such as "Mandorla" with its many repetitions would seem to be well-suited for a Jakobsonian analysis, Schulz has chosen a different method by trying to make the concept of "nothingness," which occurs both in this poem and in the poem "Psalm," credible as evidence for its autoreferentiality. "In the poems 'Psalm' and 'Mandorla' . . . it [the concept of nothingness] refers to the poem itself and its execution in language itself by resisting a direct connection to concreteness." One must admit that with the concept of "nothingness" it is not easy to establish a connection to the concrete when its content is exactly the opposite of concreteness. Still, it is extremely difficult to conclude that simply because a concept that denies concrete reality appears, it is used with the intention of referring to itself in part or whole, or that it even carries the connotation that its context refers to itself. By contrast, Jakobson's principle of equivalence does suggest this. The recurrence of similarities in places where dissimilarities normally are combined adds something to the expression which makes the contrast to a normal form of expression conspicuous and, through its very lack of referential function, emphasizes the intrinsic value of the expression. No such thing could be said about a concept. It seems to me that the contention that the concept (of nothingness) refers to the poem and to its own representation in language is based on the a priori certainty that poems are autoreferential by nature and not based on a (repeatable) observation of the poetic text.

But even an analysis that took Jakobson's second principle of poetics into account would not prove a "fundamental difference between poem and mystical experience," because even in Jakobson's view the poetic function in poetic texts is dominant but does not exclude the other functions of language, among them the referential function: "Poetic function is not the sole function of verbal art but only its dominant, subsidiary, accessory constituent." Therefore, according to Jakobson, poems with mystical references are possible without the reference having been "transformed" into a poetic function.

In addition to Jakobson's theory of the dominant autoreferentiality of language in a poem, Schulz brings up another theory of poetics, that of the poem being created out of the impulses of language. In Celan's poetry, Schulz claims, "the speaking 'I' enters the language as the dominant force" and is identical with "language, which has become the subject, . . . and which asks the question and gives the answers." This idea rests on Mallarmé's concept of the "oeuvre pure," the "pure work" whose canonical passages are to be found in *Crise de vers*: "The pure work implies the elocutionary disappearance of the poet, who yields the initiative to the words, mobilized through the shock of their inequality; they catch fire by means of reciprocal reflections like a virtual trail of flames spread over precious gems, replacing the breathing perceptible in the ancient lyrical breath or in the enthusiastic personal direction of the sentence." In opposition to the "enthusiastic personal direction" of the sentence, Mallarmé posits the impersonal inspiration from the powers of language which causes the person of the poet to disappear.

Comments from Celan himself, however, made in answer to a questionnaire sent by the Librairie Flinker in 1958, prevent us from using Mallarmé's concept of the "oeuvre pure" as proof of the "fundamental difference between poem and mystical experience." He maintains that German lyricism takes a quite different direction from the French, and that in it, "it is never language itself that is operative, but always an 'I' which speaks from a special vantage point of its existence, and which is concerned with contours and orientation. Reality does not exist, reality must be sought and won." In *Der Meridian*, Celan's direction becomes even more clear because there he uses the word "correspondence": "This . . . can only be language, but not just language generally, and presumably also not just deriving from the word 'correspondence'." In French the word "correspondance" is an important signal word in the self-commentary of lyric poets, especially Mallarmé and Valéry, and is connected with concepts like rhythm, harmony and musicality. Rhythm, harmony, and musicality are, however, characteristics of beauty, and in the name of "truth" Celan has certain reservations about "beauty." The language of lyricism which he has in mind "distrusts beauty; it tries to be true" and wants to have "its 'musicality' located where it will have nothing in common with that 'melodiousness' that resounds more or less untroubled along with or next to the terrible." That Celan has turned against Mallarmé is explicitly expressed when he asks skeptically: "should we follow Mallarmé to his logical conclusion?" That, I believe, forbids our looking for the "fundamental difference between poetry and mystical experience" in Celan in the entrance of a speaking "I" into "language which has become its own subject."

I have discussed Georg-Michael Schulz's argumentation in such detail because it seems to me symptomatic of the way critics deal with the stumbling block of mystical themes and direct citations from primary and secondary mystical literature. The cornerstone of this type of argument seems to be a *petitio principii*, that is, the premise that texts which are published under the genre of "poetry" belong to the area of art, which by nature is completely different from the area of religious experience. From a historical viewpoint this is based on classical aesthetics, according to which art is the area of "disinterested pleasure" (Kant), from which involvement with reality, truth, and orientation (all expressions Celan uses when speaking of his poetry) is banned. In order to claim these poems, which are saturated with mystical thought, for this area of art, critics seize on the most contradictory theories of poetics without regard for Jakobson's theory, which disallows any fundamental distinction between "poetic" and "engaged" language.

In light of such a pre-determined decision that every text published as a "poem" belongs to a realm of art which is strictly separated from the realm of the religious, there is justification in emphasizing a comment of Celan's in which he expresses reservations about classifying his poetry as this kind of art, an art which he believes reached its culmination in Mallarmé, who represented the quintessence of the "l'art pour l'art" standpoint. "May we," as it says in the *Meridian* in a passage that has already been quoted, "proceed from the notion (as is now often done) that art is something given, something to be taken for granted; should we, to be specific, above all—let's say—follow Mallarmé to his logical conclusion?"

Mallarmé, whom Celan has doubts about following to a logical conclusion in his particular conception of art, is an interesting case for the problem of the difference between poetry and mystical experience. I shall discuss this case in some detail because I believe it illustrates how this difference, when it actually exists, can better be established by depending on the intentions of the author in question, at least to the degree that these intentions can be reconstructed out of the author's own explanations, rather than by relying on one or the other theory of poetics that has been determined to be the only correct one for a particular author.

Since the nineteenth century, personal commentary has become an increasingly significant part of a writer's work, especially for lyric poets. It appears that such commentary has increased to the degree that agreement on the meaning and purpose of poetics (not to mention the demise of the close symbiosis between author and audience and the change this relationship has undergone) has decreased. Since this time, poets repeatedly give information about the position from which they are writing. Mallarmé discussed this problem in his letters to his friend Cazalis. From these letters we can see that his attempts at achieving the ideal purity of the "oeuvre pure," which were driven by a dissatisfaction with everything attainable, had led him into experiencing nothingness—something he understood as a religious experience, as shown by the comparison with Buddhism when he speaks of "the Nothingness at which I have arrived without knowing Buddhism" ("le Néant auquel je suis arrivé sans connaître le Bouddhisme"). This experience caused him to stop writing for a time. One year later it became clear that this acquaintance with nothingness was the "borderline case of a nihilistic mystic," a type about whom Gershom Scholem says that he views as his highest value "the demolishing of all forms" and who, in an undialectic spirit, tries to preserve this "impulse instead of using it the way other mystics do as a driving force in constructing new forms."

With such a mystic, "the destruction of all religious authority in the name of authority seems itself to be the purest representation of the revolutionary aspect of mysticism." With Mallarmé the destruction of religious authority assumes the form of a struggle with God, who is represented as an angel, and ends with the conquest of God: "my fight with that creature of ancient and wicked plumage [whom I] fortunately defeated—God" ("ma lutte avec ce vieux et méchant plumage, terrassé, heureusement, Dieu"). That the destruction of this authority is carried out in the name of authority itself can be seen from the fact that the struggle with the angel takes place on its wings, and is "winged" or carried by it. A second indication of the mystical character of this experience is the mention of the state of "external indifference" ("indifférence extérieure") into which he is transported. This appears to be the *sancta indifferentia* of the mystical tradition, where it expresses one's death from worldly things in order to concentrate on more essential matters.

After Mallarmé's experience of nothingness, however, there followed for him an "aesthetic turn," a return to writing. The "dream in its ideal nakedness" ("rêve dans sa nudité idéale"), which led into nothingness, now appears as "sin," and the remorse of the poet has the following appearance: "For me, two years ago I committed the sin of seeing the Dream in its ideal nakedness, while I ought to have amassed between it and myself a mystery of music and forgetting" ("Pour moi, voici deux ans que j'ai commis le péché de voir le Rêve dans sa nudité idéale, tandis que je devais amonceler entre lui et moi un mystère de musique et d'oubli"). And: "I want to produce for myself this spectacle of [the] matter . . . proclaiming, before the Nothing which is truth, these glorious lies" ("je veux me donner ce spectacle de la matière, . . . proclamant, devant le Rien qui est la vérité, ces glorieux mensonges"). The drama of the material world as music and lies interposed between the ego and the nihilistic mystic's experience of nothingness in order to forget ("oubli") this experience of the truth so that he can once again be a poet: that is Mallarmé's poetic position and his vocation as a poet relative to mystical experience. Thus his relationship as a poet to this experience is one of "aesthetic distance," a distance which makes turning one's attention back to the "drama of the material world" possible, that is, back to the forms of the world which have been overcome by experiencing nothingness and the "external indifference." These are forms whose "sparse beauty" ("éparse beauté") can be isolated from the poetic view and synthesized to poetic signs, but which still remain a "lie."

This is Mallarmé's position, at least in connection with the problem of the difference between poetry and the mystical experience, a position Celan has reservations about following to its logical conclusion, because for truth's sake he distrusts the beauty and musicality which are Mallarmé's means of hiding the truth of nothingness with a "beautiful" lie; it makes a certain view of art questionable for his own works. If one wants to make a credible argument for a "fundamental difference between poetry and mystical experience" in Celan's poetry, one cannot simply base one's proof on the *petitio principii* that mystical citations—which occasionally, as in the case of "Treckschutenzeit," comprise almost the entire poem—do not have the same sense their original sources do, but are meant only aesthetically. One must also harmonize Celan's skepticism toward Mallarmé and his type of art with Mallarmé's stance on art by proving, for example, similar "aesthetic distance" in Celan.

Proving this distance as a pre-condition for *aisthesis*, i.e., the aesthetic perception, seems to me the only way to dispose of the notion that mysticism in Celan's works is a stumbling block. If this proof does not succeed with the same clarity that, in my view, is possible with Mallarmé—and also Baudelaire—which is to say without applying external concepts to the poetry, concepts that cannot be rendered understandable from the text itself (who can tell by looking at a text whether or not it arose out of devotion to the sheer force of language?), then there seems to be another possible hypothesis. From Celan's theme of nothingness, which is connected to mysticism in many ways, among them direct citation, we can reach the conclusion that he tries to follow Mallarmé, perhaps not to his logical conclusion, but in the opposite direction, in the direction toward exactly this "Nothing that is truth" ("Rien qui est la vérité"), which he does not wish to hide anymore with the lie of beauty and musicality, but which he engages for the sake of truth, orientation, and reality with all its consequences. This results in the position of the one who "moves through nothingness" ("Die Liebe, zwangsjackenschön"), who knows himself to have been

> durchgründet vom Nichts,
> ledig allen
> Gebets
>
> (constituted of nothingness
> free of all
> prayer).
>   ("Wirk nicht voraus")

This is the one who sees the king in the "Nothingness in the almond," and who does not fear even the highest degree of mystical destruction:

> Todes quitt, Gottes
> quitt.
>
> (Quit of Death, quit
> of God.)

That could be the premise of the "stumbling block" of mysticism, a notion which rejects the taking of art as "something given, something to be taken for granted" and likewise rejects the reduction of religious speech to art, even if this is only a "mystical level of poetry," whatever one understands that to be. But there still remains the question of understanding how mystical experience articulates itself in the genre we call lyric poetry and which is thus in large degree suspiciously "artistic."

First of all, I would answer this question by saying that after the thematic expansion of literary genres which took place mostly during and after the Romantic era, literature became a very broad field that allowed every type of experience to be expressed and all forms to be used to articulate experience better. Secondly, I would point out that the religious, and especially the mystical aphorism, has a long tradition in poetry. The aphorism resists systematic treatment. It formulates succinctly an isolated thought, inspiration, or insight without attempting an explanation in a broader context, with no attempt at argumentation, and without trying to prove anything. It is in this way, for example, that in the seventeenth century Johannes Scheffler (Angelus Silesius) extracted isolated thoughts and insights from a systematic context of mystical tracts, mostly from Jakob Boehme, and put them into the poetic form of the epigram. Here are two examples of the paradoxes that shocked more orthodox spirits:

> Die Gottheit ist ein Nichts
>
> Die zarte Gottheit ist ein Nichts und Übernichts:
> Wer nichts in allem sicht, Mensch, glaube, dieser sichts.

(The Godhead is a Nothing

The gentle Godhead is a Nothing and Over-Nothing:
He who sees nothing in everything, believe, oh man, that he
sees this.)

With Angelus Silesius, however, the systematic essays precede the aphorism. As one commentator says, the conversion of the systematic essays into aphorisms serves the purpose of "lifting mysticism out of its dark underground to the heights of highly formalized mastery." In the use of the epigram, a form that emphasizes making points, one can recognize the intention of a "formal-aesthetic reconstruction" which does not, however, prevent even the modern reader from gaining the "impression of a dual religious/poetic nature," which has as its background both classical aesthetics and the rediscovery of Baroque literature as an artistic form. The reverse is true with Pascal, whose religious aphorisms precede a systematic treatment. One of his "pensées," whose dual "religious-poetic nature" was discovered only in this century by Paul Valéry, is famous, and for this reason I will discuss it in the form that Valéry discovered:

Le silence éternel de ces espaces infinis
M'effraye.

(The eternal silence of the infinite spaces
Terrifies me.)

Finally, in twentieth-century poets before Celan, e.g. in Guiseppe Ungaretti, we can also find aphorisms in poetic form with religious content. His famous "lyrical laconism" is not unrelated to Pascal's "pensée."

Mattina

M'illumino
d'immenso

(Morning

I illuminate myself
with the immense)

"The immense" in the context of "illumination" can certainly be understood as religious in nature, and even the "morning" in the title takes on a religious character in this context in the sense of the "sun of salvation," which rises every morning in the east ("es oriente lux"). In addition, Ungaretti answers the question he asked of himself: "Should our century therefore perhaps have a religious mission?" ("Dunque, forse, sarebbe il nostro secolo di missione religiosa?") with the concise statement: "There is no notion of liberty if not for poetic action, which gives us the notion of God" ("Lo è che non si ha nozione di libertà se non per l'atto poetico che ci dà nozione di Dio"). From the pen of a lyricist, quite an interesting statement. Thus one can see a certain relationship between Celan and the mystical aphorisms of Angelus Silesius in a number of poems which take as their base a systematic connection between mystical sermons and tracts as well as Gershom Scholem's portrayal of Jewish mysticism. To some degree he does this for personal use of what, point by point, he finds there, but scarcely, I believe, for the purpose of "highly formal mastery" or "formal-aesthetic reconstruction." If we take him seriously, the most compelling argument against this position comes from his own reservations about art.

Paul Celan in Translation:
"Du Sei Wie Du"

John Felstiner

With Paul Celan's writing I have found the translator's task at its most challenging and revealing—especially with his later poems, which fracture and obscure the lineaments of lyric form. Why do they? "Every word you speak," he said, "you owe to destruction." Born in Czernovitz, Rumania, in 1920, within a German-speaking Jewish community, Celan saw Soviet forces overrun his homeland in 1940, then a year later, Rumanian troops plundered and brutalized the Jews, followed by an SS *Einsatzgruppe* obliterating the millennium-old culture, burning, torturing, shooting, deporting. Paul's parents (he was the only child) were wrenched from the ghetto overnight; he worked 18 months at forced labor, hearing first of his father murdered, then of his mother.

After the war an exile in Paris, teaching German poetry, he also made brilliant translations from Rimbaud, Valéry, Mandelstamm, Dickinson, Shakespeare, and many others. It heartens me that Celan upheld the possibility of verse translation. Above all he dwelt in—wrote poems in—the *Muttersprache*, the German mother tongue that had passed through "a thousand darknesses of deathbringing speech," he said—the language that was literally all he had left. He became the leading postwar poet in German, though increasingly inaccessible, unattended to. In 1970 he drowned himself in the Seine River.

Paul Celan's poetry, however idiosyncratically lodged within his native tongue, still beckons to the translator, because every poem he wrote remains a work in progress—or as he himself, estranged and precarious, once put it: "a poem can be a message in a bottle . . . that may somewhere and sometime wash up on land." A poem, he said in his great speech "The

From *Studies in Twentieth Century Literature* 8, no. 1 (Fall 1983). © 1983 by *Studies in Twentieth Century Literature*.

Meridian," a poem wants to reach an other, a "thou," a poem is making toward encounter, homecoming, messianic release from exile. Is it presumptuous to see in translation a way of continuing that work in progress, of keeping the poem in motion toward attentive listeners, and toward some new beginning, following Celan's meridian around to where his poem and its translation alike have their source?

Nothing he wrote has drawn me more than one poem composed in 1969, between the Six-Day War and Celan's late journey to Israel. The poem appeared shortly before his *Freitod*, as the German has it, his "free-death":

DU SEI WIE DU, immer.

Stant vp Jherosalem inde
erheyff dich

Auch wer das Band zerschnitt zu dir hin,

inde wirt
erluchtet

knüpfte es neu, in der Gehugnis,

Schlammbrocken schluckt ich, im Turm,

Sprache, Finster-Lisene,

kumi
ori.

(YOU BE LIKE YOU, ever.

Ryse vp Ierosalem and
rowse thyselfe

The very one who slashed the bond unto you,

and becum
yllumyned

knotted it new, in myndignesse,

spills of mire I swallowed, inside the tower,

speech, dark-selvedge,

kumi
ori.)

To carry over into English and yet still respect the integrity of Paul Celan's poem, which already bespeaks enough displacement and loss, I won't leave you with my (always provisional) version but will retrace my way there and back via the to-and-fro, symbiotic exchange between interpretation and translation—the process of reading and writing.

Du sei wie du: how to preserve the tensile arc of that phrase, and the modulation of its vowels? We cannot tell yet whether the poet is speaking to God, himself, or his listener, or what has dissevered *du* from *du* so that we need this stark imperative. But we can hear how Celan's grammar moves—how it binds—one pronoun to the next through a terse articulation. I know two French versions of the poem. One begins *Toi sois comme toi*, euphonious and seemingly inevitable; yet the other says *Toi sois égale à toi-même*, "You be equal to yourself," which tips the balance of the phrase. Celan's barest utterances can make so strong a call on us that in translating, one is tempted to interpret them. Whatever we may hear in *Du sei wie du*, the simplest rendition probably holds the most potential: "You be like you." For the verbal symmetry, if nothing else, holds some promise.

What English cannot manage, though, as French can quite naturally, is a true equivalent for *du*. We have "thou" only in archaic or poetic usage, whereas the intimate pronoun marks four hundred of Celan's poems, coloring their speech and shaping their stance. Celan began to read Martin Buber intensively during the war—the lectures on Judaism, the Hasidic translations, and possibly *Ich und Du*, "I and Thou." Unfortunately a modern English version cannot reflect the charged expectancy of Celan's *du*, although it can closely mime both his rhythm and vowel-sounds: *DU SEI WIE DU, immer*, "You be like you, ever."

Stant vp Jherosalem inde
erheyff dich

Here two more imperatives enter, again in the second-person singular: literally, "Stand up Jerusalem and / raise yourself." Now, we hear that line one may also have been addressed to Jerusalem, Zion. These next two lines, bearing the emphasis of italics and strange orthography, seem to have warned off their French translators, who simply transfer the Middle High German as is. But how do the words sound to German readers of Celan's poem, and how then should they sound within an English version? These questions of translation carry straight to the heart of Celan's own poetic undertaking.

The thirteenth-century mystic Meister Eckhart first uttered the words. He would open his sermons with a Biblical text in Latin, then translate it into the vernacular as here, then go on to speculation. One such sermon caught Celan's eye, giving rise to "Du sei wie du." *Surge, illuminare, Jerusalem*, reads Jerome's Vulgate, *quia venit lumen tuum, et gloria Domini super te orta est*. We know this in the King James version of Isaiah 60, which makes a soaring alto aria and chorus in Handel's *Messiah*: "Arise, shine, for thy light is come, and the glory of the Lord is risen upon thee." The preacher's Middle High German version, *Stant vp jherosalem inde erheyff dich inde wirt erluchtet*, made its way literally into Celan's poem—having made its way, that is, from the prophet Isaiah's pre-Christian Hebrew to Saint Jerome's fourth-century Latin to Meister Eckhart's medieval German and then into Paul Celan's lyric voice, the messianic word under way and translated through time.

Eckhart considerately rendered the Latin for his flock, but Celan does not in turn adjust Eckhart's words for his own audience. Nearly every German reader would understand them, but at the same time would feel a sudden strangeness, feel displaced backward in time. Celan wanted this dialogue between one epoch and another. In carrying us back from the present, Eckhart's German preempts by seven centuries the spawning of words such as *Einsatzgruppe* and *Sonderbehandlung* and *Endlösung*. Long before *Juden raus!*, as it were, was heard *Stant vp Jherosalem inde erheyff dich*—words which, incidentally, more than one reader of Celan's poem has taken for Yiddish—a plausible yet painfully ironic mistake, given that language's European fate.

If a German listener, then, would catch the sense of Eckhart's words, they need translating into an equivalence, familiar yet slightly inaccessible. I went to the visionary Dame Julian of Norwich and to the mystic Richard Rolle of Hampole. My keenest pleasure came from seeking out the early English Bibles, and then going back to the Hebrew itself: Isaiah 60:1 and also 51:17, since Eckhart (or the scribe or congregant who wrote down his sermon) made a new blend of those two passages. Isaiah 60:1 opens, , which in John Wycliff's 1382 version from the Vulgate becomes "Rys thou . . . be thou lightned." And for the Hebrew of 51:17— —Wycliff offers a striking verb: "be rered, be rered, ris thou, ierosalem." Finally "rere" felt merely physical and I pulled out a prosodic stop to carry the metaphoric energy of Eckhart's *Stand vp Jherosalem inde / erheyff dich*: "*Ryse vp Ierosalem and / rowse thyselfe*."

Auch wer das Band zerschnitt zu dir hin

Each word here bristles with possibilities and problems, which begin to resolve as one decides how to translate the pivotal noun *das Band*. It can mean "ribbon, band, strap," so that literally the line reads, "Also the one who cut apart the band to you there." But the figurative sense of *Band*, a "link" or "bond," may come closer to what animates this poem. The German word *Band* is cognate with *Bund*, meaning "covenant," or in Hebrew , which originally meant a binding. Once Isaiah's call to God's people has rebounded off Eckhart and resounded through Celan's voice—*Stant vp Jherosalam*—the idea of breaking and renewing a convenant comes into force.

It may well be the speaker who feels he has severed himself from Jerusalem, from his people. This line might then read: "Whoever cut off the bond to you there." Always in Jewish history it was a sinful people, not their God, who broke the mutual covenant. Yet now if the poet, like Isaiah, speaks to the Jewish dead and to a people returning from exile, then the very one who slashed the bond—I need that stressful verb—may also be God. This crucial ambivalence must remain in translation.

inde wirt
erluchtet

The dialogue returns in italics to another prophetic imperative, *"and becum yllumyned,"* letting us hear that Isaiah's words, the old dispensation, have been at work all the time. I hope "yllumned" does not look merely quaint. To intensify the word I have gone from translating Eckhart's *wirt* as "be" to a more full and exact idea: "becum."

knüpfte es neu, in der Gehugnis

Whoever slashed the bond, Celan now tells us, also *knüpfte es neu*, "knotted it new." (I must have had Pound's "Make it new" in mind here.) God's knotting it new seems too much to hope for, unless it is the very persistence of the divine word that binds the covenant again. Celan found that persistence not just expressed but embodied in language. After the Holocaust, he said, "there remained in the midst of the losses this one thing: language." In exile he dwelt, he took refuge, within the mother tongue itself, and every poem he wrote he wrote in mind of the dead. So to summon up a medieval German that has the prophet's Hebrew behind it constitutes the only kind of memorial that counts for him, and lets the poet himself renew a covenant.

The same one who slashed the bond knotted it anew, and Celan can say where: *in der Gehugnis*—in a very strange word. Virtually no German reader will recognize this term from Middle High German (and rare in that lexicon, too), where its root *hügen* meant "think on, be in mind of, long for." Given the dictionary's three modern equivalents for *Gehugnis*—*Erinnerung, Andenken, Gedächtnis*—we find that the word means "memory" or "remembrance." *Gehugnis*, then, vexes translation in a revealing way. For a while I tried "memoraunce," dating from 1320 and filling out the verse rhythmically, but it came to seem too Latinate and, what's worse, too understandable. The point is, Celan leads his audience to a word they cannot know, then prints it in roman rather than italics as if they ought to know it. Possibly he wished his readers to go through something like what the translator does here. In digging for the arcane and archaic word *Gehugnis*, "remembrance," we perform an act of memory itself and of possible renewal. Not quite having the courage of Celan's conviction, I searched for remote but just barely perceptible terms and finally settled on early Middle English "myndignesse," akin to "mindedness" and meaning the faculty of memory. I still wonder if it is obscure enough or too obscure.

Schlammbrocken schluckt ich, im Turm

I've put more time into revising and refining precisely what the speaker recalls here, than into any other line of the poem. Translated simply—"I swallowed bits of mud in the tower"—it drains from Celan's verse the revulsion and anger and pain of exile. More must emerge. Impelling the line, strong drawn-out stresses pull the word *Schlamm* ("mud," "mire," "slime") into *schluckt* ("swallowed," "gulped"), then a vowel ties *schluckt* into *Turm* ("tower").

Schlammbrocken schluckt ich, im Turm, "mudclods I swallowed, in the tower": that will do, yet it still lacks something. Despite—or rather thanks to—my difficulty in finding a vital equivalent, I begin to feel myself edging closer to the experience behind Celan's line as I sound out phrase after not-quite-adequate phrase. "Hunks of muck I gulped" or "scum in lumps" or "chunks of sludge" go too far in miming the poet's disgust, while "scraps of slime" and "bits of swill I swallowed" risk sounding like tongue-twisters.

I need a deeper sense of the voice Celan is projecting. Both Luther's and Buber's German Bibles use *Schlamm* in figures of abandonment and despair: Jeremiah prophesies Jerusalem falling to the armies of Babylon and is put into a dungeon where (in the King James) "there was no water, but mire: so Jeremiah sunk in the mire." Psalm 69 makes the painfullest utterance if we remember Paul Celan's own death: "I sink in deep mire, where there is no standing: I am come into deep waters, where the floods overflow me. I am weary of my crying: my throat is dried: mine eyes fail while I wait for my God. . . . Deliver me out of the mire." So maybe Celan is saying, "mire in lumps I gulped, inside the tower." That felt all right, until one day I recognized a constraint more essential than any other, in *Schlammbrocken schluckt ich, im Turm, /Sprache.* . . . The alliteration linking *schlamm* with *schluckt* carries even further to a word in apposition. *Sprache,* "language" or "speech," supplants the mire the poet swallowed. After *Schlamm* and *schluckt* make their bitter alliteration, in *Sprache* they give way to what the poet cherishes, what "remained in the midst of the losses." Celan's language so engages with his agony that I feel obliged to alliterate these two lines, even if it means changing word order. Here then is one rendering, awaiting a better: "spills of mire I swallowed, inside the tower, / Speech. . . ."

Sprache, Finster-Lisene

Why "speech" for *Sprache,* instead of "language"? I would respect the source of *Sprache* in *sprechen,* "speak," and also bring out the influence of Buber, who made speech that act by which we identify all our realities. Since the next image describes *Sprache* as something bordering or buttressing the dark, I think Celan meant it as language in use, in action—that is, speech.

As to *Finster-Lisene,* he invented the term and had never used *Lisene* before. In Romanesque architecture, *Lisene* denotes a pilaster strip, a semiprojecting column that buttresses, and later mainly decorates, the corner of a building. *Lisene* derives from French *lisière,* "list, selvedge," a woven edge that keeps fabric from unraveling and thus by extension a margin or frontier. That figurative sense of speech as an ultimate stay against dissolution fits Celan's image, yet he loved the precise and highly unusual names of things, probably because they were not spoiled, not abused by any usage other than their own.

So if I translate *Lisene* at all familiarly, I am prying Celan away from the difficult purity he elected. He craved yet in his way resisted being understood. Still I myself dearly want him understood, and reluctantly, wrongly, I abandon the architectural sense of *Lisene* in favor of "selvedge," derived from "self" and "edge," with overtones of "savage" and of "salvage":

> spills of mire I swallowed, inside the tower,
> speech, dark-selvedge.

And here Celan's German ends.

kumi
ori
Whatever displaces—and releases!—this final Hebrew couplet from the German poem should do the same from the English poem. Like Celan, I leave untranslated these imperatives, second-person singular, feminine, of   ("rise") and   ("shine"). In Isaiah 60, *kumi ori* proclaims a new Jerusalem, renewing the covenant and returning the exiles. Since German and English transliterate the Hebrew words   identically, Celan's gesture in closing as he does allows me the choice—I would almost say the grace—to do the same and leave *kumi ori* as is.

In several earlier poems, Celan moves at the end from German into Yiddish or Hebrew, utterly transfiguring the tone of the lyric. Possibly these moments offer him a kind of refuge. (Though what happens, I wonder, when "Du sei wie du," exposing Celan's Diaspora fate, gets translated into Hebrew?) As it is, I delight in not needing to translate the poem's final words, *kumi ori*. I see him breaking free in them, renewing his bond with them in messianic speech. After a lifetime's writing dictated by loss, here at least nothing need be lost in translation—unless the very catch of breath between German and Hebrew has its own quality, distinct from that between English and Hebrew.

Celan's audience in Germany, as he well knew, had scarcely anyone left to recognize *kumi ori*. For him, Hebrew was anything but strange. He studied it as a child, after his parents' death used to recall the beauty of the language, kept a Hebrew Bible on his bookshelf in Paris, and in Jerusalem in 1969, recited Bialik to Yehuda Amichai.

In Jerusalem, Celan renewed contact with a woman he'd known when they were young in Czernovitz, and who had emigrated after the war. He wrote out "Du sei wie du" for this friend, and recently when I visited her, she gave me a photocopy. Only later, on the plane, as I was staring at this paper, did I notice that Celan had written the two closing words not in transliterated form, as the published version has them, but in a perfectly natural Hebrew script. Perhaps he could write the words that way only there, for someone in Jerusalem.

Not, anyway, for his postwar German public, who must find the Hebrew in this poem legible, barely legible and audible. Although he could expect precious few to understand *kumi ori*, I think that not only printers' limitations kept Celan from setting the words in Hebrew characters. His listener must have something at least to wonder at, and should (in a utopian world) feel spurred to seek the source.

From modern to medieval German, then back out of all this toward a yet deeper source, reversing the process of translation as if of history itself, Celan comes finally upon words that were there to begin with. "Du sei wie du," as it closes, renews, a circle, a meridian from Isaiah's
through Jerome's *Surge illuminare* to Eckhart's *Stant vp Jherosalem* and then around to the poet's (I hope also the translator's) *kumi ori*—a circle broken by the slashed bond knotted anew, the mired mouth surviving.

The Poetry of Ingeborg Bachmann:
A Primeval Impulse
in the Modern Wasteland

James K. Lyon

Ingeborg Bachmann, one of the most widely respected of recent German poets, has published two slender volumes of poetry said to be a happy fusion of traditional and modern elements. While affinities with Trakl or Hölderlin or the central line of German confessional poetry become apparent immediately, Bachmann's poems are neither fully intelligible nor meaningful unless one studies her in the light of the modern tradition to which she actually belongs.

Basic to this modern tradition is what Walther Killy calls the "private mythology" each writer constructs through his use of images. Images and symbols no longer contain "das Allgemeine" that Goethe's classical definition requires. Though remnants of traditional meaning can and do cling to them, modern poets such as Bachmann more frequently use images in a manner that has meaning only within their private mythological systems. Occasionally one can refer to traditional usage of images to understand them; generally, however, one must think of them as hieroglyphs or ciphers in a code which can only be deciphered in relation to the writer's whole private poetic world.

Several implications of this fact underlie the present study. The first implication is that no single poem of a writer can be fully apprehended without reference to everything else he has written. Another implication suggests that apparently unrelated images might be used by the writers to symbolize an identical motif, while identical images might have totally different meanings in different poems. A third implication is that poetic imagery as well as other structural devices given to obsessive repetition in a poet's work can help unlock the centre of his poetic vision.

From *German Life and Letters* 17, no. 3 (April 1964). © 1964 by Basil Blackwell Publishers Ltd.

Holthusen's essay *Kämpfender Sprachgeist: die Lyrik Ingeborg Bachmanns* has done the most to make Bachmann's private poetic world accessible. He uses the term "panegyric" and "elegiac" consciousness to describe the basic tension between hope and despair or joy and anguish found in the fabric of nearly every poem. The present study proposes to examine several recurrent image clusters in her poetry and to demonstrate how Bachmann uses them within this visionary poetic world to express either of these two basic attitudes.

In her private mythology one finds images of night, darkness, evening, rain, fog and clouds used almost exclusively as constructs for the despairing, elegiac consciousness. They nearly always fulfil a limiting or oppressive function, e.g. hindering speech, killing feeling, limiting perception and obscuring understanding. Other images of ice, snow, cold, winter, stone or a barren landscape reinforce this attitude. Bachmann despairs at the state of the modern world and modern man. Her poems are often commentaries on our time, sometimes criticizing, sometimes identifying with, sometimes trying to gain distance from it. Nearly every use of an image listed above can be related to this outlook.

In her first volume, *Die gestundete Zeit*, she refers to the symbolic coldness of the modern age:

> In den Zeitungen lese ich viel von der Kälte
> und ihren Folgen, von Törichten und Toren,
> von Vertriebenen, Mördern und Myriaden
> von Eisschollen, aber wenig, was mir behagt.

In volume two, images of what one might call a "modern ice age" increase in frequency and clarity. *Von einem Land, einem Fluss und den Seen* is a cycle describing the life cycle of one person and simultaneously the historical process which has led this figure symbolizing mankind into the modern ice age. Night, here personified as a huge oppressive being surrounding man, charts man's present condition but obscures for him all goals or purpose:

> Sie [die Nacht] schlägt den Erdplan auf, verschweigt die
>   Ziele;
> sie trägt die Zeit als eine Eiszeit ein,
> die Schotterstege über die Moränen,
> den Weg zu Grauwack und zu Kreidestein.
> . . . .
> Ins Schwemmland führt die Nacht. Es schwemmt uns
>   wieder
> ins Kellerland der kalten neuen Zeit.
> So such im Höhlenbild den Traum von Menschen!
> Die Schneehuhnfeder steck dir an das Kleid.

Glacial imagery suggests both the coldness and the hardness of a barren, benighted age. Either the night, or glacial ice, or perhaps both have dropped man in this alluvial wasteland, apparently a reference to being cast into existence in an unsheltered, cold age. Yet with the inexorability of a moving glacier, man is carried even farther in the "Kellerland der kalten neuen Zeit." To this point the poet has spoken of mankind collectively in the first person singular. The admonition in the final lines directed to a single person, perhaps the poetess herself (one might also read: "Thou, O man"), represents the panegyric consciousness which holds hope for man if he but returns to primeval existence. More will be said later about these lines.

Nearly all images of ice, snow and cold represent similar muting, stultifying, restricting elements in life. The poem "Curriculum Vitae" describes a winter landscape where a sled decorated with the events of recent history races past the speaker:

> Nicht dass ich schlief: wach war ich,
> zwischen Eisskeletten sucht' ich den Weg,
> kam heim, wand mir Efeu
> um Arm und Bein und weisste
> mit Sonnenresten die Ruinen.

Life here has been a quest for a path laid between "ice skeletons," perhaps insensitive modern men or perhaps rigid social forms. Again, the last lines represent the panegyric consciousness mollifying the despair. Ivy traditionally had mystical healing powers. Might these lines mean an attempt to heal the "remnants" of an injured self from the wounds of the age? "Sonnenresten" ties in closely with light imagery Bachmann uses so often to dispel the darkness connected with despair, and such a reading also is reinforced by the following stanzas. Numerous other passages use imagery of the modern ice age. One final example comes from the title story of her prose collection *Das dreissigste Jahr* (Munich, 1961):

> Ich bin zornig von einen Zorn, der nicht Anfang und Ende hat.
> Mein Zorn, der von einer frühen Eiszeit herrührt und sich gegen
> die eisige Zeit jetzt wendet.

Bachmann writes more poems on the love theme than any other type. Yet love, too, has become a victim of the modern age, as repeated imagery of snow, ice and cold testify. The impossibility of communication or enduring reciprocal feeling between lovers characterizes this age. The well-known poem "Nebelland," which is set in winter, illustrates the kinship of fog imagery with ice and snow. All represent the same forlorn attitude. The poem is an anguished cry lamenting love that has grown cold. Here as elsewhere Bachmann uses animal imagery to portray lovers. The lost lover is described as a fish, while the beloved says:

> [hier] steh ich am Ufer und seh,
> bis mich Schollen vertreiben.

The ice floes which make life in the beloved's presence intolerable also represent the condition described in the final lines where the joy of love has been supplanted by a benumbed, inarticulate sense of desolation:

> Nebelland hab ich gesehen,
> Nebelherz hab ich gegessen.

The taste of love has helped induce the present wretched, lonely state.

Though not a love poem, "Mein Vogel" also uses fog to symbolize the devastated modern landscape just as snow and ice do elsewhere. Critics have called attention to the wasteland theme which opens this poem ("die verheerte Welt"). Here a bird, the poet's "Beistand des Nachts" symbolizing her creative gift, flies to her through the night and fog of this wasteland. The bird's feather is her "Waffe" against the modern age. The bird itself, an owl, recalls the companion attending Minerva, goddess of wisdom.

Another group of images belonging to the same broad category and fulfilling a similar function includes sand and stone. One hears of lovers who, after losing the momentary joy, lament:

> Wir werden beisammen liegen,
> . . . .
> mit einem Steingefühl.

The fourth poem in the cycle *Von einem Land, einem Fluss und den Seen* describes both the joy of love and yet the impossibility of communication or unity of feeling between lovers:

> Und niemand sag ich, was du mir bedeutest—
> die sanfte Taube einem rauhen Stein!

A poem published separately entitled "Liebe: dunkler Erdteil" depicts love as a "dark continent" with a black panther as its king. The symbolic internal landscape alternates between jungle growth and scorching, barren sands, the latter representing suffering under the oppression of love.

For Bachmann, love is a cyclical progression from one love to another which never ceases. *Lieder auf der Flucht*, which deals with this flight from love to love, uses a number of images familiar from previous examples. At the outset desolation has "frozen" man:

> Ich aber liege allein
> im Eisverhau voller Wunden.
> . . . .
> Niemand liebt mich und hat
> für mich eine Lampe geschwungen.

Later in the cycle summer dispels winter. Now love appears as an inversion of the familiar stone imagery, for it is molten stone where the intense heat of the love experience has fused separate identity and feeling into a fluid:

> Eingeweiht in die Liebe
> aber erst hier—
> als die Lava herabfuhr
> und ihr Hauch uns traf

am Fuss des Berges,
als zuletzt der erschöpfte Krater
den Schlüssel preisgab
für diese verschlossenen Körper—.

Still later when the stone cools and the lovers regain their individual identity which separates them, love is extinguished:

O Liebe, die unsre Schalen
aufbrach und fortwarf, unseren Schild,
den Wetterschutz und braunen Rost von Jahren!

O Leiden, die unsre Liebe austraten,
ihr feuchtes Feuer in den fühlenden Teilen!
Verqualmt, verendend im Qualm, geht die Flamme in sich.

The oxymoron "feuchtes Feuer" suggests tears and fire combining to form the steam or smoke which envelopes the lover in obscurity. This steam or smoke which remains is another familiar image of desolation related to ice, cold, fog, stone and sand which symbolize barrenness, isolation, inability to perceive or feel, and suffering attendant on love ("Liebesleiden"). Here it corresponds closely to the "Nebelherz" which the deserted love in "Nebelland" still tasted. This condition is the inescapable consequence of having loved.

Despite the frequency of these negative image clusters, Bachmann's love poetry also manifests a strong panegyric impulse. A poem such as "Erklär mir, Liebe" laments man's inability to find love, but it also praises love so strongly that one critic calls it "ein Lobgesang mit schmerzverzerrten Lippen." For Bachmann, love represents one of man's great primeval experiences. "Tage in Weiss" fuses the panegyric and elegiac impulses to illustrate the anguish and joy arising simultaneously from love:

In diesen Tagen steh ich auf mit den Birken
und kämm mir das Weizenhaar aus der Stirn
vor einem Spiegel aus Eis.

Mit meinem Atem vermengt,
flockt die Milch.
So früh schäumt sie leicht.
Und wo ich die Scheibe behauch, erscheint,
von einem kindlichen Finger gemalt,
wieder dein Name: Unschuld!
Nach so langer Zeit.

In diesen Tagen schmerzt mich nicht,
dass ich vergessen kann
und mich erinnern muss.

Ich liebe. Bis zur Weissglut
liebe ich und danke mit englischen Grüssen.
Ich hab sie im Fluge erlernt.

In diesen Tagen denk ich des Albatros',
mit dem ich mich auf-
und herüberschwang
in ein unbeschriebenes Land.

Am Horizont ahne ich,
glanzvoll im Untergang,
meinen fabelhaften Kontinent
dort drüben, der mich entliess
im Totenhemd.

Ich lebe und höre von fern seinen Schwanengesang.

Again this poem portrays the condition of love which dies as it flourishes.
This explains both the "days in white," i.e. snow and cold surrounding
the love, and the mirror of ice, i.e. reflection on or recall of dying passion.
The frost which the breath of lovers forms on the window evokes a frequent
motif in Bachmann's poetry: nostalgia for a primeval state of child-like
innocence, a condition prior to the guilt incurred through love and human
existence generally. Stanza three suggests that while the memory of love
lingers, one must forget in order to live, though this, too, is impossible.
Somehow the coldness of desolation brought on by love has a pain-killing
effect which makes recollection bearable.

"Weissglut" is an interesting word play on the white-hot passion of
love and the coldness which surrounds this relationship. "Englische
Grüsse" is difficult to interpret, but it might be the archaic use of this word
meaning "angelic" to portray the exalted feeling love brings. The albatross
in the following stanza, another use of white imagery, supports this reading, for love has been an exalted flight into an "undescribed" or "indescribable" land.

The concept of "land" here is fundamental to the primeval experience
of man. It is "das für die menschliche Existenz Grundlegende." Repeatedly
Bachmann's poems and prose represent someone leaving one land and
fleeing into another. It is even the central theme in the two long cycles,
Von einem Land, einem Fluss und den Seen and *Lieder auf der Flucht*. Here flight
into this land as a symbol for the love experience is but one phase of a
constant progression of journeys. For Bachmann they ultimately lead back
to the "fabled continent" of the penultimate stanza, the primordial condition similar to the child-like innocence in stanza two. The love experience
awakens her nostalgia for this condition from whence she came into a land
of death, i.e. contemporary existence.

In "Curriculum Vitae" flight from one land to another signifies the
essence of meaningful existence:

> In einer grosspurigen Zeit
> muss man rasch von einem Licht
> ins andere gehen, von einem Land
> in andere . . .

Light imagery, a sharp contrast to the darkness seen so often over the desolate landscape of the modern ice age, refers to the primeval condition man might attain. In order to regain it, one must move constantly to new experiences such as love. Whereas enduring love leads to isolation, barrenness and silence, each new love experience brings man in contact again with the elemental situation of primordial human life.

Poem 4 in the cycle *Von einem Land, einem Fluss und den Seen* describes lovers who have just experienced the power of love as a primeval experience:

> Wir kamen in das Land mit seinen Quellen.
> Urkunden fanden wir. Das ganze Land,
> so grenzenlos und so geliebt, war unser.

Poem 5 of this cycle then points out why love is the primordial experience. Man has set up barriers against man and isolated himself in the modern ice age. Love, temporarily at least, transcends these barriers; it is "grenzenlos":

> Wo anders sinkt der Schlagbaum auf den Pässen;
> hier wird ein Gruss getauscht, ein Brot geteilt.
>
> . . . .
>
> Wir aber wollen über Grenzen sprechen,
> und gehn auch Grenzen noch durch jedes Wort:
> wir werden sie vor Heimweh überschreiten
> und dann im Einklang stehn mit jedem Ort.

Significantly "Heimweh" here is the power which enables lovers to shatter the barriers of speech. This nostalgia for the primeval condition is inherent in love. Love may not endure, but while it does it comprises an experience reminiscent of primordial innocence and joy.

When the panegyric consciousness prevails and love or poetry are praised as aspects of primitive human experience, a totally different cluster of images is used. Sunlight either supplants or dominates over darkness, while warmth, summer, water, plant growth and images related to childhood or primitivism appear in greater frequency. *Lieder auf der Flucht* illustrate the interplay of these images of hope with the antitheses. The cycle progresses from desolation of winter and ice to new love symbolized by summer weather and hot lava. As passion cools, wasteland imagery reappears, and the subsequent suffering is attended by smoke and ice. Poem 14 depicts the joyous song of love which escapes again as the ice melts and its water renews the wasteland. But this is not the only song of love—it is the poet's song of joy:

> Die Liebe hat einen Triumph und der Tod hat einen,
> die Zeit und die Zeit danach.
> Wir haben keinen.
>
> Nur Sinken um uns von Gestirnen. Abglanz und Schweigen.
> Doch das Lied überm Staub danach
> wird uns übersteigen.

Love's triumph is as temporary as death's. Neither has permanence; only the poetic song which springs from the primordial experience of love has immortality.

For Bachmann poetry is the most basic primeval act, while love, one means of experiencing the primeval state of mind, nourishes this creative sensibility. Earlier a poem urged a man to escape the modern ice age:

> So such im Höhlenbild den Traum von Menschen!
> Die Schneehuhnfeder steck dir an das Kleid.

The act of making one's vision of mankind a primeval vision refers to the primitive impulse one must cultivate to write poetry. The feather recalls "Mein Vogel," a poem about the poetic gift, where the writer identifies the bird as ". . . mein Waffe, mit jener Feder besteckt, meiner einzigen Waffe!" This archetype of a writing instrument apparently has the same meaning in the verses above. They exhort the poet to commit himself to the primeval act of poetic speech in order to escape the modern wasteland.

The poem "Landnahme" illustrates most clearly the primeval impulse which motivates Bachmann to resist or escape the modern ice age:

> Ins Weideland kam ich,
> als es schon Nacht war,
> in den Wiesen die Narben witternd
> und den Wind, eh er sich regte.
> Die Liebe graste nicht mehr,
> die Glocken waren verhallt
> und die Büschel verhärmt.
>
> Ein Horn stak im Land,
> vom Leittier verrannt,
> ins Dunkel gerammt.
>
> Aus der Erde zog ich's,
> zum Himmel hob ich's
> mit ganzer Kraft.
>
> Um dieses Land mit Klängen
> ganz zu erfüllen,
> stiess ich ins Horn,
> willens im kommenden Wind
> und unter den wehenden Halmen
> jener Herkunft zu leben!

This deceptively difficult poem refers to taking possession of a piece of land for purposes of cultivation or inhabitation. It is a variation on the theme of progression from land to land as the basic human experience. The benighted landscape and the desolation wrought by a "love animal" which previously grazed there (the meadows have been denuded by grazing, leaving only clumps or tufts of grass in the soil) announce the familiar wasteland theme. When the speaker enters the land it is already night; love no longer flourishes in the landscape symbolizing existence.

One remnant of the "love animal," however, remains: its horn. Though not specifically identified, the "lead animal" of the herd which overgrazed this land and left only this trace is most probably love, as the first stanza suggests. The poet's act of raising the horn, blowing and creating the most primitive form of music symbolizes the primeval nature of the poetic calling. This primitive instrument corresponds to the feather which was described in "Mein Vogel" as a "weapon." Once the horn, too, functioned as an animal's weapon; now the same weapon also serves to create poetic sound. Thus love has contributed to the creation of poetry by providing the instrument.

The final stanza summarizes Bachmann's attitude towards the poetic calling in modern life better than any other single poem. It describes a posture of defiance, or resistance, of the will not only to endure future uncertainty ("Wind"), but to do something to change it. Her office is to fill the land completely with sound. If she follows this primeval impulse, she can transform the modern wasteland.

Though the acute awareness in Bachmann's poetry of a bleak modern age prevents it from being called "utopian," its recurrent note of hope, joy and praise sets it apart from much contemporary German verse. The panegyric strain evident in her imagery testifies how well she has held the balance against despair and disillusion so prevalent among her contemporaries.

Doppelgänger Motif and Two-Voiced Poem in the Works of Hans Magnus Enzensberger

William S. Sewell

Although the term "Doppelgänger" appears explicitly in only one of Enzensberger's poems—"gewimmer und firmament"—it has been seized upon by Dieter Schlenstedt in two articles as being a major key to "das Wesen des lyrischen Ichs Hans Magnus Enzensbergers." The "Doppelgänger" figure which Schlenstedt discovers in the volume *landessprache*, in the poems "der gefangene" and "der schlafende schlosser," as well as in "gewimmer und firmament," is said to represent the poet's direct or indirect involvement in an arid commercialized world and his humanistic rebellion against it ("Aufschrei und Unbehagen"). But his interpretation of this literary persona as it appears in its most distinct form in "lachesis lapponica," from the later volume *blindenschrift*, goes one step further: "[das Bild vom Doppelgänger] entspricht dem Zwiespalt zwischen bürgerlicher Existenz und humanem Anspruch, dem Zwiespalt auch zwischen dem Wunsch nach Aktivität und der Erfolglosigkeit der Bemühungen." Here the dimension of the conflict between political action and political resignation is added, a conflict which has in fact pervaded Enzensberger's poetry from the very outset. For on the one hand Enzensberger is clearly a committed poet, concerned with "die politische Alphabetisierung Deutschlands," who as Germany's first Angry Young Man attempted to alert his readers to grave deficiencies in the Federal Republic of Germany and indeed the world at large; and who, on seeing the situation deteriorate, went so far as to advocate revolutionary solutions. On the other hand, there have always been signs in his poetry that all political activity is a Sisyphean labor, doomed from the start, that those he is attempting to "alphabeticize" are worthy only of bitter contempt, that the poet's sole remaining course is to withdraw

From *The German Quarterly* 52, no. 1 (January 1979). © 1979 by the American Association of Teachers of German.

into a solipsistic exile. It is the purpose of the present article, therefore, not only to demonstrate that this conflict lies at the heart of Enzensberger's use of the "Doppelgänger" motif—and of the related two-voiced structure—but also to conduct a rather deeper investigation of the phenomenon than Schlenstedt and others have attempted.

It was Jean Paul who originated the term "Doppelgänger" (originally "Doppeltgänger") in the novel known by its abbreviated title, *Siebenkäs*, and the motif subsequently became a popular feature of German Romantic literature and eventually of European literature in general, found not only in the stories of E. T. A. Hoffmann (*Die Elixiere des Teufels*), for example, but also in Dostoevsky's *The Double*, Maupassant's *Le Horla*, and R. L. Stevenson's *The Strange Case of Doctor Jekyll and Mr Hyde*. Perhaps because of its wide application, however, there are a number of distinctions that need to be made when considering the "Doppelgänger" as a literary device. In order to make these distinctions, it is necessary to draw to some extent on the terminology of psychoanalysis.

The notion of an individual having a double or multiple nature is not peculiar to literature or to psychoanalysis: it appears to be a universal human phenomenon, finding its expression in the body-soul dichotomy, Man's dualistic tendencies towards good and evil (reflected in the function of the Devil as the evil opposite of God), and in the superstitions connected with mirrors and shadows. This phenomenon was given a scientific application by Freud who insisted that the "division of the psychical into what is conscious and what is unconscious is the fundamental premise of psychoanalysis." Psychoanalysts have also recognized that the single components of the psyche may become split or fragmented from each other: this process is known as fragmentation or "decomposition." In a literary context, such "decomposition" may be implicit or explicit. If it is implicit, the splitting is expressed in a subtle form, not openly acknowledged by the author; whereas, in explicit fragmentation, the double is overtly identified by the author as a dissociation of personality. A second distinction is to be made between "subjective" and "objective" doubling, where the former is associated with conflicts within an individual, the latter with an individual's conflicting attitudes towards others. Finally, one must discriminate between a situation in which the "Doppelgänger" appears in a "subjective-realistic" capacity, issuing from the subconscious self, and in a symbolic guise as an expression of the "complex and disharmonious nature of man."

What is possibly the closest literary antecedent to Enzensberger's adoption of the "Doppelgänger" motif—the man with the axe in caputs 6 and 7 of Heine's *Deutschland. Ein Wintermärchen*—has already been pointed out by Schlenstedt:

> Verschwunden ist der vorher noch mögliche aktive Held (vergleichbar dem Doppelgänger in Heines *Wintermärchen*, der mit

dem Richtbeil dem Dichter folgte); geblieben ist die Ausglie-
derung aus der Gessellschaft, Gleichgültigkeit und Passivität als
Alternative.

("Die schwierige Arbeit des Hans Magnus Enzensberger")

However, a brief consideration of Heine's version will enable us to determine in what precise sense we may expect Enzensberger to make use of
the device. Heine pokes much fun at his literary contemporaries in the
Wintermärchen. Owing to its frequent and popular use in the Romantic
literature of which Heine became so wary, we can assume that there is an
element of satirical intent in his inclusion of the "Doppelgänger" in his
poem. But there is a more serious purpose to Heine's "schwarzer, ver-
mummter Begleiter": he compensates for a character deficiency in the poet;
he is "von praktischer Natur," the complementary active side to a man
content with the world of thought:

> Und gehn auch Jahre drüber hin,
> Ich raste nicht, bis ich verwandle
> In Wirklichkeit, was du gedacht;
> Du denkst, und ich, ich handle.

This shadow with the "Richtbeil," then, is a counterpart to Heine's reluc-
tance to submit himself wholeheartedly to a political cause. Its insertion in
the poem also reveals Heine's thorough recognition of his own problem.
We may thus conclude that the fragmentation here is explicit, rather than
implicit, since the man with the axe is openly acknowledged as a dissociated
part of the poet's personality, though not in any pathological sense; that
by the same token the function of Heine's "Doppelgänger" is largely symbolic; and that the doubling that takes place here is of the "subjective"
variety, since it arises from an internal conflict. As will become apparent,
Enzensberger's "Doppelgänger" fulfills an essentially similar role.

The double in Enzensberger's poems does not have a consistent shape.
It is variously referred to as "mein schatten," "mein feind . . . mein bruder," "der hund," "ein mann mit löwenhänden," "der schlafende schlosser," "der andere," and "der vogel in meinem kopf." Only in one poem
does he make direct use of the word "Doppelgänger," not in its customary
singular form, but in the plural: "meine doppelgänger." Notwithstanding
the frequent change in appearance, such "Doppelgänger" may be said to
operate in a more or less explicit fashion; but there is another group of
poems in which the "Doppelgänger's" presence is registered only in the
structure of the poem. These poems are most conveniently classified as
"two-voiced," because they involve a clearly indicated dialogue situation.
Although it is more usually confined to drama and prose fiction, the use
of dialogue in poetry is scarely an innovation on Enzensberger's part. When
employed in poetry it tends to add a certain dramatic tension and is thus
particularly suited to conveying a state of inner conflict, as well as to the

ballad-type poem, which traditionally includes a dramatic, as well as a narrative element. The ballad as such will not concern us further here, but as far back as the Middle High German period we are provided with an excellent example of a dialogue poem which conveys inner tension: Walther von der Vogelweide's "Vrô Welt, ir sult dem wirte sagen. . . . " The tension in this case is between worldly temptations and heavenly redemption, and the dialogue takes place on a symbolic level, that is, the poet projects one side of his conflict onto an allegorical figure, "Vrô Welt," whom he then engages in conversation. That the "Vrô Welt" figure is herself two-sided in medieval thought, complicates the issue even further. A more recent example of this structure may be taken from Enzensberger's own *Museum der modernen Poesie* , in a poem by Constantine Cavafy entitled "Die Stadt." Here a "Doppelgänger" is apparent only in the two-voiced shape of the poem: each of the two strophes is governed from the perspective of the "ich," which quotes in the first strophe a lengthy utterance of the "du," and in the second comments directly on this utterance. The tension arises between the desire of the "du" to escape to another environment and start afresh, and the prediction of the "ich" that escape will afford no solutions.

Enzensberger's dialogue poems are for the most part independent of those poems of his in which the "Doppelgänger" is present in its own right, although both fulfil similar functions. There is, however, one outstanding exception where the two are combined: the poem "lachesis lapponica." Before this poem is subjected to a detailed examination, we shall follow separately the development of the individual strands, "Doppelgänger" motif and two-voiced poem, up to the point of their combination and beyond.

verteidigung der wölfe contains two poems which come into question as vehicles for the "Doppelgänger": both are examples of "objective" doubling, since they concern the poet's attitude to others—although this may in turn reflect his own divided situation. "hôtel fraternité" is a picture of deprivation and despair, conjured up in the first strophe by a series of relative clauses which are seemingly independent of any main clause:

> der kein geld hat um sich eine insel zu kaufen
> der vor dem kino wartet auf die königin von saba
> der sein letztes hemd zerreisst vor zorn und trauer . . .

In the second strophe the subject of the poem and thus of the absent main clause is suddenly revealed in the paradoxical combination "mein feind . . . mein bruder," who communicates with the lyrical self through the medium of the eyes: "die augen auf mich gerichtet." The conflict element arises in "mein feind . . . mein bruder," which seems to echo the phrase "stinkender bruder" from a poem of the same vintage, "an einen mann in der trambahn." In this latter poem, Enzensberger's loathing and contempt of the man in the street is uttered: in "hôtel fraternité" fear and distance are still present, but the fact that the poem ends with the statement "mein bruder" indicates a measure of rapprochement. The rapprochement, however, has not yet reached the stage where a complete identification can be made, as in a later poem which will be discussed separately, "der andere," where the other is merged with the lyrical self: "der andere . . . das bin ich." The other in "hôtel fraternité" is a "Doppelgänger" only by virtue of its dogged ubiquitousness:

> mein feind
> hockt auf den simsen
> auf dem bett auf dem schrank
> überall auf dem fussboden . . .

and the poem is included in this discussion only because it represents an earlier stage in the development of the phenomenon in Enzensberger's work. "rast und gedanken" uses the figure of the shadow ("mein schatten und ich") to embody a decaying past:

> meine liebe rostet im kalten gebirg
> mein gesell ist in der zisterne verdurstet
> meine freundschaft unters geröll gekommen . . .

a past which is still part of the poet, if only in a dissociated form. His attitude towards it is therefore one of acceptance:

> wärmen wir uns, mein schatten und ich
> und trinken wir derer
> die nicht mehr dürsten
> finsteren wein

In this poem the shadow has the rare opportunity to operate in harmony with the lyrical self.

In *landessprache* the figure of "niemand," which haunts a good half of the volume ("oden an niemand"), takes on qualities of the "Doppelgänger," particularly in "schaum," when in its closing stages the poet expresses the desire to detach himself from the civilized world, exclaiming: "ich bin keiner von uns! ich bin niemand!" Since the detachment from the collective "uns" is impossible, the poet is compelled to substitute a "niemand" representing a projection of his unattainable wish to opt out, while he himself must remain involved in a world abhorrent to him. Another type of "Doppelgänger" with a marked similarity to Heine's dark companion is evident for the first time in the same volume: in "dies ist der hund" the poet describes a dog which "jaulend sprang mit mir aus dem mutterleib," an odious creature incorporating an evil, repugnant, but equally *active* side of his nature. It, too, is referred to as a "schatten," and just as it accompanies the poet at his birth, so it accompanies him at his death: "und stösst mich, wie ein sterbender schatten das licht, / . . . in meine mitgeborene grube." In "der gefangene" repugnance is transformed into violence, locked up inside the poet and straining for release:

> verschüttet in meinem fleisch
> ist ein mann mit löwenhänden
> mit zarten gewaltigen augen . . .
> der atmet in meinem gebein
> und wird es zerbrechen

Schlenstedt interprets this violent alter ego rather paradoxically as "das bessere Ich, der menschliche Mensch" and links this poem with that immediately following it in *landessprache*, "der schlafende schlosser." Here the poet depicts a search, under extremely arduous conditions, for a locksmith, whose task it is to bring the poet some relief:

> dass er aufschweisse die finsternis!
> dass er die schollen sprenge!
> dass er mir öffne mein knirschendes herz!

Two things are particularly noteworthy in this poem: first, the repetition of the verb "schlafen" in its present participle form; secondly, the fact that the locksmith appears to be external to the poet, rather than incarcerated inside him, as in "der gefangene." The locksmith, then, would seem scarcely qualified to be a "Doppelgänger," were he not connected with the recurrent motif of sleep in the title. For the "lyrisches Ich" of the poem is also in a sleeping state: "schlafend wate ich in meinem kettenhemd/durch das eismeer." The likelihood is therefore that an internal search is in operation here, a search for a side to the poet's personality which has yet to be aroused. The locksmith represents an active, capable and effective character: "Die Gestalt des Schlossers ist eine Chiffre für die Figur des Helfers, von dem erhofft wird, dass er das Krumme gerade, Heilloses heil macht und die Not des Leidenden wende." A being both "zart" and "gewaltig," in the sense of "der gefangene," he is the subjective double of the poet.

The final poem in *landessprache* to include a "Doppelgänger" and the only one in Enzensberger's entire output to do so in a direct fashion is "gewimmer und firmament." Strangely though, it does not have the expected significance here. The term appears seven times in all in the course of this long poem, and refers not so much to a conflicting facet of the poet's personality as, in the sense of "hôtel fraternité," to his fellow beings. It is these external "Doppelgänger" who are responsible for the proliferation of "gewimmer" on the earth—"und schon gehn sie wimmernd/. . . meine zahllosen doppelgänger"—but since the poet is intimately bound to them and the world they inhabit, his identity is interchangeable with theirs:

> ich als nicht ich, ich
> als vollakademiker, ich als sucher
> nach transzendenz in mülleimern und in bibeln,
> ich als hausherr mit schnapstränen in den augen
> als einer, der einigermassen schläft,
> als bluthund, als privatpatient,
> als sozialdemokratischer staubsauger . . .

Such "Doppelgänger" are the antithesis of the "niemand" figure, confounding the poet's attempts to detach himself from the collective.

The influence of the Spanish poet, Juan Ramón Jiménez, is to be found in "der andere," from *blindenschrift*, where the process of dissociation is manifested in the deliberate confusion of the first and third persons singular:

> einer lacht
> kümmert sich
> hält mein gesicht mit haut und haar unter den himmel
> lässt wörter rollen aus meinem mund
>
> . . . .
>
> aber nicht ich
> ich bin der andere . . .

A similar dissociation is evident in Jiménez's "Yo no soy yo" ("Ich bin nicht ich"), which Enzensberger included in his *Museum der modernen Poesie*:

> Ich bin nicht ich.
> Ich bin jener,
> der an meiner Seite geht, ohne dass ich ihn erblicke . . .

Here the "Doppelgänger" acts in a diametrically opposed manner to the lyrical self—"Jener, der ruhig schweigt, wenn ich spreche, / der sanftmütig verzeiht, wenn ich hasse." Enzensberger establishes a parallel contrast in his poem. The lyrical self in "der andere" wishes to behave like a normal human being, but overwhelmed by a faceless, speechless and indifferent "other," lacking all human sensitivity, it is able only to observe from a distance itself performing such active functions as laughing, fighting, even worrying. The influence of "der andere" has become so dominant that the lyrical self has become dislocated from its body—now referred to in the third person as "einer"—and is beginning to lose its separate identity in the other. Perhaps we are witnessing here the eclipsing of the younger, more volatile Enzensberger by the withdrawn Norwegian exile.

There are several poems amongst Enzensberger's lyrical works which might be described as *two-voiced*. At its broadest, this term could apply to any poem of his which clearly differentiates between two or more voices. Into this category, therefore, would go poems which could only in the very remotest sense be connected with the "Doppelgänger" phenomenon. These are poems with fragments of dialogue, used illustratively rather than in a dialectical manner, such as the words of the shepherd in "für lot, einen makedonischen hirten," those of the war veterans in "konventioneller krieg" or in the snatches of telephone conversation in "Aus dem Bandarchiv eines Telefonspitzels"; or those which make use of direct quotation from outside sources, indicated often by italic print, such as the advertising jingles in "bildnis eines spitzels," the scraps of radio broadcasts in "abgelegenes haus," or the brief extracts from letters in "karl heinrich marx." In a few poems, however, italic print has been stipulated by the poet as the indicator of a second voice functioning as the mouthpiece of the poet's alter ego: it is in this sense that we shall use the term *two-voiced*.

Even though Enzensberger has recourse to italics in "telegramm-schalter null uhr zwölf," their role is not to maintain a sharp distinction between two opposed voices, but to isolate them from a third voice that comments. The poem arises out of the confrontation of a genuine human emotion with the brutal matter-of-factness of a world run on a commercial basis in which even telegrams announcing a death must be pruned to the bare outline sufficient for a commercial transaction: "hier gilt allein / die harte poetik fester tarife." Two sample telegrams are supplied in the poem, the first one being the death announcement:

> mit allen tröstungen unsrer religion
> sanft entschlafen

the second, instructions for a commercial transaction:

> dringend aufkauft malakka zinn loco
> limit zwohundertsiebzig das picul

Both are isolated from the rest of the poem by being printed in italics. Directly related to each of the telegrams are two phrases, also emphasized by italic print, "mi dulce amor," which may be associated with the emotional aspect, and "fasse dich kurz," with the financial aspect. The contours of a double are not manifest in this poem, yet a dialogue of sorts does result from the conflict of the ideal—unlimited expression of emotion—and reality—"60 pfennig pro wort nach valladolid." In another poem from *verteidigung der wölfe*, "option auf ein grundstück," a similar contrast between the real and ideal is made, the latter represented by the standard print in the first two lines of each stanza, and the former by the italics in the remaining lines. But here two voices only are present and these are kept strictly apart in the alternation of standard and italic print, and even when, as in the final stanza, the pattern is broken, the identities of the two voices are not in any way confused. The first voice expresses in elegant terms a longing for a world which is aesthetic, unmechanized and undivided:

> ich wünsche, ich wünsche mit ziegenhirten im regen zu
> > kauern
> und mich mit ballerinen und korbmachern zu besprechen

but this voice is continually interrupted by a cynical alter ego which ridicules the world sought after by the first voice by confronting it relentlessly with a less attractive world, portrayed in a harsh, contemporary, synthetic vocabulary:

> bete zu den kybernetischen göttern, erwirb
> raketen, börsenblätter und brillen

In the final stanza, however, the second voice is able to contribute only the words "saboteur!" and "feigling!" and the musings of the first voice are then allowed to continue uninterrupted to the end of the poem. As in the later poem "lachesis lapponica" it is the first voice which has the last word, and the second voice here has more than a little in common with the "vogel in meinem kopf" of the latter.

"zweifel" qualifies in essence if not in form as a two-voiced poem. The very title suggests an inner dialogue, since the process of doubt involves the interaction of two conflicting standpoints. Enzensberger does not, however, formalize the conflict here to the extent of creating two distinct voices with a more or less equal weight, preferring instead to use the device of the question directed against himself and supplemented on two occasions by the affirmative replies of what he calls "meine feinde":

> meine wünsche sind einfach.
> einfach unerfüllbar?
>
> ja, sagen meine feinde.

Such a structure provides perhaps the barest statement in Enzensberger's poetry of the altercation which gives rise to the two-voiced technique and "Doppelgänger" motif. In these three short lines we find the ideal, represented by "wünsche," reality, represented by "unerfüllbar," and the urgings of a tempter: the resigned attitude of society, represented by the "feinde." The conflict is set into motion by the poet's urge to question, his application of the principle of doubt, the necessity of viewing each proposition from more than one side.

Two poems, written subsequently to "lachesis lapponica" and numbered among the new poems of *Gedichte 1955–1970*, also show evidence of a two-voiced structure, if in a modified form. "An Niccolò Machiavelli geboren am 3. Mai 1469" is the prototype for the later ballads in *Mausoleum*, all of which share a common feature: the interpolation in greater or lesser number of quotations originating from the personage who is the subject of the ballad or from his contemporaries. Once again the change in perspective is clearly marked by italics, in the *Mausoleum* version at least. Such a structure endows the poem with an objective, documentary aspect, bringing it into contact not so much with academic methods as with those of broadcasting journalism. For the journalistic style affected in *Mausoleum* is akin to that employed in television or radio documentaries: fast-moving narrative with snippets of quotation. When, as in the case of "Niccolò Machiavelli," quotations are applied with sufficient frequency and consistency, they may also constitute a second voice in opposition to that of the poet. In this particular poem the world-weary and realistic side of the poet's internal conflict is projected on to the historical figure of Machiavelli and his political theories, thus creating the second voice, while the first voice mounts a fierce attack on his character: "Und abends die lyrische Seele: Bettelsonette

an den Gangster vom Dienst." This dialogue combined with paradox—
"Und dass deine Lügen / so oft die Wahrheit sagen . . . "—produces a tension between feelings of admiration and contempt for this Renaissance
figure, but also for the poet's own conclusions, which are admired for their
essential truth and despised for the attitude of mind they engender. Two
voices and paradox do not provide the only interesting formal features of
this poem. Close study reveals that it is divided into five segments, the
outer two of which place Machiavelli in a general context, the other three
encompassing specific periods in his life. The latter begin with the seventh
couplet ("Kleiner Krautjunker . . .") and concern his private life, the years
of power in Florence from 1498–1512 ("Keine Angst, Niccolò . . .") and his
retirement ("Zehn Jahre später die Katastrophe . . ."). The outer segments
frame the biographical details and consist of the first six and the last five
couplets: it is here that the principal interaction between the poet and
Machiavelli, alias the poet's alter ego, takes place, while the three central
segments allow Machiavelli to express himself in word and deed with less
interference from the poet. In the other poem from the same period, "Das
wirkliche Messer," the lyrical self appears to be eliminated altogether. Two
voices clash, but both are external to the lyrical self, which has no more
than observer status. However, the conflict portrayed here—between an
ideology of commitment postulated by "Der eine," using terms such as
"Der Mehrwert," "Das Proletariat und die Revolution," and the more skep-
tical, individualistic approach of "der andere," expressed in the words "Ich
liebe nur dich / und nicht alle"—may occur both externally and internally
and does not take account of numbers:

> Es waren aber Abertausend in einem Zimmer
> oder einer allein mit sich oder zwei
> und sie kämpften gegen sich miteinander . . .

It is the second of the three possibilities which is applicable to Enzensberger's own situation.

   Enzensberger does not abandon his fondness for the "Doppelgänger"
and its associated forms with "Niccolò Machiavelli" and "Das wirkliche
Messer." Although *Mausoleum*, with its almost total exclusion of the lyrical
self, obscures for the most part the expression of personal conflict, in *Der
Untergang der Titanic* Enzensberger exposes this conflict once again as one
of his major themes. It is not surprising, therefore, that the "Doppelgänger"
reappears, this time in a more explicit guise. For among other things in
this highly complex "epic" poem, Enzensberger is concerned to compare
his optimistic, politically aggressive self of ten years ago, during his Cuban
sojourn, with a resigned, slightly bitter and more mature self of the present.
Three early cantos in the poem (3, 4 and 6) clearly reveal a tension, not
only between the past and the present, but also between the differing
geographical locations of Havana and Berlin: Enzensberger contrasts "die
sonderbar leichten Tage der Euphorie," when "Es schien uns, als stünde

etwas bevor,/etwas von uns zu Erfindendes," with a cold and sober present, "Wo Europa am hässlichsten ist/. . . in der bitteren/angstvollen vaterländischen Schäbigkeit." So remote is this past from him now that his former self becomes dissociated, almost unrecognizable, and here we encounter the latest manifestation of his "Doppelgänger":

> Und jener dünne Mensch, unterwegs
> in Habana, aufgeregt, zerstreut, verwickelt in Streitereien,
> Metaphern, endlose Liebesgeschichten—war ich das
>   wirklich?
> Ich könnte es nicht beschwören . . .

"Untergang" for Enzensberger is not confined to its nautical meaning: it is also used as a universal metaphor for what he calls elsewhere the "negative Utopie," and in a personal sense it alludes to the frustration of his political ideals after his experiences in Cuba, the result of which is a radical development in personality. The most convincing evidence that the "Doppelgänger" motif and the two-voiced poem fulfil one and the same function is to be found in "lachesis lapponica," where Enzensberger identifies the second voice as belonging to "der vogel in meinem kopf" and thus recognizes it as a dissociated part of his own being:

> lachesis lapponica
>
> hier ist es hell, am rostigen wasser, nirgendwo. hier,
> das sind die grauweiden, das ist das graue gras,
> das ist der düstere helle himmel, hier stehe ich.
>
> (*das ist kein standpunkt,* sagt der vogel in meinem kopf.)
>
> hier wo ich stehe, das weisse im wind sind die moordaunen,
> sieh wie es flimmert. die leere lautlose wildnis hier ist die
>   erde.
>
> (*¡viva!* ruft der düstere vogel: (*¡viva fidel castro!*))
>
> was hat castro damit zu schaffen! (*was hast du damit zu*
>   *schaffen,*
> *mit dem wollgras, dem pfeifengras am düsteren wasser?*)
>
> nichts, ich habe nichts, vogel, hörst du? und kein vogel,
> vogel. kräht nach mir. (*das ist wahr.*) lass mich in ruhe.
> hier kämpfe ich nicht. (*es wird ein brachvogel sein.*)
> dort ist norden, dort wo es dunkel wird, siehst du,
> das moor wird sehr langsam dunkel. hier habe ich nichts,
> hier habe ich nichts zu tun. das weisse im norden
> sind seine geister, die hellen geister des moores.
>
> (*das ist kein standpunkt, das sind keine geister,*
> *das sind birken,* schreit er, *hier ist nichts los.*)

das ist gut. ich kämpfe nicht. lass mich. ich warte.

mit der zeit, sehr langsam, schält sich die rinde,
(*ich mache mir nichts daraus*) und das weisse dort,
das weisse dort unter dem weissen, siehst du,
das will ich lesen. (*und hier*, sagt er, *die genaue zeit:*
dreiundzwanzig uhr fünfzig.) hier, im rostigen moos.

ich glaube an geister (*das gibts nicht!*) leer wild lautlos.
auch ich bin ein geist. auch dieser schreiende vogel da
in meinem lautlosen kopf. (*sag das nicht.*)

wir blicken beide nach norden. mitternacht. (*am times square*
stehst du, toter, ich kenne dich, sehe dich wie du kaufst,
verkaufst und verkauft wirst, du bist es, auf dem roten platz,
auf dem kurfürstendamm, und blickst auf deine rostige uhr.)

(ein brachvogel wird es sein, oder ein regenpfeifer,
sag das nicht, schlag dir das aus dem kopf.)

ich schlag dir den kopf ab, vogel. (*es ist dein eigner.*
¡viva fidel! lieber tot als rot! mach mal pause! ban the bomb!
über alles in der welt!) sag das nicht. (*das alles bist du,*
sagt der vogel, *stell dir das vor, du bist es gewesen, du bist es.*)

wie meinst du das? (*allen ernstes*, sagt der vogel und lacht.)
ein brachvogel kann nicht lachen. (*du bist es*, sagt er,
der lacht. du wirst es bereuen. ich weiss, wer du bist,
totenkopf auf dem kurfürstendamm.) im moor.

weiss, düster, grau. hier sind keine siege.
das sind die moordaunen, das sind die grauweiden,
das ist der helle vogel am düsteren himmel.

jetzt ist es mitternacht, jetzt springt die rinde,
(*die genaue zeit:*) es ist weiss, (*null uhr zwei*)
dort im rauch, wo es dunkel wird, ist es zu lesen,
das unbeschriebene blatt. die leere lautlose wildnis.
hier ist nichts los. (*sag das nicht.*) lass mich allein.

(*bist du einverstanden, totenkopf, bist du tot?*
ist es ein regenpfeifer? *wenn du nicht tot bist,*
worauf wartest du noch?) ich warte. ich warte.

es ist am äussersten rand dieser fläche, sumpfgras,
wollgras, pfeifengras, wo es schon düster ist, vogel,
(*wie meinst du das?*) siehst du? die weisse schrift?

(*feigling*, sagt er, *machs gut. wir sprechen uns noch.*)
lass mich im unbeschriebenen. (*totenkopf.*)

sieh wie es flimmert. (und der düstere vogel
in meinem kopf sagt zu sich selber: *er schläft, also ist er
einverstanden.*)
                    aber ich schlafe nicht.

This poem, as Enzensberger informs us in a note at the end of *blin-denschrift*, takes its title from Carl von Linné's account, also entitled *Lachesis Lapponica*, of an expedition to Lapland undertaken in 1732, and published posthumously in 1811. The link with Linné is established in the first instance by the setting of the poem—"die leere lautlose wildnis," the northern wastes—and by the precision in the wildlife terminology that one might expect from such a meticulous classifier as the Swedish naturalist: "woll-gras," "pfeifengras," "sumpfgras," "brachvogel," "regenpfeifer." The reader is also given some hint in the note as to the significance of "lachesis": this is the name of one of the three classical fates, the one who distributes the thread of life, as opposed to Klotho who spins it and Atropos who determines its span. That the lyrical self is not prepared to resist any external influences (what we may broadly call "Fate")—in contrast to the *internal* influence of the "vogel in meinem kopf" with whom it does contend, if somewhat distractedly—is borne out by such utterances as "hier kämpfe ich nicht," "hier habe ich nichts zu tun" and "ich warte." The situation of the lyrical self in this poem is perhaps made clearer by citing three lines from a poem in the same volume, "ufer," which is set against a similar isolated background:

                am anderen ufer, im grauen morgen
                entscheidet sich wer ich bin
                in einem rauch.

It is the preoccupation of several of the poems in *blindenschrift* that Fate, or more specifically the course of political events, is remote, obscure and out of the hands of the individual; and they record the tension which results from this realization, a tension between an attitude of acceptance and one of considerable disquiet.

In "lachesis lapponica" the lyrical self has accepted this condition and withdrawn from the sphere of human activity to an environment almost totally devoid of human traces. So bare is this environment that the poet is compelled to describe it and his existence there in predominantly negative terms: it is "nirgendwo," "leer" and "lautlos," he possesses nothing, is unoccupied ("hier habe ich nichts, / hier habe ich nichts zu tun."), is unre-sisting ("hier kämpfe ich nicht"). Even the colors of the surroundings are not of the vivid kind, but are without distinction: "weiss," "grau," "hell," "düster." These colors and shades of light and dark underline the empty and negative quality of the landscape, white in particular: "Da Weiss ja eigentlich keine Farbe ist, sondern als das Fehlen jeder Farbe gedeutet werden kann, haftet dem Motiv von vornherein etwas Negierendes an."

It would indeed be a fitting landscape for that "negated" human being in *landessprache*, the "niemand" figure. But despite this state of deficiency, there is one decisive advantage which this landscape holds for the lyrical self, a fact expressed in the cliché "das unbeschriebene blatt." The negative side of whiteness becomes the positive virtue of purity, that which is in its original, untouched state. The world has been reduced to a minimum of variables—"die leere lautlose wildnis hier ist die erde"—and it seems as if the lyrical self is waiting ("ich warte") for some positive development to arise out of these modest beginnings.

The situation of the lyrical self is an unnatural one, however; total isolation causes strange behaviour in human beings, and an irritating companion identified as "der vogel in meinem kopf" materializes. The German expression "er hat einen Vogel" signifies eccentricity or an obsession in an individual: in this instance the "vogel" has the task of interrupting the lyrical self's flow of thought and peace of mind, with continual intrusions, questions and reminders of the world from which the lyrical self has attempted to escape. It is realistic where the lyrical self is romantic—"ich glaube an geister (*das gibts nicht!*)"—precise where the lyrical self is vague:

> jetzt ist es mitternacht, jetzt springt die rinde,
> (*die genaue zeit:*) es ist weiss, (*null uhr zwei*)

It also appears to be a habitual companion, not one who emerges only for the duration of the poem, because it is referred to as "*der* vogel in meinem kopf" from the outset, and not "*ein* vogel in meinem kopf," suggesting some measure of familiarity. Initially, the second voice is ignored, but after enduring the irrelevancy of the slogan "*viva fidel castro!*", the lyrical self feels goaded into retorting "was hat castro damit zu schaffen!", provoking a counter-retort from the "vogel": "(*was hast du damit zu schaffen . . . ?*)." Thus a dialogue of sorts results, which is not wholeheartedly pursued by the lyrical self. Although it does attempt to bring the "weisse schrift" to the notice of the second voice, it appears to be more concerned with the developments in the external situation than with what is taking place inside its head. It is, however, once aggravated to the point of anger, in the threat "ich schlag dir den kopf ab, vogel." And although the lyrical self tries to dismiss the second voice as a particular species of bird, either a "regenpfeifer" or a "brachvogel," a note of uncertainty creeps in as to its origin in the realization: "ein brachvogel kann nicht lachen." This indicates an incipient awareness in the lyrical self that the existence of the "vogel" is very closely tied up with its own.

Schlenstedt is correct in commenting that "Die Übertreibungen des Vogels lassen es nun allerdings als unglaublich erscheinen, dass er, der Doppelgänger, eine wirkliche Alternative des quietistischen wie des zeitlichen Ichs sein könnte . . ." ("Die schwierige Arbeit des Hans Magnus Enzensberger"); but this impertinent second voice does perform the important task of throwing into doubt the passive isolation of the lyrical self by confronting it with elements of the populated world. These elements relate principally to a political context, in the slogans *"viva fidel! lieber tot als rot! ban the bomb! über alles in der welt!"* and the inclusion of geographical locations which allude to political power or points of tension: Times Square in New York, Red Square in Moscow and the Kurfürstendamm in West Berlin. The lyrical self is placed in these surroundings by the second voice, not in an effective capacity, but as a "toter" or "totenkopf" (*"totenkopf auf dem kurfürstendamm"*), the inference being that the present inactivity of the lyrical self is in a political sense tantamount to death, a logical consequence of the slogan *"lieber tot als rot!"* In "option auf ein grundstück" the second voice addresses the first voice as "feigling," for hankering after an ideal world. Here the second voice repeats this accusation and prepares to abandon for the present the lyrical self "(*machs gut. wir sprechen uns noch.*)" with a certain satisfaction: " 'er schläft, also/ist er einverstanden.' " But the lyrical self has the last word, with the ambiguous "aber ich schlafe nicht." To some extent, therefore, the "vogel in meinem kopf" has fulfilled its task of maintaining a state of political awareness in the lyrical self, but in spite of the haranguing at the hands of the former, this awareness seems slyly self-determined.

The ambiguities of "lachesis lapponica" are not easily resolved. One thing may be stated with certainty, however, and it is upon this one factor that the poem is constructed: two conflicting attitudes, each one representing an extreme, are engaged in direct and indirect dialogue. This dialogue must be interpreted in the light of other poems in the same volume, poems such as "abgelegenes haus," "camera obscura" and "ufer," in which we see the poet's will to resigned isolation thwarted by external and internal intrusions from the populated world. In "lachesis lapponica" the intrusion comes from an internal source—as opposed to "abgelegenes haus," for instance, where it originates from a transistor radio—but the poet chooses to objectify this by creating an explicit subjective double in the form of the "vogel in meinem kopf." It is not a pathological symptom or a hallucination, but merely a convenient literary mode of expressing a divided nature which must contend incessantly with the conflicting impulses of political involvement and a profound political skepticism; it is a means of harnessing the paradox pointed out by Reinhold Grimm:

> Gerade darin, dass Hans Magnus Enzensberger an jeglicher politischen Realität verzweifelt und dennoch leidenschaftlich zum politischen Handeln drängt und aufruft, liegt das Paradox dieses Schriftstellers.

Like Heine in his *Wintermärchen*, Enzensberger is able to acquit himself in "lachesis lapponica" with a certain amount of humor. In the midst of a serious personal crisis the poet is able to distance himself by developing a witty and familiar repartee between the lyrical self and its "Doppelgänger," between two sides of his nature, which despite their differences are intimately linked.

Biographical Notes

René Karl Wilhelm Josef Maria Rilke was born in Prague in 1875. At the age of eleven he was sent to a military school in St. Pölten. The young Rilke, however, proved to be seriously unsuited for life as an officer. He studied at the School of Commerce in Linz and Prague University but did not complete his studies at either. In 1896 he moved to Munich to dedicate himself to writing. He met Lou Andreas-Salomé and the two travelled to Russia in 1899 and 1900. Rilke came away from the journeys much impressed by the Russian people, having made the acquaintance of Tolstoy and L. O. Pasternak, Boris Pasternak's father. In 1901 he married Clara Westhoff and the couple had a daughter, Ruth Rilke. When the marriage broke up one year later Rilke travelled to Paris, where he became the personal secretary of Auguste Rodin. He spent much time in Rodin's studio and the hard clarity of Rilke's visual imagery is often attributed, at least in part, to this experience. In 1909 he visited Spain and North Africa. Between 1911 and 1912 Rilke was the guest of Princess Marie von Thurn und Taxis-Hohenlohe at Duino Castle, where he spent much of the winter alone beginning his *Duino Elegies*. In 1915 he was conscripted to the Austrian army, but he was quickly given a position in the Military Records Office. With the help of a Swiss patron, W. Reinhard, Rilke established himself in a castle at Muzot after the war. There he spent the rest of his time finishing the Elegies and, in the span of three weeks in 1923, wrote all of the Orpheus sonnets. He died of leukemia in 1926.

Rilke's first volume of poems, *Leben und Lieder*, appeared in 1894. Other early collections include *Larenopfer* (1896), *Traumgekrönt* (1897) *Das Stunden-Buch* (1905), and the two-volume *Neue Gedichte* (1907–8). The *Duineser Elegien* appeared in 1923 as did *Die Sonette an Orpheus*. His works have been collected in the twelve volumes of *Gesammelte Werke* (1927) and *Sämtliche Werke* (1955–56). He is one of the German poets most widely translated into English.

Gottfried Benn was born in Mansfeld in 1886. He studied medicine and in 1912 qualified for military service. He served as an army medical officer in Belgium and after the war he set up a private practice in Berlin. Benn returned to the army, however, in 1935 and once again served as a medic for the duration of the Second World War. In 1948 he established himself in private practice in East Berlin, where he remained until his death in 1956.

Benn's early works include *Morgue und andere Gedichte* (1910), *Söhne* (1913), and *Fleisch* (1917), among others. His later, more experimental work includes *Fragmente* (1951), *Destillationen* (1953), and *Aprèslude* (1955). He is the author of several plays, a novel, *Der Ptolemäer* (1945), and two works of criticism, *Goethe und Naturwissenschaften* (1932) and *Probleme der*

233

Lyrik (1951). He was awarded the Büchner Prize in 1951. One collection of his work, *Primal Vision* (1971), has appeared in English.

Georg Trakl was born in Salzburg in 1887. While studying pharmacology he became addicted to drugs. Trakl's sister, to whom he was exceptionally close, was similarly addicted. In 1910 he served as a volunteer in the army medical service for one year. Trakl was later called up to serve as a reserve officer in the medical corps. Whether his drug addiction, personal problems, or wartime duty serving dying men in battles such as Grodek caused his rapid decline is difficult to say. He died of a cocaine overdose in Cracow in 1914.

Trakl published one collection of poems during his lifetime, *Gedichte* (1913). A three-volume *Gesammelte Werke* appeared between 1948 and 1951. Among Trakl's early admirers was Rilke, and he exerted considerable influence upon the Expressionists. *Georg Trakl: A Profile* (1983) remains the only edition of his work in English.

Eugen Bertolt Friedrich Brecht was born in Augsburg in 1898. In 1917 he entered Munich University intending to study medicine, but left after his first year. He returned to Augsburg and worked as an orderly in a military hospital. He spent the following ten years writing plays and poems. By 1922 he had established a reputation for himself in the theater and was awarded the Kleist prize. In 1928 he married Helen Weigel. He moved to Berlin and began an association with Max Reinhardt of the Deutsches Theater. It was also at this time that he began collaborating with composer Kurt Weill. Brecht was blacklisted by the NSDAP, a political organization of which Adolf Hitler was a key member. He consequently went into exile in Switzerland and then in Denmark, where he remained until 1939. He moved to Finland, then to Russia, and then to California where he spent the years between 1941 and 1947 working with such performers as Charlie Chaplin and Charles Laughton. He settled in Berlin finally in 1949. Brecht spent the remainder of his life working with the Berliner Ensemble, which sought to sharply contrast its theater with the Weimar theater of Goethe and Schiller. He died in East Berlin in 1956.

Whether as a dramatist, poet, novelist, or essayist, Brecht was enormously prolific. His major works for the theater include *Baal* (1922), *Aufstieg und Fall der Stadt Mahagonny* (1929), and *Die Dreigroschenoper* (1930), among countless others. *Dreigroschenroman* (1934) remains among the best known of his four novels. A considerable selection of his poetry may be found in the seven-volume *Gedichte* (1961). His works are generally available in English.

Günter Eich was born in Lebus/Oder in 1907. He studied Chinese and law at the universities of Leipzig, Berlin, and the Sorbonne. He later translated the work of Li Tai Pe as well as numerous other poets of the Orient. Eich's own early poetry appeared in *Anthologie jüngster Lyrik* (1927) under the name of Erich Günter. He also composed a number of radio plays during this time and is generally recognized as one of the pioneers of the medium in Germany. While serving in the army during the Second World War, Eich was taken prisoner by the Americans. The experience spawned his poem *Inventur*. After his release in 1948 he settled in Bavaria and married Ilse Aichinger in 1953. Eich lived in Austria until his death in 1972.

Gedichte (1930) was Eich's first collection of poems. Subsequent volumes include *Abgelegene Gehöfte* (1948), *Untergrundbahn* (1949), and *Botschaften des Regens* (1961). His "moles" have appeared in *Maulwürfe* (1968) and *Ein Tibeter in meinem Büro* (1970). His *Selected Poems* appeared in English in 1975.

Paul Celan, pseudonym of Paul Antschel, was born in Czernovitz in 1920. A Jew in German-occupied Romania, Celan lost both of his parents in a concentration camp. He went to Vienna in 1947 and then settled in Paris in 1948. As many of his poems indicate, Celan was haunted his whole life by his wartime experiences. He was awarded the Büchner Prize in 1960. In 1970 he took his own life in Paris.

Celan collections include *Der Sand aus den Urnen* (1948), *Mohn und Gedächtnis* (1952), and *Die Niemandsrose* (1963), among others. His *Gesammelte Werke* appeared in five volumes in 1983. Michael Hamburger published a volume of translations in English in 1981.

Ingeborg Bachmann was born in Klagenfurt in 1926. She attended Graz, Innsbruck, and Vienna universities. In 1959 she was appointed Lecturer in Poetry at Frankfurt University, a position she held for one year and which spawned many of the essays, poems, and stories in *Ingeborg Bachmann: Gedichte, Erzählungen, Hörspiele, Essays* (1964). She wrote numerous radio plays, opera libretti, and a novel, *Malina* (1971). She was awarded the Büchner Prize in 1964. Bachmann died in Rome in 1973.

A four-volume collection, *Werke*, appeared in 1978. Her work has not been widely translated.

Hans Magnus Enzensberger was born in Kaufbeuren in 1929. A student of philosophy and literature, he attended Erlangen, Hamburg, Freiburg, and Paris universities. The restlessness of his student days has become his lifestyle. He has lived in the United States, Mexico, the Near East, Norway, and Italy. Enzensberger's poetry traffics in foreign words, neologisms, and terms from popular culture. He has compiled a number of anthologies of modern poetry that deliberately seek to break away from the traditions that attend such books. His novel, *Der kurze Sommer der Anarchie* (1972), takes the Spanish anarchist Durriti as its hero. He won the Büchner Prize in 1963. Enzensberger lives alternately in Norway and Berlin.

Enzensberger's collections include *verteidigung der wölfe* (1957), *Beschreibung eines Dickichts* (1979) and, most recently, *Die Gedichte* (1983). Five volumes of his work are available in English.

Contributors

Harold Bloom, Sterling Professor of the Humanities at Yale University, is the author of *The Anxiety of Influence, Poetry and Repression*, and many other volumes of literary criticism. His forthcoming study, *Freud: Transference and Authority*, attempts a full-scale reading of all of Freud's major writings. A MacArthur Prize Fellow, he is general editor of five series of literary criticism published by Chelsea House. During 1987–88, he served as Charles Eliot Norton Professor of Poetry at Harvard University.

Erich Heller was Professor of Humanities at Northwestern University, Evanston. He is the author of *The Ironic German, The Poet's Self and the Poem*, and *Die Wiederkehr der Unschuld*.

Paul de Man was, until his death in 1983, Sterling Professor of Comparative Literature at Yale University. He is the author of *Blindness and Insight: Essays in Contemporary Criticism, Allegories of Reading, Figural Language in Rousseau, Nietzsche, Rilke, and Proust*, and *The Rhetoric of Romanticism*, and posthumously of the forthcoming collections *The Resistance to Theory, Aesthetic Ideology*, and *Fugitive Essays*.

Michael Hamburger has been key in presenting German poetry to the English-speaking world, whether as a critic or translator. His books include *Reason and Energy, From Prophecy to Exorcism, Art as Second Nature*, and *A Proliferation of Prophets*.

Martin Heidegger was Professor of Philosophy at Marburg and Freiburg. His most influential books are *Sein und Zeit, Kant und das Problem der Metaphysik*, and *Nietzsche*.

Brigitte Peucker, Professor of German at Yale University, is the author of *From Arcadia to Elysium*.

Reinhold Grimm is Professor of German and Comparative Literature at the University of Wisconsin, Madison. He is the author of *Brecht und Nietzsche*.

Anselm Haverkamp is Professor of German and Comparative Literature at the University of Konstanz. He is the author of *Typik und Politik* and *Second Readings*.

Joachim Schulze, Professor of French at the University of Bochum, is the author of *Celan und die Mystiker, Enttäuschung und Wahnwelt*, and *Charles Nodier*.

John Felstiner is Professor of English at Stanford University. He is the author of *Translating Neruda: The Way to Macchu Picchu*.

James K. Lyon is Professor of Germanic Languages and Literature at the University of California, San Diego. He is the author of *Bertolt Brecht and Rudyard Kipling* and *Lyrik am Rande der Sprache*.

William S. Sewell has written numerous articles on contemporary German literature.

Bibliography

GENERAL

Adorno, Theodor W. "Lyric Poetry and Society." *Telos* 20 (Summer 1974): 56–71.

Allemann, Beda. "Non-Representational Modern German Poetry." In *Reality and Creative Vision in German Lyrical Poetry*, 71–79. London: Butterworth, 1963.

Bienek, Horst. "German Poetry since 1945." *United Asia* 12 (1960): 42–57.

Closs, August. "Poetry." In *Twentieth Century German Literature*, 1–61. New York: Barnes & Noble, 1969.

Demetz, Peter. *Postwar German Literature: A Critical Introduction*. New York: Pegasus, 1970.

Exner, Richard. "German Poetry 1950–60: An Estimate." *Berliner Byzantinistische Arbeiten* (1962): 245–54.

Hamburger, Michael. *The Truth of Poetry*. London: Weidenfeld; New York: Harcourt, Brace, 1969.

Hamburger, Michael, and Christopher Middleton, eds. *Modern German Poetry 1910–1960*. London: Macgibbon & Klee, 1962.

Haverkamp, Anselm. "Saving the Subject: Margins of Lyrical Precision." *Poetica* 14 (1982): 70–91.

Holthusen, Hans Egon. "German Lyric Poetry since 1945." *Poetry* 88 (1956): 257–66.

Prawer, Siegbert. "Reflections on the Numinous and the Uncanny in German Poetry." In *Reality and Creative Vision in German Lyrical Poetry*, 153–73. London: Butterworth, 1963.

Raulet, Gerard. "The Logic of Decomposition." *New German Critique* 7 (1980): 81–111.

Schwebell, Gertrude Clorius, ed. *Contemporary German Poetry*. New York: New Directions, 1962.

RAINER MARIA RILKE

Allemann, Beda. *Zeit und Figur beim späten Rilke—Ein Beitrag zur Poetik des modernen Gedichts*. Pfuhlingen: Neske, 1961.

239

Batterby, Kenneth A. J. *Rilke and France*. London: Oxford University Press, 1966.

Belmore, H. W. *Rilke's Craftsmanship*. Oxford: Blackwell, 1954.

Bollnow, Otto Friedrich. *Rilke*. Stuttgart: Kohlhammer, 1951.

Bradley, Brigitte. *Rainer Maria Rilkes Neue Gedichte: Ihr zyklisches Gefüge*. Munich: Francke, 1968.

Brodsky, Patrick Pollock. "The Russian Source of Rilke's *Wie der Verrat nach Russland kam*." *Germanic Review* 54 (1979): 72–77.

Buddeberg, Else. *Rainer Maria Rilke, eine innere Biographie*. Stuttgart: J. B. Metzlersche Verlagsbuchhandlung, 1954.

Butler, Eliza Marian. *Rainer Maria Rilke*. Cambridge: Cambridge University Press, 1941.

Demetz, Peter. *Réné Rilkes Prager Jahre*. Düsseldorf: Diederichs, 1953.

Franklin, Ursula. "The Angel in Valery and Rilke." *Comparative Literature* 35 (1983): 215–46.

Fuerst, Norbert. *Phases of Rilke*. Bloomington: Indiana University Press, 1958.

Gadamer, Hans Georg. "Mythopoetische Umkehrung in Rilkes Duineser Elegien." *Kleine Schriften* 2 (1979): 194–209.

Graff, Willem Laurens. *Rainer Maria Rilke—Creative Anguish of a Modern Poet*. Princeton: Princeton University Press, 1956.

Guardini, Romano. *Zu Rainer Maria Rilkes Deutung des Daseins*. Bern: Francke, 1946.

Hamburger, Käte. *Philosophie der Dichter: Novalis, Schiller, Rilke*. Stuttgart: Kohlhammer, 1966.

Hartman, Geoffrey H. "Rilke." In *The Unmediated Vision*, 70–96. New York: Harcourt, Brace & World, 1966.

Holthusen, Hans Egon. *Portrait of Rilke*. New York: Herder & Herder, 1958.

Jacobs, Carol. "The Tenth Duino Elegy or the Parable of the Beheaded Reader." *MLN* 89 (1974): 978–1002.

Kramer, Lawrence. "The Return of the Gods: Keats to Rilke." *Studies in Romanticism* 17 (1978): 483–500.

Latimer, Dan. *The Elegiac Mode in Milton and Rilke: Reflections on Death*. Bern: Lang, 1977.

Mason, Endo C. *Rilke, Europe and the English-Speaking World*. Cambridge: Cambridge University Press, 1961.

Mood, John L. *Rilke on Love and Other Difficulties: Translation and Considerations of Rainer Maria Rilke*. New York: Norton, 1975.

Rolleston, James. *Rilke in Transition—An Exploration of His Earliest Poetry*. New Haven: Yale University Press, 1970.

Schoolfield, George C. *Rilke's Last Year*. Lawrence: University of Kansas Libraries, 1969.

Schwarz, Egon. *Poetry and Politics in the Works of Rainer Maria Rilke*. New York: Frederick Ungar, 1981.

Shaw, Priscilla Washburn. *Rilke, Valery, and Yeats—The Domain of the Self*. New Brunswick, N.J.: Rutgers University Press, 1964.

Steiner, Jacob. *Elegies*. Bern: Francke, 1962.

Stewart, Corbet. "Rilke's *Neue Gedichte*: The Isolation of the Image." *Publications of the English Goethe Society* 48 (1977/78): 81–103.

Thum, Reinhard. "The Medieval City: A Motif in Rilke's *Neue Gedichte*." *Colloquia Germanica* 15 (1982): 331–44.

Tucker, Cynthia Grant. "The Rilkean Lover and His Laurel—The Orpheus Poems and Petrarcan Tradition." *Philological Quarterly* 53 (1974): 256–74.

Wood, Frank Higley. *Rainer Maria Rilke—The Ring of Farns*. Minneapolis: University of Minnesota Press, 1964.

GOTTFRIED BENN

Adams, Marion. *Gottfried Benn's Critique of Substance*. Assen: Van Gorcum, 1969.
Alter, Reinhard. *Gottfried Benn: The Artist and Politics*. Bern: Lang, 1976.
Manyoni, Angelika. *Consistency of Phenotype: A Study of Gottfried Benn's Views of Lyric Poetry*. New York: Lang, 1983.
———. "*Das Gedicht aus Worten, die sie faszienierend montieren*: Gottfried Benn's Conception of Poetic Montage." *German Life and Letters* 36 (1982/83): 329–46.
Seidler, I. "Art and Power: An Expressionist Dilemma and Gottfried Benn's 'Solutions.' " *Michigan German Studies* 2 (1976): 169–82.

GEORG TRAKL

Calbert, Joseph P. *Dimensions of Style and Meaning in the Language of Trakl and Rilke*. Tübingen: Niemeyer, 1974.
Casey, Timothy John. *Manshape That Shone: An Interpretation of Trakl*. Oxford: Blackwell, 1964.
de Man, Paul. *Blindness and Insight*. New York: Oxford University Press, 1971.
Killy, Walter. *Über Georg Trakl*. Göttingen: Vandennoeck & Ruprecht, 1967.
Kurrik, Maire Jaanus. *Georg Trakl*. New York: Columbia University Press, 1974.
Lincoln, P. "Religious Dualism and Aesthetic Mediation in the Work of Georg Trakl." *Orbis Litterarum* 32 (1977): 229–46.
Lindenberger, Samuel Herbert. *Georg Trakl*. New York: Twayne, 1971.
Methlagl, Walter, and William E. Yuill. *Londoner Trakl—Symposion*. Salzburg: Müller, 1981.
Ritzer, Walter. *Neue Trakl Bibliographie*. Salzburg: Müller, 1983.
Sharp, Michael. *The Poet's Madness: A Reading of Georg Trakl*. Ithaca: Cornell University Press, 1981.
Stern, Howard. "Verbal Mimesis: The Case of 'Die Winzer.' " *Studies in Twentieth Century Literature* 8 (1983): 23–39.
Weiss, Walter, and Hans Weichselbaum. *Salzburger Trakl Symposion*. Salzburg: Müller, 1979.

BERTOLT BRECHT

Birkenhauer, Klaus. *Die eigentümliche Lyrik Bertolt Brechts: Theorie eines kommunikativen Sprachstils*. Tübingen: Niemeyer, 1971.
Bohnert, Christiane. *Brechts Lyrik im Kontext*. Königstein/Taunus: Athenäum, 1972.
Bronnen, Arnolt. *Tage mit Bertolt Brecht*. Darmstadt: Luchterhand, 1960.
Demetz, Peter, ed. *Brecht: A Collection of Critical Essays*. Englewood Cliffs, N.J.: Prentice-Hall, 1982.
Esslin, Martin. *Bertolt Brecht*. New York: Columbia University Press, 1969.
Gray, Ronald D. *Brecht*. Edinburgh: Oliver & Boyd, 1961.
Hartinger, Christel. *Bertolt Brecht: Das Gedicht nach Krieg und Wiederkehr*. Berlin: Brecht Zentrum der DDR, 1982.
Hill, Claude. *Bertolt Brecht*. Boston: Twayne, 1975.
Killy, Walter. *Über Gedichte des jungen Brecht*. Göttingen: Vandennoeck & Ruprecht, 1967.
Lyon, James K. *Bertolt Brecht's American Cicerone*. Bonn: Bouvier, 1978.
Mayer, Hans. *Bertolt Brecht und die Tradition*. Pfuhlingen: Deutscher Taschenbuchverlag, 1961.

Needle, Jan. *Brecht*. Oxford: Blackwell, 1981.

Pietzcker, Carl. *Die Lyrik des jungen Brecht*. Frankfurt am Main: Suhrkamp, 1974.

Schuhmann, Klaus. *Der Lyriker Bertolt Brecht*. Munich: Deutscher Taschenbuch-verlag, 1964.

Thomson, Philip. "Exegi Momentum: The Fame of Bertolt Brecht." *German Quarterly* 53 (1980): 337–47.

Völker, Klaus. *Brecht: A Biography*. New York: Seabury, 1978.

Whitacker, Peter. *Brecht's Poetry*. Oxford: Clarendon Press, 1985.

GÜNTER EICH

Foot, Robert. *The Phenomenon of Speechlessness in the Poetry of Marie Luise Kaschnitz, Günter Eich, Nelly Sachs and Paul Celan*. Bonn: Bouvier, 1982.

PAUL CELAN

Binder, Hartmut. *Kafka-Handbuch*. Stuttgart: Kroner, 1979.

Glenn, Jerry. "Celan's Transformation of Benn's *Südwort*: An Interpretation of the Poem *Sprachgitter*." *German Life and Letters* 21 (1967): 11–17.

———. "Nightmares, Dreams and Intellectualization in the Poetry of Paul Celan." *World Literature Today* 51 (1977): 522–25.

———. *Paul Celan*. New York: Twayne, 1973.

Menninghaus, Winfried. *Paul Celan: Magie der Form*. Frankfurt am Main: Suhrkamp, 1980.

Meyerhofer, Nicholas J. "Ambiguities of Interpretation: Translating the Late Celan." *Studies in Twentieth Century Literature* 8, no. 1 (1983): 9–22.

Petuchowski, Elizabeth. "Bilingual and Multilingual *Wortspiele* in the Poetry of Paul Celan." *Deutsche Vierteljahresschrift* 52 (1978): 635–51.

———. "A New Approach to Paul Celan's *Argumentum e Silentio*." *Deutsche Vierteljahresschrift* 52 (1978): 111–36.

Steiner, George. "A Terrible Exactness." *Times Literary Supplement* (June 11, 1976): 709–10.

Studies in Twentieth Century Literature 8, no. 1 (1983). Special Paul Celan issue.

Szondi, Peter. *Celan—Studien*. Frankfurt am Main: Suhrkamp, 1972.

Yates, W. E. "Mythopoetic Allusion in Celan's Poem *Die Krüge*. *Neophilologus* 65 (1981): 594–99.

INGEBORG BACHMANN

Lyon, James K. " 'Nature': Its Idea and Use in the Poetic Imagery of Ingeborg Bachmann, Paul Celan and Karl Krolow." Ph.D. diss., Harvard University, 1962.

Schoolfield, George C. "Ingeborg Bachmann." In *Essays on Contemporary German Literature*, edited by Brian Keith-Smith. London: Oswald Wolff, 1966.

HANS MAGNUS ENZENSBERGER

Grimm, Reinhold, and Bruce Armstrong, eds. *Critical Essays*. New York: Continuum, 1982.

Acknowledgments

"Rilke and Nietzsche: Orpheus, Dionysus and the Revision of Thought and Feeling" (originally entitled "Rilke and Nietzsche") by Erich Heller from *The Disinherited Mind* by Erich Heller, © 1959 by Meridian Books. Reprinted by permission of Barnes & Noble Books, Totowa, New Jersey, and Bowes & Bowes Ltd.

"Tropes (Rilke)" by Paul de Man from *Allegories of Reading* by Paul de Man, © 1979 by Yale University. Reprinted by permission of Yale University Press.

"The Expressionist Mode" (originally entitled "1912") by Michael Hamburger from *Reason and Energy* by Michael Hamburger, © 1957 by Routledge & Kegan Paul Ltd. Reprinted by permission of Routledge & Kegan Paul Ltd.

"Gottfried Benn" by Michael Hamburger from *A Proliferation of Prophets* by Michael Hamburger, © 1983 by Michael Hamburger. Reprinted by permission of the author, Carcanet Press, Manchester, and St. Martin's Press, New York.

"Georg Trakl: Language in the Poem" (originally entitled "Language in the Poem") by Martin Heidegger from *On the Way to Language,* translated by Peter D. Hertz, © 1971 in the English translation by Harper & Row Publishers, Inc. Reprinted by permission of Harper & Row Publishers, Inc.

"Georg Trakl: The Revisionary Language of Descent" (originally entitled "The Poetry of Repetition: Trakl's Narrow Bridge") by Brigitte Peucker from *Lyric Descent in the German Romantic Tradition* by Brigitte Peucker, © 1987 by Yale University. Reprinted by permission of Yale University Press.

"Confessions of a Poet: Poetry and Politics in Brecht's Lyric" by Reinhold Grimm from *From Kafka and Dada to Brecht and Beyond*, edited by Reinhold Grimm, Peter Sprycher, and Richard A. Zipser, translated by Francis G. Gentry, © 1982 by the Board of Regents of the University of Wisconsin System. Reprinted by permission of the University of Wisconsin Press.

"Marxist Emblems: Bertold Brecht's *War Primer*" by Reinhold Grimm from *Comparative Literature Studies (Special Issue: Media and Society)* 12, no. 3 (September 1975), © 1975 by the Board of Trustees of the University of Illinois. Reprinted by permission of the author and the University of Illinois Press.

"Laura's Metamorphoses: Eich's 'Lauren' " by Anselm Haverkamp from *Comparative Literature* 36 (Fall 1984), © 1984 by Anselm Haverkamp. Reprinted by permission.

"Celan and the 'Stumbling Block' of Mysticism" by Joachim Schulze from *Studies in Twentieth Century Literature* 8, no. 1 (Fall 1983), © 1983 by *Studies in Twentieth Century Literature*. Reprinted by permission of *Studies in Twentieth Century Literature*.

"Paul Celan in Translation: 'Du Sei Wie Du' " by John Felstiner from *Studies in Twentieth Century Literature* 8, no. 1 (1983), © 1983 by *Studies in Twentieth Century Literature*. Reprinted by permission of *Studies in Twentieth Century Literature*.

"The Poetry of Ingeborg Bachmann: A Primeval Impulse in the Modern Wasteland" (originally entitled "The Poetry of Ingeborg Bachmann") by James K. Lyon from *German Life and Letters* 17, no. 3 (April 1964), © 1964 by Basil Blackwell Ltd. Reprinted by permission of the author and Basil Blackwell Ltd.

"Doppelgänger Motif and Two-Voiced Poem in the Works of Hans Magnus Enzensberger" by William S. Sewell from *The German Quarterly* 52, no. 1 (January 1979), © 1979 by the American Association of Teachers of German. Reprinted by permission of the American Association of Teachers of German.

Index